M000237183

MASQUERADE

MASQUERADE

QUEER POETRY IN
AMERICA
TO THE END
OF WORLD WAR II

SELECTED AND EDITED BY JIM ELLEDGE

INDIANA UNIVERSITY PRESS
Bloomington and Indianapolis

This book is a publication of

Indiana University Press
601 North Morton Street
Bloomington, IN 47404-3797 USA

http://iupress.indiana.edu

Telephone orders   800-842-6796
Fax orders   812-855-7931
Orders by e-mail   iuporder@indiana.edu

© 2004 by Indiana University Press

All rights reserved

No part of this book may be reproduced or utilized in any form or by any means,
electronic or mechanical, including photocopying and recording, or by any
information storage and retrieval system, without permission in writing from the
publisher. The Association of American University Presses' Resolution on
Permissions constitutes the only exception to this prohibition.

The paper used in this publication meets the minimum requirements of American
National Standard for Information Sciences—Permanence of Paper for Printed
Library Materials, ANSI Z39.48–1984.

Manufactured in the United States of America

Library of Congress Cataloging-in-Publication Data

Masquerade : queer poetry in America to the end of World War II / selected and
edited by Jim Elledge.
p. cm.
Includes bibliographical references (p.) and index.
ISBN 0-253-34326-7 (alk. paper)—ISBN 0-253-21634-6 (pbk. : alk. paper)
1. American poetry. 2. Gays' writings, American. 3. United States—Literatures.
4. Lesbians—Poetry. 5. Gay men—Poetry. I. Elledge, Jim, date
PS591.G38M37 2004
811.008'0920664—dc22
2003015571

1 2 3 4 5 09 08 07 06 05 04

For David

He aikāne ka mea aloha, ē.

CONTENTS

PREFACE

The chief goal of this volume is to make visible what has been made invisible. The poems that it presents are not just literary artifacts, they are also important evidence of, and monuments to, those gay, lesbian, bisexual, and transgendered persons who were creating texts decades, even centuries, before our time. Those of us who, for many, many decades now, have demanded that society become sensitive to issues of diversity must listen to our own message. Diversity must be extended to include Native American creation myths of the oral tradition as well as the formalist poetry of Dunstan Thompson, the undecorated chants of voodoo practitioners as well as the academic poetry of Katherine Bates—and everything between.

To that end, I have elected to expand the definition of what we typically think of as gay, lesbian, bisexual, or transgendered poetry to include work that is not necessarily sexual in content—although it may be—and work that may be subtly gay, lesbian, bisexual, and transgendered in theme, not only overtly so. My first criterion was to include work by all persons whom various scholars have identified as being gay, lesbian, bisexual, or transgendered. This includes those who engaged in actual same-sex experiences or those who only experienced homoerotic emotions. Emily Dickinson, for example, probably never had a sexual relationship with her sister-in-law, yet she wrote extraordinary lines about her love for Susan:

> Precious to Me—She shall be—
> Though She forget the name I bear—
> The fashion of the Gown I wear—
> The very Color of My Hair—

Similarly, T. S. Eliot's brief, but extraordinarily important, encounter with Jean Verdenal made him a candidate for inclusion.

I also set out to include poetry by writers known not as poets but as fiction writers, such as Glenway Wescott and Gale Wilhelm; as playwrights, such as Lynn Riggs; or as writers of nonfiction, such as Margaret Fuller. I wanted to include representative selections from all races; from unexpected quarters, such as from cowboys and voodoo practitioners; and from a broad representation of genres, including not only free verse, the variety that would be most familiar to contemporary readers, but also chants, prayers, songs, limericks, prose poems, and poems in traditional forms. For the same reason, I have included work from the secular as well as the sacred realms of human existence.

In selecting poems by individuals or by anonymous authors, I have tried to include those that offer recurring gay, lesbian, bisexual, or transgendered themes, images, and iconography when possible. I worked against including large numbers of love or sex poems, although there are many in the anthology. I wanted the anthology to be diverse thematically as well as racially and ethnically.

The anthology opens with some of the earliest poems of U.S. literary history, the anonymous texts—chants, prayers, songs—from the oral traditions of Native America and the Hawaiian Islands. I have also included chants to various transgendered voodoo deities and anonymous poems and songs by cowboys. I have added explanatory titles to a number of the Native American, Hawaiian, and voodoo texts that were published without titles. I have added notes to some of the songs, poems, and chants in this section to help allay any confusion that may arise due to differences in cultures. The second and largest section includes work by gay, lesbian, bisexual, and transgendered persons who lived after 1776 primarily, but not exclusively, in the continental U.S. I have arranged the poets chronologically, on the basis of year of birth. When two or more poets were born in the same year, I have arranged them alphabetically by last name within that year. Most of the poets had collections published before the end of World War II, although there are some exceptions.

While most of the poets will not be familiar to contemporary readers, those who are posed a problem. I had to decide whether to reprint their well-known poems or the lesser-known, but perhaps more gay, lesbian, bisexual, and transgendered. I choose the latter. I hope that by placing these works by famous poets in an openly gay, lesbian, bisexual, and transgendered context, they will be more intriguing to the reader, and simultaneously open themselves up to interpretations never before imagined.

In all cases, I have attempted to include poems that are successful as poems and representative of the time in which the poet wrote as well as representative of the poet's abilities and oeuvre. My selection was never based on literary reputation per se. While a number of those whose work I included were "household names" during their time, many are unknown today. As I noticed while compiling this anthology, their decline in popularity—another brand of "invisibility"—is often unfounded. Among them I would include George Boker, Witter Bynner, Charles Henri Ford, Angela Weld Grimké, Hasteen Klah, Rose O'Neill, Lynn Riggs, Jessie B. Rittenhouse, and Dunstan Thompson. I hope this volume draws attention to their and others' work and affords them a new visibility. There are a few whose work is going to seem quaint, at best, to contemporary readers, and while readers may bemoan their inclusion, I chose to keep them because they are as important as any ancestor is. I had hoped at the beginning of my research to include as many women poets as men. That has not happened. The patriarchy of U.S. society at large, and particularly within U.S. literary history, is a powerful force. Far fewer women poets have been published than their male counterparts. However, I have included work by all the women whom I have been able to identify as lesbian, bisexual, or transgendered.

In essays and books by anthologists Will Roscoe, an unflagging specialist in the role of the two-spirit in Native America, and Stephen O. Murray, who has pioneered the study of oceanic homosexualities, I discovered many sources or leads to sources of texts by indigenous peoples. Without the pioneering efforts of Roscoe and Murray, I could not have embarked on this project. In books such as Claude J. Summers's *The Gay and Lesbian Literary Heritage* and *Cassell's Encyclopedia of Queer Myth, Symbol and Science*, edited by Randy P. Connor, David Hatfield Sparks, and Mariya Sparks, I was able to find many leads to the poetry of authors from early or usually ignored eras of U.S. literary history and often pinpointed their most important work. To these scholars and editors I owe a great deal of thanks.

I also owe gratitude for the support of my friends—to Kristy Nielsen and Keith Humphreys and to Susan Swartwout, Jonathan Budil, and Ben Foster—for their encouragement. I owe special thanks to Romayne and Damon Dorsey, who, over the course of several years, checked out many hundreds of volumes of poetry from the library at Indiana University on my behalf, gave me room, board, and access to a computer, and never once complained. This volume owes its life to them.

INTRODUCTION

Typically, when we speak of the poetry of a gay, lesbian, bisexual, or transgendered person, we are alluding to a body of work written after 1969, the year of the precipitous Stonewall Riots. The "riots" took place at the Stonewall Inn, a gay bar in Greenwich Village, beginning the evening of June 28, 1969, and lasting for several days while police harassed the management and clientele of the bar. As an event, it marks for most scholars in queer studies the birth of gay liberation.[1] It has become, in essence, the date on which queer persons began to struggle to make themselves and their culture (including their literature, art, and music) visible in the United States. The metaphor of invisibility suggests that the queer lives and artifacts are right before our very eyes but are simply "not seen." They have always existed, but they weren't always noticed. In terms of literary history, the metaphor of invisibility is more apt than the more ubiquitous metaphor of the "closet."

It is crucial to the study of U.S. literary history as a whole to be aware that a literature existed long before Europeans arrived to colonize the peoples of the "New World," which includes the mainland of North America and the Hawaiian Islands, and that within that precolonial literature there was a strong and pervasive queer tradition. This literature was not a collection of written texts, but a series of myths and legends[2]—including narratives, songs, chants, and prayers—that were memorized by specific individuals and passed down from one generation to the next orally. The myths and legends were completely integrated into the societies and cultures of the indigenous peoples here and were an integral part of daily and liturgical life. Much of this literature was lost through what has amounted to genocide waged by Europeans against the indigenous peoples. Yet some of the literature remains with us because of anthropologists, missionaries, and others who translated it into English and recorded it, thereby preserving it for future generations. What we have traditionally called "mythology" is the most readily available literature of indigenous peoples, and like its ancient Greek counterpart, it is rich with queer characters and experiences—often uncensored. Some early colonizers took

note of such myths, especially nineteenth-century Christian mission-
aries to the Hawaiian Islands and the anthropologists who studied
Native American life during the late 1800s and the first decades of
the 1900s.[3]

U.S. anthropologists such as Alfred Kroeber, Elsie C. Parsons, Les-
lie Spier, and Matilda C. Stevenson spent a great deal of time on
reservations west of the Mississippi River and built their careers on
observing, evaluating, and reporting the cultures of various Native
American nations. Some were aware of a group of men and women
who differed from the typical Native American individual but who,
more often than not, held a respected and important role in the native
community.

While today we often use the term "two-spirit"[4] to denote these
individuals whom we would identify as queer, their own people used
a variety of terms to refer to them, depending on the nation to which
they belonged. The Mohave called them *alyha* or *alyha:* (the female
two-spirit was *hwami* or *hwame:*), while the Cheyenne called them
he'eman (the female two-spirit was *hetaneman*). What is crucial to their
identification is not the exact word that Native Americans used to
designate the two-spirit, but what the terms tended to mean to the
Native Americans. As anthropologist Will Roscoe, the most noted
authority on the two-spirit in history, has revealed, the names used by
Native Americans tend to suggest an individual of neither of the two
sexes that our polarized view (of men at one end and woman at the
other) permits. Their names for two-sprit individuals often translate
into English as denoting a person whose identity falls somewhere be-
tween the sexes or who combines the two sexes into one. The Western
Shoshone, for example, used *tangwuwaip* (and several versions of this
word) or "man-woman" to refer to both male and female two-spirits,
while the Tlingit used *wⁿcitc*, or "boy whose sex changes at birth," to
refer to male two-spirits. The Aleut called them *ayagigux'*, or "man
transformed into a woman" (females were called *tayagigux'*, or "woman
transformed into a man").

The problem one faces when trying to uncover the literature of the
two-spirit is twofold. First, most of the literature was initially pub-
lished in anthropological journals and monographs many decades ago.
Second, not only are the sources difficult to locate, but anthropologists
of the time used no single word or phrase in their published articles
and reports to refer to the two-spirit individuals. Fifteen or so different
terms can be found, ranging from "two-spirit," the most recent, and
probably the most apropos, to "hermaphrodite," the longest-lasting
and most often used. Because so many Native Americans' terms for

two-spirited persons meant "changing from man to woman," "man-woman/woman-man," or some similar phrase, Europeans often translated the Native American term as "hermaphrodite," not understanding that the "changing" from one sex to another or the combination of two sexes into one that the two-spirit had undergone was spiritual, an inner transformation or union, and that the cross-dressing that often, but not always, accompanied two-spirit status was a physical, external symbol of their nonphysical, inner state.[5] For example, the European wrongly thought the Apache's *ndé'sdzan,* or "man-woman," had both male and female genitals. What one discovers and is overwhelmed by immediately is not only a lack of access to the source materials, but a confusion of language. Together, these create their special brand of invisibility.

Other language problems helped to create a state of invisibility for the two-spirit person. Native Americans' terms for "two-spirit" individuals differed from nation to nation, from tribe to tribe. The Crow, for example, used *boté,* while the Lakota used *winkte.* Even within a particular nation or tribe, there might be a variety of words used to identify a queer person. The Navajo used seven: *nutlys, natle, nu'tle, nadle, nádle, nadleeh,* and *nadleehi.* Confusing matters even more is the fact that both Native American terms and the terms anthropologists used vary in spelling. For example, the word for the Western Shoshone two-spirited individual was spelled *tangewuwaip, tangowaip, tango-waipu, tainna'wa'ippe,* and *taikwahni tainnapa',* while *hermaphrodite,* a term common among anthropologists, was bastardized into four different words—*morphy, morphodite, murfidai,* and *morphdites*—all of which were used at one time or another in the anthropological sources. In many cases, the broad array of terms was a matter of different peoples having different languages, and there was no malicious intent involved. Native America had many languages each with its own term—or terms—for two-spirited persons, and European colonists were often simply ignorant of Native American cultures and of two-spirit individuals in general. Yet these helped to make invisible an entire people and literature. A contemporary researcher trying to untangle the many knots that a lack of knowledge and a misunderstanding of others' cultures created is frustrated at almost every turn.

Male and female same-sex relationships also permeate the annals of the earliest Hawaiian literature—again myths transmitted orally from generation to generation—although these relationships were often made invisible by those who initially collected and translated them into English. The myths often use the term *aikāne* to indicate both male and female same-sex relationships, a word created by the combination of two others: *ai*, meaning "sexual intercourse," with *kane*, or "man." (The word *ai* suggests a pun, since its homophone *'ai* means "food" and "to eat." The pun suggests an even further sexual euphemism, one that parallels similar phrases in English in which eating is a metaphor for sexual contact.[6]) *Aikāne* simultaneously suggests a sexual role undertaken by individuals, as well as the individuals themselves who engaged in the role.

The first record of the Hawaiian *aikāne* appears not in anthropological studies, but in journal entries written by members of the crew of Captain James Cook's third voyage to the Hawaiian Islands. The journals were penned between January 19 and May 5, 1779. While the various men[7] who wrote the entries called the *aikāne* with whom they had contact a number of different and bastardized versions of the word (including *t'akanee*, *takanee*, *i'car'nies*, and *ikany*[8]), their reports agree on several important and relevant points despite their heterocentricism: that the *aikāne* were involved in sexual contact of some sort; that having *aikāne* status was not considered shameful or something to be hidden, but was as honorable as any role in Hawaiian society; and that although noticed through the class-conscious English eyes only in the upper rungs of Hawaiian society, and only among men, *aikāne* undoubtedly also extended to lower societal classes and existed among women.

However, once the newness of the first encounters with the Hawaiians wore off and Polynesia was no longer fetishized—or at least the fetishization of it had lessened[9]—Europeans began to make the *aikāne*—both the person and the once-acceptable role—invisible. In the earliest literature of the Hawaiians that is extant, a large and very complex cycle of interrelated and interdependent myths, male and female *aikāne* are apparent throughout. In fact, in contrast to most literature of other cultures, the *aikāne* seems to be common rather than an exception.

While the characters who populate ancient Hawaiian myths are, for the most part, demigods, to use a Western concept, who are more than the typical human being but are less than divine, several are indeed deities. Some are exclusively opposite-sex-focused, while others are exclusively same-sex-focused. Many of the characters fall somewhere between those polar opposites, sometimes being *aikāne* and at other times not. What is apparent is that one's sexual orientation as illustrated by the mythology is not necessarily static—although it may be—and does not necessarily shift focus—although it may. Most important is the fact that "orientation" is the individual's prerogative, not a social dictum.

However, if we were to read the Hawaiian myths solely as they were translated by Europeans and Americans of European descent, we would see absolutely no evidence of a queer presence, making the journal entries of Cook's men—Clerke, King, Samwell, and Ledyard— seem at the very least odd.

Among the first to collect and translate the Hawaiian myths was Abraham Fornander. His monumental *Collection of Hawaiian Antiquities and Folk-Lore*, an encyclopedic compendium of the myths, was published with facing texts, so that the original version of the myth in Hawaiian appears on the left-hand page and the text in English translation is on the right-hand page. However, Fornander's "translation" is not as valid as one might hope. He always translated *aikāne* as "friend," "close friend," "bosom friend," or any number of other words or phrases to disguise—and thereby make invisible—the sexual content of the myths and of their characters' sexual roles. If, when reading the English text, we run across the word *friend* (or its many synonyms), we need to glance across to the opposite page to see what word the Hawaiians themselves had used. The original word is often *aikāne*. It's perfectly obvious, then, that Fornander heterosexualized texts throughout the three volumes of his work.[10]

What is both odd and ironic—and deserving of attention—are two facts: that Fornander never suppressed the evidence that he had censored and corrupted the translations on purpose, although he was perfectly free to do so, and that he left the evidence for us to find, also on purpose—or so we might assume. It would have been easy for him to change the original Hawaiian so that it did not contain *aikāne* and so obliterate any clue of same-sex activities or relationships in the myths and to use some other unrelated word instead. He didn't. Fornander left *aikāne* in the original in full view of anyone who wanted to see it, for anyone who would take the time to look for it, and for anyone who was lucky enough to know what to look for in the first place.

The question is: Why?

One expects that Fornander corrupted his English translation for one of two reasons—perhaps for both. He undoubtedly was reacting to what was then perceived as sanctions in Scripture (in both the Hebrew and the Christian bibles) against queer persons and same-sex sexual activities by attempting to protect a people and their literature. He would have known that had the world at large learned of the overt and pervasive queer focus of much of Hawaiian mythology, which in turn would have thrown suspicion on their culture and society at large, the Hawaiians would have paid the price.[11] By using "friend" rather than "lover" or some other possible English equivalent of *aikāne*, it's possible that he was being protective. One would like to believe that he retained *aikāne* in the original so that in some future day the myths might be afforded their original intent and the *aikāne* be made visible when it was safe. Of course, that's mere conjecture. It's just as probable—perhaps even more likely than not—that Fornander simply didn't think anyone would take the time or effort to review the myths and the record of his dishonesty and simply didn't bother to cover his tracks.

Or perhaps he didn't realize what *aikāne* actually meant.

The way that Europeans and Americans of European descent dealt with the poetry of indigenous queer peoples illustrates one form of invisibility. Yet that form of invisibility is no less insidious than the version that their counterparts with European backgrounds experienced. This is the case beginning with Fitz-Greene Hallack (1803–1882) and continuing into our time.

Most queer poets who lived during the centuries before Stonewall wrote for two audiences simultaneously, combining the public and the private in an attempt to be visible *and* invisible—also simultaneously. They strove for ambiguity.[12] On one hand, they wrote for society at large, a heterosexual world, the one in which they found themselves and with which they negotiated daily, often for their very survival. They wanted their work read by family, neighbors, and friends, as well as the reading public in general. They wanted their work to sell.[13] To be successful in the public—which always means heterosexual—sphere, then, meant that a queer poet had to accept what many contemporary scholars have rightly called "compulsory heterosexuality." This simply meant that the poets should be married with children to guarantee that they would "pass" as heterosexual in their everyday lives. In terms of their literary careers or aspirations, this also meant they had to be discreet to the extent of obliterating from their work all hints of any sort of same-sex desire, point of view, or content, however small. Compulsory heterosexuality also meant that, regardless of what the poets may have wanted to investigate or discuss in their work, their subjects had to be anchored somehow in a heterosexual context. In short, compulsory heterosexuality dictated compulsory invisibility.

On the other hand, queer poets wanted to write for themselves and for others like them, attempting to put into words their actual feelings, thoughts, experiences, dreams—not those camouflaged by a thin veneer of heterosexuality. In order to negotiate compulsory heterosexuality safely, they learned to encode the personal aspects of their lives into an acceptable—i.e., heterosexual—context. For example, a large

number of queer poets lamented the deaths of their beloved, or the
break-up of their relationships, by adopting any of several models of
what heterosexuals considered to be only deeply emotional friendships
between individuals of the same sex. Two of the best-known of these
models are, ironically, from Scripture: David's lament for Jonathan and
the story of Ruth's loyalty to Naomi.[14] Because most heterosexuals
have traditionally presumed that the Hebrew Bible rejects, even con-
demns, homosexuality, the love shared by these same-sex "couples"
could not, from their point of view, be sexual, although it may have
been deeply emotional and felt by both. Knowing their heterosexual
counterparts' point of view, queer poets used heterosexuals' point of
view to their advantage. If Scripture could recount a deeply felt emo-
tion between men or between women, and if that, therefore, was ac-
ceptable in God's sight, even if a sexual relationship between them
was not, then queer poets would simply use the models to express the
emotion that they felt and to hint at the sexual intimacy they expe-
rienced.

Queer readers have traditionally seen David's elegy for Jonathan or
Ruth's promise to Naomi as a glimpse of same-sex couples expressing
a love that was not only emotional but also sexual. When a gay poet
cast his concerns in a poem employing David's lament for Jonathan,
he wrote ambiguously, acceding to, while rebelling against, compulsory
heterosexuality. He was able to make its gay content invisible to the
heterosexual world around him, while simultaneously revealing its gay-
ness to others like him because they, too, agreed that David and Jon-
athan were more than friends. The same is true for lesbians who have
relied on the Ruth/Naomi narrative.[15] Consequently, most heterosex-
uals who have read, for example, "2. Samuel I. 26" by George Sylvester
Viereck (1884–1962) have presumed that the poem is about a strong,
friendly bond between persons of the same sex, while gay men who
have read the poem see their own lives reflected in the scriptural mod-
els, especially when David cries out, "greatly beloved were you to me;
/ your love to me was wonderful, / *passing the love of women*" (NRSV;
italics added). Viereck's use of the elegy allowed him to write a poem
that heterosexuals would see as a poem about friendship, albeit one
founded on deep emotional ties, but which gay men would recognize
immediately as a sexual relationship between two men. The allusion
to David's love for Jonathan that the poem's title and last line provide
keeps the poem from being subsumed by heterosexuality, and thus the
love his narrator feels for the poem's "you"—"the great flame heaven-
lit" when they met "soul to soul"—is rescued from invisibility, if one
is willing or able to read it ambiguously.

While not borrowing the David/Jonathan model outright, but its heterosexualized theme of "friendship," Fitz-Greene Halleck (1803–1882) could express his life-long, and unrequited, love for Joseph Rodman Drake—with whom he had collaborated on many poems—and could lament Drake's death in an elegy entitled "On the Death of Joseph Rodman Drake of New York, Sept., 1820," which is as eloquent and passionate as the biblical David's for Jonathan. Whether or not it is overtly linked to the David/Jonathan model, the heterosexualized theme of friendship allows very complex feelings to emerge from the poets, lending itself to other related, deeply felt expressions. In "Indeed, indeed, I cannot tell" by Henry David Thoreau (1817–1862), the narrator admits to his "dear friend,"

> O, I hate thee with a hate
> That would fain annihilate;
> Yet sometimes against my will,
> My dear friend, I love thee still.

It expresses a central conflict of his life. He hates that whom he loves *because he loves him*. His "dear friend" is a source of both joy and despair simultaneously. Similarly in "Friends," Scudder Middleton (1888–1959) relies on the metaphor of two men—farmers and neighbors of one another—plowing fields together to suggest a deeper relationship than simply friendship between them. Before his "friend's" death, the narrator reveals that

> my hand and his
> Were closer linked than now,
> And by that doubled strength of ours,
> These fields were light to plow.

The fields that once provided a symbolic union for their relationship now "yield [him] less." Without his beloved, life has diminished.

For centuries, poets have adopted a number of figures from myth, legion, and history as codes that, like the models of David/Jonathan or Naomi/Ruth, allowed the poet to be both visible and invisible simultaneously. St. Sebastian, for example, adopted by T. S. Eliot (1888–1965) in his "The Love Song of St. Sebastian," allows Eliot's narrator to explore the complexities of love between men during his time, a love that is both devotional and destructive. Indeed, in his poem, the beloved becomes a murderer to preserve his love: ". . . I should love you the more because I had mangled you / and because you were no longer beautiful / To anyone but me." Willa Cather (1873–1947) alludes to a figure from classical history in "Antinous."

Beloved of Roman emperor Hadrian (76–138), the beautiful Greek youth Antinous (c.110–130) drowned mysteriously, and Hadrian had him deified. Their love has become a code of unconditional devotion within a same-sex relationship: "Antinous, beneath thy lids, though dim, / the curling smoke of altars rose to thee, / Conjuring thee to comfort and content."

Poets also adopted other sorts of codes, including specific colors (for example, purple—and its various shades, especially lavender) and even stereotypes. The cowboy wannabe of the anonymous "The Lavender Cowboy" might wear the clothes and practice the mannerisms of the "he-men" he so admires, he might even die with his "six-gun a-smokin'," but he'll never be a real cowboy, only a lavender one (i.e., gay). In short, he might disguise—or in other words: make invisible—the truth about himself (that he is lavender), but he is what he is. Even if the world doesn't see it, his gayness is a fact of his life. The image of the hermaphrodite has also been a code to indicate queer persons. The figures in Elizabeth Bishop's (1911–1979) "The Gentleman of Shalott" and in Natalie Clifford Barney's (1876–1972) "Double Being" inform readers that the person in question is gay or lesbian or bisexual or transgendered and in all likelihood not hermaphroditic at all. Barney recognizes a value in the combination of the male and the female:

> A natural being, yet from nature freed,
> Like a Shakespearean boy of fairy breed—
> A sex perplexed into attractive seeming
> —Both sex at best, the strangeness so redeeming!

However, poets have often revealed the truth of their lives more subtly. The concluding couplet of "Flowers in the Dark," by Sarah Orne Jewett (1849–1909), does exactly that: ". . . what surprise could dearer be than this: / To find my sweet rose waiting with a kiss!" The pun on *rose*—Is it simply a flower, or might it not also be a woman's name, albeit not capitalized by the poet?—allows for, even requires, a lesbian reading. For many, many other poets, addressing a poem to a gender-nonspecific "you" allowed them to speak directly to their beloved or about their love while retaining their invisibility. Heterosexual readers would simply assume that the poem's "you" was someone of the opposite sex, but to a queer reader the "you" would suggest just the opposite.

Since 1969, events such as the Stonewall Riots have allowed queer literature—and its writers—to become more and more visible not only to the world at large but, as important—one could argue, more important—to themselves. Pre-Stonewall authors had no similar public event on which they might build community. For post-Stonewall poets, community provided support and the strength they needed to become visible—to write their lives and its varied experiences outside of compulsory heterosexuality. While certainly some "community" existed for pre-Stonewall poets—the Transcendentalists of New England, nineteenth-century poet Bayard Taylor's circle of exclusively male friends (who were often former lovers of one another), Gertrude Stein's and similar salons in Paris, and the various coteries associated with the Harlem Renaissance are a few—such groups were restricted in terms of number and location. The groups were always small and always located in large metropolitan areas or other centers of sophistication.

I have compiled this book to show for the first time in U.S. literary history the continuum of queer literature that exists in this country—and existed here long before it became a "country." By showing it, I hope to make visible what has been invisible since the first European set foot in this hemisphere more than five centuries ago. If nothing else, this anthology is a document of the existence of a literature created by an entire people—the queer individuals of the territory now known as the United States, a people within a people, a group as diverse in race, gender, and socio-economic status as humanly possible, but a people united by the fact of their invisibility. This anthology makes obvious and undeniable two simple facts: that the study of U.S. literature must begin with the oral tradition of the indigenous peoples of Native America and Hawaii, and that queer persons and their texts have been an integral part of that literature's history since its beginning. Indeed, queer poets have been among its forerunners.

NOTES

1. By gay liberation, I am in no way meaning or attempting to exclude lesbians, bisexuals, or transgendered persons. Hereafter, I will use *queer* to refer to gay, lesbian, bisexual, and transgendered persons.

2. Readers interested in such myths should consult my *Gay, Lesbian, Bisexual, and Transgender Myths from the Arapaho to the Zuñi: An Anthology* (New York: Lang, 2002).

3. I have relied on a number of sources for the facts and concepts that appear in this introduction. These can be found in the reference list that follows these endnotes.

4. For quite some time, anthropologists and nonanthropologists alike used the word "berdache," but in recent years it has fallen into disrepute among some scholars. According to them, it is a derogatory word, and they have convincingly argued for the adoption of "two-spirit" as more representative of the Native American view of the queer individual's existence. Readers interested in the debate over what English phrase or word should be adopted should consult Roscoe's *The Changing Ones*, pp. 108–12, and *Two-Spirit People: Native American Gender Identity, Sexuality, and*

Spirituality, ed. Sue-Ellen Jacobs, Wesley Thomas, and Sabine Lang (Urbana: University of Illinois Press, 1997).

5. Readers wanting a more in-depth investigation into the Native American two-spirit should see especially the work by Will Roscoe, Paula Gunn Allen, Beatrice Medicine, and Walter L. Williams in the reference list that follows these endnotes.

6. It may seem tempting to take the easy way out and claim that *ai* plus *kane*—or *ʻai* plus *kane*—equals "cannibalism." However, the context of the texts in which *aikāne* appears has nothing to do with that sort of "eating." *Aikāne* often appears along with phrases such as *noho pu* or *moe pu*, denoting two men cohabitating or sleeping with one another. Readers wanting a more in-depth investigation into the Hawaiian aikane should see especially the work by Robert J. Morris in the reference list that follows these endnotes.

7. The men were James King, a second lieutenant; Charles Clerke, Cook's second in command; ship's surgeon David Samwell; and an American and Marine corporal, John Ledyard. Samwell mentions that when several Hawaiian men noticed a handsome young man among Cook's crew, the Hawaiians asked if he was involved in an *aikāne* relationship with another of the crew. Later, Samwell notes that Kalanikoa offered to give six hogs to Clerke (who became the captain after Cook's death) if Clerke would allow an unidentified young and handsome man to become his *aikāne*, if only for a little while. King admits not only that both Kalaniʻopuʻu, a king of the Islands, and another Hawaiian man named Koa asked Cook to leave King behind for them when the English left for home, but also that he had also received a number of proposals from the Hawaiian men to run away from the English.

8. Another word, *kikuana*, was also used, but it seems to have been a word of endearment used between same-sex siblings, and it may suggest incest between brothers or sisters.

9. For many poets and fiction writers of the 1800s, and occasionally even now, things "Polynesian" and related to the "East" became extremely exoticized and idealized and became codes for a variety of liberations. For queer male authors, the most noteworthy among these "liberations" was sexual freedom. A number of male authors of European descent wrote poems, stories, and novels set in the Hawaiian Islands, in Tahiti, in the Middle East, etc.—areas that they believed offered a freedom of sexual orientation. Herman Melville's novel *Omoo*, Charles Warren Stoddard's collection of stories *South-Sea Idyls*, and Bayard Taylor's *Poems of the Orient* are perfect examples of the fetishization of "the East." In our own time, Paul Bowles lived in Tangier most of his life, with frequent visits from queer authors Allen Ginsberg, Peter Orlovsky, and William S. Burroughs.

10. Fornander was not the only person to heterosexualize texts. Among those translators of Hawaiian mythology who did not properly translate *aikāne* are Martha Beckwith, Padraic Colum, Nathaniel B. Emerson, and William D. Westervelt.

11. One has only to look at the extant records of early contact with the peoples of Native America to see how those armed with Christianity and its ideals dealt with the queer peoples they encountered there. For example, in the 1540s Girolamo Benzoni published an account of Conquistador Vasco Núñez de Balboa, who had his dogs attack then eat alive a number of two-spirited persons.

12. As I use it here, *ambiguous* doesn't mean that a text is confusing, but rather that a text may be interpreted in at least two different ways, with both making sense.

13. Ironically, the "best seller" of gay poetry is Badger Clark's *Sun and Saddle Leather*. During Clark's life, his collection of "cowboy poetry" went through three different editions between 1915 and 1919. We can only assume that the heterosexual readership was unwilling to read lines such as

> We loved each other in the way men do
> And never spoke about it, Al and me,
> But we both knowed, and knowin' it so true
> Was more than any woman's kiss could be

as anything other than a deep friendship between men. Clark's obvious reliance on the David/Jonathan model no doubt helped.

14. A number of articles, chapters of books, and entire monographs have recently been devoted to the investigation of the stance of both the Hebrew Bible and the Christian Bible on homosexuality, both male and female. Among the most illuminating and astute of these studies are John Boswell's *Christianity, Social Tolerance, and Homosexuality* (Chicago: University of Chicago Press, 1980) and his *Same-Sex Unions in Premodern Europe* (New York: Vintage, 1994); Gary David Comstock's *Gay Theology Without Apology* (Cleveland: Pilgrim, 1993); John J. McNeill's *The Church and the Homosexual*, 4th ed. (Boston: Beacon, 1993); Martti Niesinen's *Homoeroticism in the Biblical World*, trans. Kirsi Stjerna (Minneaplis: Fortress, 1998); and Robin Scroggs' *The New Testament and Homosexuality* (Philadelphia: Fortress, 1983).

15. It is ironic and extraordinarily hypocritical that, on one hand, heterosexual couples have employed Ruth's oath to Naomi—

> . . . wherever you go, I shall go,
> wherever you live, I shall live.
> Your people will be my people,
> And your God will be my god.
> Where you die, I shall die
> And there I shall be buried.
> Let Yahweh bring unnameable ills on me
> And worse ills, too,
> If anything but death
> Should part me from you! (Ruth 1:16–17 NJB)

—on their wedding announcements or during their wedding liturgies while simultaneously denying that what the two women felt for one another could be sexual.

REFERENCES

Allen, Paula Gunn. "Hwame, Koshkalaka, and the Rest: Lesbians in American Indian Cultures." *The Sacred Hoop: Recovering the Feminine in American Indian Traditions.* Boston: Beacon, 1986. 245–61.

Charlot, John. *The Kamapua'a Literature: The Classical Tradition of the Hawaiian Pig God as a Body of Literature.* La'ie, Hawai'i: Institute for Polynesian Studies, Brigham Young University, 1987.

Conner, Randy P., David Hatfield Sparks, and Mariya Sparks. *Cassell's Encyclopedia of Queer Myth, Symbol and Spirit: Gay, Lesbian, Bisexual and Transgender Lore.* New York: Cassell, 1997.

Hogan, Steve, and Lee Hudson. *Completely Queer: The Gay and Lesbian Encyclopedia.* New York: Holt, 1998.

Katz, Jonathan. *Gay American History: Lesbian and Gay Men in the U.S.A.: A Documentary.* New York: Crowell, 1976.

Martin, Robert K. *The Homosexual Tradition in American Poetry*. Austin: University of Texas Press, 1979.

Medicine, Beatrice. "Warrior Women: Sex Role Alternatives for Plains Indian Women." *The Hidden Half: Studies of Plains Indian Women*. Ed. Patricia Albers and Beatrice Medicine. Lanham, Md.: University Press of America, 1983. 270–74, 278.

Morris, Robert J. "Aikāne: Accounts of Hawaiian Same-Sex Relationships in the Journals of Captain Cook's Third Voyage (1776–80)." *Journal of Homosexuality* 19 (1990): 21–54.

———. "Same-Sex Friendships in Hawaiian Lore: Constructing the Canon." *Oceanic Homosexualities*. Ed. Stephen O. Murray. New York: Garland, 1992. 71–102.

Robertson, Carol E. "The Māhū of Hawai'i." *Feminist Studies* 15 (1989): 313–326.

Roscoe, Will. "Bibliography of Berdache and Alternative Gender Roles Among North American Indians," *Journal of Homosexuality* 14.3/4 (1987): 81–171.

———. *The Changing Ones: Third and Fourth Genders in Native North America*. New York: St. Martin's, 1998.

———. *The Zuñi Man-Woman*. Albuquerque: University of New Mexico Press, 1991.

Summers, Claude J. *Gay and Lesbian Literary Heritage: A Reader's Companion to the Writers and Their Works, from Antiquity to the Present*. New York: Holt, 1995.

Williams, Walter L. *Spirit and the Flesh: Sexual Diversity in American Indian Culture*. Boston: Beacon Press, 1992.

Woods, Gregory. *A History of Gay Literature: The Male Tradition*. New Haven, Conn.: Yale University Press, 1998.

MASQUERADE

ANONYMOUS SONGS AND CHANTS

HAWAII

Paoa's Proclamation to Hiiaka

The world is convulsed; the earth-plates sink
To the nether domain of Wakea;
Earth's rooted foundations are broken;
Flame-billows lift their heads to the sky;
The ocean-caves and reefs, the peopled land
And the circle of island coast
Are whelmed in one common disaster:
The gleam of it reaches Kahiki:—
Such blush encircles the pale apple's eye.
Heaven's blotted out, the whole sky darkened;
Hoali'i's cliffs are shadowed with gloom.
Now bellows the thunder of Winter;
Ku-lani-ha-ko'i's banks are broken;
Down pours a pitiless deluge of rain;
There's rumble and groan of the earthquake,
The reverberant roar of thunder,
The roof-stripping swoop of the tempest,
Tearing the thatch over Ele-uä,
Tearing the thatch over Ele-ao.
The freshet makes home for the water-fowl,
Flooding the thickets at Kehau,
The wide-spread waters of Kula-manu.
O Pele, fold back the curtains of heaven;
Thou Woman, consumer of Puna woods,
Swift thy foray in Hopoe's fields:
The land of contending rains is wiped out,
And the lands that border Keäau.
Up springs the steam from her caldron,
A white cloudy mountain of smoke:
She's consuming the bowlders of Long-rock,
The treacherous paths of Lau-ahea.
A flash of lightning rends the sky!
O Ku-kuena, 'tis for you to dwell

In the flaming Eastern Gate of the Sun.
The plateau of Uwé-kahuna
Breathes the reek of burning woods;
There's pelting of heads with falling stones
And loud the clang of the smitten plain,
Confused with the groan of the earthquake.
Yet this cools not the rock-eater's rage:
The Goddess grinds her teeth in the Pit.
Lo, tilted rock-plates melt like snow—
Black faces that shine like a mirror—
Sharp edges that bite the foot of a man,
The traveler's dread in the glare of the sun.
The fire-flood swells in the upland—
A robber-flood—it dries up the streams.
Here's cliff for god's jumping, when wild their sport;
Deep the basin below, and boiling hot.
The Goddess gnashes her teeth and the reek
Of her breath flies to the farthest shore.
Thine was the fault, O Goddess, thine, a
Jealous passion at all times and places—
The snap and spring of a surly dog.
Let your gnashing range to its limit,
Till it reaches the fringe of your skirt,
Your hot paü at Wai-welawela.
Trample down, O Ku, these ominous clouds;
Let them sag and fall at Ulu-nui.
They flatten, they break; look, they spread.
White loom, now, the clouds of Ulu-lani;
Fierce blazes the Sun, and Thunder
Unrolls his black curtains on high.
Then bellows his voice from the cloud—
The ominous cloud that swallows the trees.
From the crest of Moku-aweö
Pele pours out her body, her self—
A turmoil of rain and of sea-fowl.
Now boils the lake of the Goddess:
In Kau-ú an oasis-park remains;
Her smoke covers Puna with night.
What a robbery this, to crush the flowers!
My bodily self, my lehuas, gone!
My precious lehuas, clean down to Puna!
And Puna—the land is trenched and seared!
The smoke that o'erhangs it, that I can see.

High surf in the Pit, turmoiling the sky—
The god who ate Puna's Lehuas,
She 'twas laid waste green-robed Hawaii.
The heavens—let them rend, Hiiaka!
Plunge you in the wild tossing sea;
And you, who delight in the calm sea;
Hiiaka, thou thatcher of towns,
Hiiaka, soul of the flame-bud;
Hiiaka, emblemed in ti-bud;
Hiiaka, who dwells on the headland;
Hiiaka, who parts heaven's curtains;
Hiiaka—of Pele's own heart!
These tears well from eyes hot with weeping,
The eyes of this scion, this herald:
I proclaim that he's outcast, and exiled.
'Tis I, Paoä announce this:
He speaks what is meet for your ear!

NOTES

Paoa, a male *aikāne*, beloved of Lohiau, describes the effect of the volcano goddess Pele's destructive anger aimed toward her sister, Hiiaka, an *aikāne* to Hopoe. Pele had killed Hopoe.

Line 13: *Ku-lani-ha-ko'i*. The old Hawaiians imagined that somewhere in the heavens was an immense reservoir of water, and that a heavy downpour of rain was due to the breaking of its banks. When the clouds of storm and rain gathered thick and black, they saw in this phenomenon a confirmation of their belief, which gained double assurance when the clouds discharged their watery contents.

Lines 18–19: *Eleua . . . Eleao*. When a Hawaiian house had a door at each end, the door at one end was named Ele-ua, that at the other end Ele-ao.

Lines 20–21: *Kula-manu*. A plain or tract of land that was flooded in wet weather, and thus converted for a time into a resort for waterfowl, was termed a *kula-manu* or bird plain.

Line 31: *Lau-ahea*. This was a deceitful voice, a vocal Will-o'-the-wisp, that was sometimes heard by travelers and that enticed them into the wilderness or thicket there to be entrapped in some *lua meke* or fathomless pit.

Line 33: *Kuku-ena*, a sister of Pele who, like Kahili-opua, was a physician and of a benevolent disposition. She was wont to act as the guide to travelers who had their way in the mazes of a wilderness. So soon, however, as the traveler had come clear into a clear place and was able to orient himself, she modestly disappeared.

Line 70: *Kuahiwi haoa*, a term applied in Kau to a forest-clump which a devastating lava flow has spared, after having laid waste the country on all sides of it.

Shark Hula for Ka-lani-'ōpu'u

Ka-lani-'ōpu'u, the right to impose the kapu on the land is yours:
   the right of a shark with arched dorsal fin to bare teeth

of a coral reef to house a great stingray
of a *koaʻe*-bird to take wing for the upland
of an *aku*-fish to leap and plunge in the sea
of a certain mottled bird, a swift snatcher,
    to pounce alike on the small billow and the huge
and the right to bar and baffle the pathway of Ke-pani-lā,
    streaked like a tattoo, sacred marked shark of Kaʻula Island.

Now answer us, Ka-lani-ʻōpuʻu, fierce Island-Piercer!
This is your name chant:

You are a white-finned shark riding the crest of the wave,
    O Ka-lani-ʻōpuʻu:
a tiger shark resting without fear
a rain quenching the sun's eye-searing glare
a grim oven glowing underground:
    towering Ka-welo lighted it
        who caused Ka-lani-kau-lele, the Chosen, to blaze.

Their child was flaming Ka-pū-likoliko-ka-lani
she with the shark's face and flashing eyes
she of the restless questing gaze.

O Ka-lani-ʻōpuʻu, stingray as fish, man-of-war as bird
in stillness lurking or poised aloft in flight
O ʻIwa, you do unite with hooked claw the royal kapu.

Your sovereign sway surveys this island and beyond
    over the multitudinous children of Ke-aka-mahana
        by whose name you do inherit and wear by right
        the shining feather cloak.

NOTES

This is a chant of celebration for Ka-lani-ʻōpuʻu, who was a local chief during one of
Capt. Cook's expeditions to Hawaii. Ka-lani-ʻōpuʻu's *aikāne*, Palea, was the individual
with whom Cook and his officers often dealt during that voyage. Demigod Kawelo
was Kamalama's *aikāne*.

    Line 4: *koaʻe-bird:* The white-tailed or red-tailed tropicbird or bo'sunbird.
    Line 5: *aku-fish:* Skipjack, Striped tuna.
    Line 8: *Ke-pani-lā:* A shark-god of Puna said to be so huge that when he rose
to the surface of the sea his back was higher than the tiny island of Kaʻula, southwest
of Niʻihau, named for the red-tailed bo'sunbird.
    Line 17: *Ka-welo:* A warrior-hero of Kauaʻi who was a kupua (demigod) and who
performed prodigious feats of strength and bravery—throwing spears, hurling rocks,
catching giant fish. Ka-welo's elder brother was Ka-welo-mahamaha-iʻa, a great chief

of Kaua'i whose *heiau* (temple) was dedicated to the king of the shark-gods, Ka-moho-ali'i, and who was himself worshiped as a shark-god after his death.

Line 18: *Ka-lani-kau-lele:* Half sister of Keawe, father of Ka-lani-'ōpu'u; she became the wife of Ke-kau-like, ruler of Maui.

Line 19: *Ka-pū-likoliko-o-ka-lani:* A daughter of Ka-mehameha I; literally, "the conch shell burning in the sky." It is possible also to interpret the name as Kapu-likoliko-o-ka-lani, "the chiefess with the burning kapu."

Line 26: *Ke-aka-mahana:* Great-grandmother of Ka-lani-'ōpu'u, a ruling chiefess of Kona; a kapu chiefess descended from Lono-i-kamakahiki of the royal line of Hawai'i and also from royal chiefs of Kaua'i. She was thus an illustrious female ancestor of all five members of the Ka-mehameha dynasty who successively ruled the Hawaiian Kingdom for more than seventy years.

Chant of Welcome for Ka-mehameha

You, O heavenly chief, Ka-mehameha,
great warrior, hero who hooked the islands together,
you we greet in welcome: "Come in!"

Dawn has not begun to break, night has not departed,
torches still burn.
Beloved ruler, leave the rain of Hā'ao as it flies above 'Au'au-lele,
enter the home of a people who love their chief.
Bathe in the sacred pool of Pōnaha-ke-one.
Drink the *'awa* planted by Kāne in Hawai'i.

You are an emblem of life, a tribute to gods.

NOTES

Ka-mehameha I (1736?-1819) was king during one of Cook's expedition to the Hawaiian Island. His *aikane* were Kikane and Ulumaheihei.

Line 6: *'Au'au-lele:* "Flying raindrops," name of upland above Wai-o-hinu in Ka'ū.
Line 8: *Pōnaha-ke-one:* "Sandy circle," a bathing pool in Hilo. Its location is unknown today, probably because many such small springs and sea pools on major islands have been filled with town refuse, plantation trash, and other waste materials.
Line 9: *'awa:* A drink used in Polynesian ceremonies, as in the worship of Kāne. It is made of the of a shrub, the kava, native to many Pacific islands.
Line 9: *Kāne:* The leading god among the great gods; a god of creation and the ancestor of chiefs and commoners.

Kawelo's War Chant

A few are consumed, many are consumed,
All are consumed in a short space of time.

Your lehua blossoms are consumed by the birds,
They are being eaten by the birds,
The lehua blossoms that are partly eaten by the birds,
The children are sporting with your men.
The people are gathering on the sand,
They take up their boards to ride the surf.
Kamalama is like a full-grown cock.
Thou art the piercing rod; I will keep the record.
After they are slain, the record will surely be great.
Yes, gather up the spoils.
Kamalama's knees are bent down,
The food will soon be prepared,
The nose is bitten by the barking dog,
The pig will attack its master.
The shark will attack the *kala* fish,
The eel will attack the bait,
The plover will shake its tail,
Bend the knees, make him sit,
Kuahilau our opponent.
Straighten out the hair, and thus double your points.
There is a day when one is brave and a day when one is routed.
This is a cool day, Kamalama,
For the spear is darting backwards and forwards from the hand.
The spear is stringing the cliffs of lehua.
The down of a young chicken stands up,
The feathers of the cock are ruffled.
Kamalama is like a hidden reef which breaks the canoes of Wailua
Loaded down with warriors.
The highways are filled with the fleeing soldiers
Scattered and peeping like young chicks in the brush.
Forbear of the great slaughter,
Beware of thine inwards, Kamalama.
Eat up the points of the spears
Made from the rafters of Mamalahoa,
The *kauwila* wood of Puukapele,
The *hapupue* of Haalelea,
The *kee* of Kalalau.
They are as playthings for Kamalama.
Kamalama, my younger brother, come back.

NOTE

Addressed to his *aikāne*, Kawelo describes Kamalama's ferocity in battle. The phrase "younger brother" is a code used to indicate a romantic partnership between the two men.

Song

I will not chase the mirage of Maná,
That man-fooling mist of god Lima-loa,
Which still deceives the stranger—
And came nigh fooling me—the tricksy water!
The mirage of Maná is a fraud; it
Wantons with the witch Koolau.
A friend has turned up at Wailua,
Changeful Kawelo, with gills like a fish,
Has power to bring luck in any queer shape.
As a stranger now am I living,
Aye, living.
You flaunt like a person of wealth,
Yours the fish, till it comes to my hook.
I am blest at receiving from you:
Like fire-sticks flung at Ka-maile—
The visitor vainly chases the brand:
Fool! he burns his flesh to gain the red mark,
A sign for the girl he loves, oho!

NOTES

The demigod Kawelo was *aikāne* to both 'Aikanaka and Kamalama.

Line 15: *Ka-maile:* A place on Kauai where prevailed the custom of throwing firebrands down the lofty precipice of Nuololo. This amusement made a fine display at night. As the fire-sticks fell they swayed and drifted in the breeze, making it difficult for one standing below to premise their course through the air and to catch one of them before it struck the ground or the water, that being one of the objects of the sport. When a visitor had accomplished this feat, he would sometimes mark his flesh with the burning stick that he might show the brand to his sweetheart as a token of his fidelity.

Kamapuaa's Chant

Kipu is quite a little cliff, that is being traveled,
The distance to Makuaiki has not been spanned,
And I have not yet trodden its length,
Nor have I walked its width.
It is a double cliff, high and lofty,
To Mauea that is at the top.
The voice of man is at the top,
The voice of Kaiwikui is at the bottom.
Where it is pleading to the cliff of Mahukona,

For such is Kona.
Kona the small, Kona the large.
For such is man when in love,
He is overcome with love, he is ill at ease,
Ill at ease, as the women by the cliff,
Kukuiahinahina together with Kukuiahalua.
The red bosom and the white bosom,
The daughters of Kaneiki,
What are the two doing here?
Whiling away time in the uplands,
Making love. Our greetings to you two.

NOTE

Kamapuaa, who was part pig, part human, was *aikāne* to Limaloa and Nihooleki. He
chants about discovering two women making love.

Hiiaka's Lament for Hopoe

My journey opens to Kauai.
Loving is my thought for my aikane,
My bosom friend—
Hopoe—my sweet-scented hala.
Far will we go;
Broad is the land;
Perhaps Kauai is the end.

NOTE

Pele, the volcano goddess, killed Hopoe, her sister Hiiaka's *aikāne*.

Paoa's Lament for Lohiau

You've encased him tight in a lava shell,
Scorched him with tongues of flame.
Puna, the place of thy landing,
First impact of winter rain—
Sweet rain, feeding the perfume,
Drunk by vine and firm-rooted tree—
The wilderness-robe of the gods.
Here am I, too, eye-flash of flame;
As for them, no friends they of mine:

Companions mine of the stormy coast,
My love goes forth to my toil-mate
Of the mist, cold rain and driving storm;
A blazing hearth our garment then,
And to bask in the sun at Oma'o-lála.
Those seeming friends, they went with us,
And then, they left us in Puna—
Land dear to the heart of Kane:
Who eats of your soul is your true friend.
Woe is me, woe is me!

NOTE

Paoa laments the death of his *aikāne* Lohiau.

NATIVE AMERICA

Békotsĭdi's Song of Blessing

Now Békotsĭdi, that am I. For them I make.
Now child of Day Bearer am I. For them I make.
Now Day Bearer's beam of blue. For them I make.
Shines on my feet and your feet too. For them I make.
Horses of all kinds now increase. For them I make.
At my finger's tips and yours. For them I make.
Beasts of all kinds now increase. For them I make.
The bluebirds now increase. For them I make.
Soft goods of all kinds now increase. For them I make.
Now with the pollen they increase. For them I make.
Increasing now, they will last forever. For them I make.
In old age wandering on the trail of beauty. For them I make.
To form them fair, for them I labor. For them I make.

NOTES

Békotsĭdi, be'gočidi, and *Begocidi* are different spellings of the name of a Navajo creator
god. A *nadle,* the Navajo term for a "two-spirit" person, he appears in many myths.
Hasteen Klah, whose work appears later in this volume, was an especially strong
devotee of Békotsĭdi, who was son of the Sun, patron of hunters, etc. Some myths

describe Békotṣĭdi as blonde and blue-eyed. (See the introduction for a brief discussion of Native American concepts of gay, lesbian, bisexual, and transgendered individuals.)

"Békotṣĭdi and Sun Bearer (Tṣinihanoai) made all the animals while they were sitting together in the same room—Békotṣĭdi in the north, Tṣinihanoai in the south. While the former was making a horse, the latter was making the antelope, and this is why the antelope is so much like a horse. It has a mane and no small back toes as the deer has. Both of the gods sang while they were at work, and this was the song that Békotṣĭdi sang to bless all that he was making. It was the first song which he sang at his work." (Matthews)

A Stalking Song of Be'gočidí

I am starting toward it
I am as be'gočidí
I am walking toward it
As be'gočidí
Game of all kinds
I am walking toward it
I have arrived
I am being as the young of the game

Three Songs of Initiation

1. Song of the Alyha's Skirt

We weave shredded
bark into a skirt
that she may tie in front of herself.
She tells about it.
When we finish,
she wants it.
She holds the light skirt,
wraps it around her waist,
then ties it in front.
She takes it.
She tells everyone about it.
Everyone listens.
We all hear.
All the people gather
there, all do, to hear
her tell all
about it,
standing in front of us.

2. Song of the Hwame

When people stare
at the hwame,
he's proud
and struts around,
this way and that.
Then they hear the steps
in his dance
across the damp,
flat stretch of ground,
he dances
back and forth, back
and forth.
He feels it.
Even if he's a girl,
he dances that way.

3. Song of the Boy Who Paints Dice

He advances stalking.
He advances furtively.
He advances sneakingly
and reaches the willow.
He stands there
and takes it, takes it,
and furtively cuts branches
into pieces then gathers
them up and backs
away from the tree.
He comes back here.
He tells what he's done.
He divides the pieces
up, he tosses them up,
and he tells a girl
about it.
He dances.
He gathers the pieces.
He splits them into dice
and paints them. The girl
hears about
him painting the dice
and can't make *her*
do otherwise.

NOTE

The "initiation" of "Three Songs of Initiation" is the ritual Mohave young people undertook to mark the beginning of their lives as two-sprit persons. An *alyha* is a male two-spirit; the *hwame* is a female two-spirit. The first discusses the cross-dressing *alyha*'s skirt. The second describes a *hwame*'s pride. Making dice was a woman's occupation, and when a male did it, he was expressing his two-spirit nature.

A Hogan-Building Song of Be'gočidí

1.
My hogan he is making for me
I being the Talking God
My hogan he is making for me
On top of the dark mountain
He is making my hogan
With dark piñon boughs
He is making my hogan
The finest of black bucks
Are standing on the four sides of my hogan
In that way, he is making my hogan
Its death will obey me as it stands on the four sides of my hogan
In that way he is making my hogan
Its death blood in colors of red this day it shall obey me

2.
My hogan he is making for me
I being the Black God
My hogan he is making for me
On top of the blue mountain
He is making my hogan
With blue piñon boughs
He is making my hogan
The finest of the does
Are standing on the four sides of my hogan
In that way, he is making my hogan
Its death will obey me as it stands on the four sides of my hogan
In that way he is making my hogan
Its death blood in colors of red this day it shall obey me

3.
My hogan he has made for me
I being the Talking God
My hogan he has made for me

On top of the dark mountain
He has made my hogan
With dark piñon boughs
He has made my hogan
The finest of black bucks
Are standing on the four sides of my hogan
In that way, he has made my hogan
Its death will obey me as it stands on the four sides of my hogan
In that way he has made my hogan
Its death blood in colors of red this day it shall obey me

4.
My hogan he is making for me
I being the Black God
My hogan he is making for me
On top of the blue mountain
He is making my hogan
With blue piñon boughs
He is making my hogan
The finest of the does
Are standing on the four sides of my hogan
In that way, he is making my hogan
Its death will obey me as it stands on the four sides of my hogan
In that way he is making my hogan
Its death blood in colors of red this day it shall obey me

5.
He is building for me
I being the Talking God
He is building for me
On top of the dark mountain
He is building for me
With dark mirage stone
He is building for me
The finest of black bucks
Are standing on the four sides of my hogan
In that way he is building for me
Its death will obey me as it stands on the four sides of my hogan
In that way he is building my hogan
Its death blood in colors of red this day it shall obey me

6.
He is building for me
I being the Black God

He is building for me
On top of the blue mountain
He is building for me
With blue mirage stone
He is building for me
The finest of female game
Are standing on the four sides of my hogan
In that way he is building for me
Its death will obey me as it stands on the four sides of my hogan
In that way he is building my hogan
Its death blood in colors of red this day it shall obey me

7.

He has built for me
I being the Talking God
He has built for me
On top of the dark mountain
He has built for me
With dark mirage stone
He has built for me
The finest of black bucks
Are standing on the four sides of my hogan
In that way he has built for me
Its death will obey me as it stands on the four sides of my hogan
In that way he has built my hogan
Its death blood in colors of red this day it shall obey me

8.

He is building for me
I being the Black God
He is building for me
On top of the blue mountain
He is building for me
With blue mirage stone
He is building for me
The finest of female game
Are standing on the four sides of my hogan
In that way he is building for me
Its death will obey me as it stands on the four sides of my hogan
In that way he is building my hogan
Its death blood in colors of red this day it shall obey me

NOTES

Talking God and Black God are two different aspects of Be'gočidí.

"According to ancient beliefs, Be'gočidí taught this song to the Navajo." (Hill)

COWBOY

Three Limericks

1.
There was a cowboy named Hooter,
   Who packed a big six-shooter,
   When he grabbed the stock
   It became hard as a rock,
   As a peace-maker it couldn't be cuter.

2.
A cowboy named Bill from Dallas,
   Sported a tremendous phallus,
   Mainly of callous,
   He worked without malice,
   In a Fort Worth sporting palace.

3.
Young cowboys had a great fear,
   That old studs once filled with beer,
   Completely addle'
   They'd throw on a saddle,
   And ride them on the rear.

The Lavender Cowboy

He was only a lavender cowboy,
   The hairs on his chest were two.
He wanted to follow the heroes
   To do as the he-men do.

But he was inwardly troubled
   By dreams that gave no rest:

When he heard of heroes in action
  He wanted more hairs on his chest.

Herpicide and many hair tonics
  He rubbed in morning and night,
But when he looked into the mirror,
  No new hairs grew in sight.

He battled for Red Nellie's honor
  And cleaned out a hold-up nest.
He died with his six-gun a-smokin'
  But only two hairs on his chest!

The Little Bunch of Cactus on the Wall

In my old bunkhouse tonight there's a spot that is so bright,
  To my memory the time I can recall,
It was little Joe the wrangler, my cowboy so true,
  That hung that bunch of cactus on the wall.

There never was a cowboy who could ride a bronc like Joe,
  As true and dear a friend as he was brave;
Now his bronc is in the stall and his chaps hang on the wall,
  And his saddle lies a-moldering in his grave.

(Yodel)

Little Joe, his eyes were fading; on his face there was a smile,
  He said: "My pals, I'm tellin' you goodbye.
I can hear the Boss a-callin', 'Please come home, Joe, my boy,
  For you're goin' to join the roundup in the sky.' "

Little Joe, he passed away on one bright September day,
  We buried him early in the fall,
And I wouldn't take a fortune or nothing in this world
  For that little bunch of cactus on the wall.

NOTE

"The yodel suggests that we are dealing with a text from the 1930s." (Thorp)

Riding Song

Let us ride together,—
Blowing mane and hair,

Careless of the weather,
Miles ahead of care,
Ring of hoof and snaffle,
Swing of waist and hip,
Trotting down the twisted road
With the world let slip.

Let us laugh together,—
Merry as of old
To the creak of leather
And the morning cold.
Break into a canter;
Shout to bank and tree;
Rocking down the waking trail,
Steady hand and knee.

Take the life of cities,—
Here's the life for me.
'Twere a thousand pities
Not to gallop free.
So we'll ride together,
Comrade, you and I,
Careless of the weather,
Letting care go by.

VOODOO

Devotee's Song

ALegba, try to walk.
Papa Legba, I am telling you to try to walk.
When you get tired, I will carry you on my back.
Old man, I will carry you, I will carry you on my back.
If you break your legs, I will carry you on my back.
If you lose your sight, I will carry you on my back.
Atibon Legba, try to walk.
When you get tired, I will be nearby and will carry you on my back.

I say: ALegba is an old man.
Papa Legba, you are an old man.

Papa Legba, your legs are broken *sian gondo.*
Papa Legba, your legs are broken *sian gondo.*
Atibon Legba, your legs are broken *sian gondo*
Papa Legba, your legs are broken *sian gondo.*

NOTES

ALegba, Papa Legba, and Atibon Legba are different names for the same deity of the cross-roads. Embodying polar opposites—such as male/female and old age/youth—ALegba is associated with the sun's creative power and with fire and often carries a walking stick.

This song "describes the closeness and familiarity of the congregation with Legba. A devotee asks him to walk for physical fitness and makes himself available to help. He urges the *loa* to do some exercises for his health. Legba is so old that he has lost his sight, his legs are weak, and he gets tired very quickly." (Laguerre 49)

Lesson Song

I am entering the *lakou.*
I am asking if there is any adult in, Ago-e.
I am asking if there is any adult in, Ago-e.
Good morning, mother, good morning, my dear son.
Good morning, mother, good morning, my dear son.
I am still asking if there is any adult here.
O God, if there is no adult here,
I shall get in and do whatever I want.
I shall leave the *lakou* afterwards and nobody will be there to ask me:
What have you been doing here?
I will leave the place with my reputation being untouched.

NOTE

"In the beginning of any Voodoo ceremony, the congregation may call upon Legba for a possession-trance. He will appear to greet them and to engage in conversation with adult males and females. In this scene, the domain is no long the Voodoo temple, but a *lakou.* He is greeted by the congregation as 'mother' and he refers to them as children. This is a dialogue song in which the spirit and the congregation engage in conversation. Legba is reminding the people that they must watch over their property, for if they do not, it may be stolen or destroyed and the perpetrator will go unpunished." (Laguerre 52)

Invisibility Song

I called them, I did not see them.
They call me, I did not see them.

They call me for a possession trance
And I turn into wind.
They call me into the sea,
I turn into a sea-snake.
Who is going to be able to see me?

NOTES

Danbala—or Damballah—is the male aspect of the Rainbow Serpent. (Aido Hwedo is its female aspect.) She/he lives in rivers and other watery places and is associated with happiness.

"Danbala is not visible outside of possession trance, and he does not always reveal himself to the public when called upon to possess an individual. He may turn himself into wind or a sea-snake, depending on the circumstances." (Laguerre 87)

Priest's Song

I say to Guédé Nibo, here is some money for you.
I want to give you some money to protect the temple for me.
Guédé Nibo, here is some money for you.
Guédé, I say, here is some money for you.
I give it to you precisely so that you can protect my temple.
Guédé, I say, Guédé, I say, here is some money for you.
Look at this money I give you to protect the temple for me.
Guédé, Guédé Nibo, here is some money.
I give you this money precisely
So that you can protect the temple for me, Guédé.

NOTES

Guédé Nibo (also Ghede Nibo) is leader of the dead who often cross-dresses and is considered transsexual, gay, or pansexual, depending on the context in which he is depicted.

"A Voodoo priest supplicates Guédé Nibo to accept money from him and to become one of the spirit protectors of the temple. This is a way to avoid having dead ancestors come back to annoy the members of the congregation. The power of Guédé Nibo over the dead makes him well suited to this kind of job." (Laguerre 99)

Song Announcing Death

Someone is sick in my family.
They ask me to come over.
Someone is sick in my family.

One of my associates is leaving.
One of my associates is leaving.
He may come to see where I am living.
He may come to see where I keep my magical spells.

NOTES

Father of Guédé Nibo, Baron Samedi is the bisexual (occasionally transgendered) leader of the barons and the guides, of the dead, and husband of Maman Brigitte.

"When someone is dying, his relatives may announce the news to Baron Samedi and ask him to take care of the person after death. In this poem, it is said that a Voodoo priest is about to die. Baron Samedi welcomes him to be one of his subjects." (Laguerre 101)

Song of Reproach

I am not a sheet, if I were one,
I would let them use me as their cover.
Some day they will need me,
Some day they will need me.
I am Guédé Nibo, I am not a sheet.
When they are sick,
They all love me.
When they are healthy, they say Guédé is no good.
When they are healthy, they say Guédé is no good.

NOTE

"Guédé Nibo reproaches the congregation because the people exploit him during life crises; and when everything is all right, they forget about him." (Laguerre 101)

Song of Allegiance

I say good or not,
You are my spirit protector.
You are my spirit protector, Guédé Nibo.
Guédé Nibo, you are my spirit protector.
Troublemaker, you are my spirit protector.
Fighter, you are my good spirit.
Good or not, Guédé Nibo,
You are my spirit protector.

NOTE

"Devotees confirm their allegiance to Guédé Nibo; they do not pay attention to the good or bad comments people make about Guédé Nibo's behavior. They cling to Guédé Nibo as their spirit protector and want him to be aware of that." (Laguerre 102)

Song Requesting Protection

The tree falls down and the nightingale starts flying.
The tree falls down and the nightingale starts flying.
I am begging.
I am begging.
The master of the cemetery, the keeper of the crosses,
The spirit who can get everything, the good priest,
Do something for us before we leave.
We are orphans and are begging.
I shall work, I shall work for them,
I shall work in front of the cemetery.
We are going to ask where are you.
We are going to ask where are you.
We call you seven times and you do not show up.
Malfectè lacoa, you are a good priest.
They call you seven times and you do not show up.
As the guardian of the cemetery and the crosses,
You must be a very old spirit.
They call you seven times and you do not show up.

NOTE

"The congregation asks Baron Samedi for protection. The number seven in Voodooism is a symbol of multitude." (Laguerre 103)

FITZ-GREENE HALLECK
1790–1867

[To Carlos Menie]

Though stormy billows roll between,
  And raging winds unite;
And leagues of ocean intervene,
  To hide you from my sight:

Though days and months have rolled away,
  And many a circling year,
Since that lamented, mournful day,
  That caused the parting tear:

Yet still, by fond remembrance taught,
  Your pleasing form I view;
And in my hours of lonely thought
  I muse and think of you.

Time, whose destroying, wasting hand
  Bears all before its sway,
As marks imprinted on the sand
  The ocean sweeps away—

Yet hath its circuit rolled in vain
  Your memory to efface;
Still every feature I retain,
  And every gesture trace.

Oft in the stillness of the night,
  When slumbers close mine eyes,
Your image bursts upon my sight;
  I gaze in glad surprise!

And oft when evening's mantle gray
  Is o'er the valleys spread,
With pensive steps I musing stray
  By roving fancy led.

Her wild, romantic flights unfold
  Events of former days;

And scenes on memory's page unrolled,
  Her backward glance surveys:

When, by youth's cheering smiles caressed,
  We passed the social hours;
When calm enjoyment, sportive, dressed
  Life's opening path with flowers.

And say, my friend, does memory bring
  These pleasure to *your* heart?
Can thoughts, which from remembrance spring,
  A rapturous charm impart?

Ah, yes! that gentle heart I know,
  At friendship's touch it beats;
I feel the sympathetic glow,
  My breast the throb repeats.

Then let us cherish well the flame
  Of friendship and of love;
Let peaceful virtue be our aim,
  Our hopes be placed above.

There, in affliction, may we find
  A refuge ever nigh;
May time our friendly union bind,
  And years cement the tie.

Wherever on life's varied stage—
  A devious maze—you go,
Whether where winter's tempests rage
  Or summer's breezes blow:

Yet in your hours of solitude,
  When the calm mind is free,
Let the remembrance oft intrude
  Of friendship and of me.

Secure along Life's winding stream,
  Calm may your moments glide;
And may the Almighty Power supreme
  Your wavering footsteps guide.

May He preserve you free from woe,
  Through time's few fleeting years;
And never-ending bliss bestow
  Beyond the vale of tears!

Carlos, adieu! within my heart
  Your memory firm shall dwell;
Till, pierced by death's unerring dart,
  I bid the world farewell!

Song

By Miss ****
Air: "To ladies' eyes a round, boy."
—MOORE

The winds of March are humming
  Their parting song, their parting song,
And summer skies are coming,
  And days grow long, and days grow long.
I watch, but not in gladness,
  Our garden-tree, our garden-tree;
It buds, in sober sadness,
  Too soon for me, too soon for me.
    My second winter's over,
      Alas! and I, alas! and I
    Have no accepted lover:
      Don't ask me why, don't ask me why.

'Tis not asleep or idle
  That Love has been, that Love has been;
For many a happy bridal
  The year has seen, the year has seen:
I've done a bridemaid's duty,
  At three or four, at three or four;
My best bouquet had beauty,
  Its donor more, its donor more.
    My second winter's over,
      Alas! and I, alas! and I
    Have no accepted lover:
      Don't ask me why, don't ask me why.

His flowers my bosom shaded
  One sunny day, one sunny day;
The next they fled and faded,
  Beau and bouquet, beau and bouquet.
In vain, at balls and parties,
  I've thrown my net, I've thrown my net;

This waltzing, watching heart is
    Unchosen yet, unchosen yet.
        My second winter's over,
            Alas! and I, alas! and I
        Have no accepted lover:
            Don't ask me why, don't ask me why.

They tell me there's no hurry
    For Hymen's ring, for Hymen's ring;
And I'm too young to marry:
    'Tis no such thing, 'tis no such thing.
The next spring-tides will dash on
    My eighteenth year, my eighteenth year;
It puts me in a passion,
    Oh, dear, oh dear! oh dear, oh dear!
        My second winter's over,
            Alas! and I, alas! and I
        Have no accepted lover:
            Don't ask me why, don't ask me why.

On the Death of Joseph Rodman Drake, of New York, Sept., 1820

> "The good die first,
> And they, whose hearts are dry as summer dust,
> Burn to the socket."
>
> —WORDSWORTH

Green be the turf above thee,
    Friend of my better days!
None knew thee but to love thee,
    Nor named thee but to praise.

Tears fell when thou wert dying,
    From eyes unused to weep,
And long, where thou art lying,
    Will tears the cold turf steep.

When hearts, whose truth was proven,
    Like thine, are laid in earth,
There should a wreath be woven
    To tell the world their worth;

And I who woke each morrow
    To clasp thy hand in mine,

Who shared thy joy and sorrow,
  Whose weal and woe were thine:

It should be mine to braid it
  Around thy faded brow,
But I've in vain essayed it,
  And feel I cannot now.

While memory bids me weep thee,
  Nor thoughts nor words are free,
The grief is fixed too deeply
  That mourns a man like thee.

RALPH WALDO EMERSON
1803–1883

From Frodmer's Drama *The Friends*

Malcolm, I love thee more than women love
And pure and warm and equal is the feeling
Which binds us and our destinies forever
But there are seasons in the change of times
When strong excitement kindles up the light
Of ancient memories

Love and Thought

Two well-assorted travellers use
The highway, Eros and the Muse.
From the twins is nothing hidden,
To the pair is nought forbidden;
Hand in hand the comrades go
Every nook of Nature through:
Each for other they were born,
Each can other best adorn;
They know one only mortal grief

Past all balsam or relief;
When, by false companions crossed,
The pilgrims have each other lost.

Friendship

A ruddy drop of manly blood
The surging sea outweighs,
The world uncertain comes and goes;
The lover rooted stays.
I fancied he was fled,—
And, after many a year,
Glowed unexhausted kindliness,
Like daily sunrise there.
My careful heart was free again,
O friend, my bosom said,
Through thee alone the sky is arched,
Through thee the rose is red;
All things through thee take nobler form,
And look beyond the earth,
The mill-round of our fate appears
A sun-path in thy worth.
Me too thy nobleness has taught
To master my despair;
The fountains of my hidden life
Are through thy friendship fair.

NATHANIEL PARKER WILLIS
1806–1867

To—

Thy love is like the thread of a new moon
Drawn on the faint blue of a break in clouds:—
The thunder of a storm not surely o'er

Murmurs beneath it, and the lightning gleams
Brokenly still, in one mass dark and near,
As if it would close turbulently o'er,
And make all black again. But, motionless,
As 'twere an angel's shallop in a calm,
The bent moon floats, and its round freight of hope
Lies in its breast—to unbelieving eyes
A shadow that can never grow more fair,—
But, to the clearer-sighted stars, a promise
Of brightness that will wax to fill a heaven.

The Annoyer

> Common as light is love,
> And its familiar voice wearies not ever.
> —SHELLEY

Love knoweth every form of air,
    And every shape of earth,
And comes, unbidden, everywhere,
    Like thought's mysterious birth.
The moonlit sea and the sunset sky
    Are written with Love's words,
And you hear his voice unceasingly,
    Like song in the time of birds.

He peeps into the warrior's heart
    From the tip of a stooping plume,
And the serried spears and the many men
    May not deny him room.
He'll come to his tent in the weary night,
    And be busy in his dream;
And he'll float to his eye in morning light
    Like a fay on a silver beam.

He hears the sound of the hunter's gun,
    And rides on the echo back,
And sighs in his ear, like a stirring leaf,
    And flits in his woodland track.
The shade of the wood, and the sheen of the river,
    The cloud and the open sky—
He will haunt them all with his subtle quiver,
    Like the light of your very eye.

The fisher hangs over the leaning boat,
  And ponders the silver sea,
For Love is under the surface hid,
  And a spell of thought has he.
He heaves the wave like a bosom sweet,
  And speaks in the ripple low,
Till the bait is gone from the crafty line,
  And the hook hangs bare below.

He blurs the print of the scholar's book,
  And intrudes in the maiden's prayer,
And profanes the cell of the holy man,
  In the shape of a lady fair.
In the darkest night, and the bright daylight,
  In earth, and sea, and sky,
In every home of human thought,
  Will Love be lurking nigh.

The Confessional

When thou hast met with careless hearts and cold,
Hearts that young love may touch, but never hold—
Not changeless, as the loved and left of old—
  Remember me—remember me—
  I passionately pray of thee!

—Lady E.S. Wortley

I thought of thee—I thought of thee,
  On ocean many a weary night—
When heaved the long and sullen sea,
  With only waves and stars in sight.
We stole along by isles of balm,
  We furl'd before the coming gale,
We slept amid the breathless calm,
  We flew beneath the straining sail—
But thou wert lost for years to me,
And, day and night, I thought of thee!

I thought of thee—I thought of thee,
  In France—amid the gay saloon,
Where eyes as dark as eyes may be
  Are many as the leaves in June—
Where life is love, and even the air
  Is pregnant with impassion'd thought,

And song and dance and music are
　　With one warm meaning only fraught—
My half-snared heart broke lightly free,
And, with a blush, I thought of thee!

I thought of thee—I thought of thee,
　　In Florence,—where the fiery hearts
Of Italy are breathed away
　　In wonders of the deathless arts;
Where strays the Contadina down
　　Val d'Arno with a song of old;
Where clime and woman seldom frown,
　　And life runs over sands of gold;
I stray'd to lone Fiesolé
On many an eve, and thought of thee.

I thought of thee—I thought of thee,
　　In Rome,—when on the Palatine
Night left the Caesars' palace free
　　To Time's forgetful foot and mine;
Or, on the Coliseum's wall,
　　When moonlight touch'd the ivied stone,
Reclining, with a thought of all
　　That o'er this scene has come and gone—
The shades of Rome would start and flee
Unconsciously—I thought of thee.

I thought of thee—I thought of thee,
　　In Vallombrosa's holy shade,
Where nobles born the friars be,
　　By life's rude changes humbler made.
Here Milton framed his Paradise;
　　I slept within his very cell;
And, as I closed my weary eyes,
　　I thought the cowl would fit me well—

The cloisters breathed, it seem'd to me,
Of heart's ease—but I thought of thee.

I thought of thee—I thought of thee,
　　In Venice,—on a night in June;
When, through the city of the sea,
　　Like dust of silver slept the moon.
Slow turn'd his oar the gondolier,
　　And, as the black barks glided by,

The water to my leaning ear
   Bore back the lover's passing sigh—
It was no place alone to be—
I thought of thee—I thought of thee.

I thought of thee—I thought of thee,
   In the Ionian isles—when straying
With wise Ulysses by the sea—
   Old Homer's songs around me playing;
Or, watching the bewitch'd caique,
   That o'er the star-lit waters flew,
I listen'd to the helmsman Greek,
   Who sung the song that Sappho knew—
The poet's spell, the bark, the sea,
All vanish'd—as I thought of thee.

I thought of thee—I thought of thee,
   In Greece—when rose the Parthenon
Majestic o'er the Egean sea,
   And heroes with it, one by one;
When, in the grove of Academe,
   Where Lais and Leontium stray'd
Discussing Plato's mystic theme,
   I lay at noontide in the shade—
The Egean wind, the whispering tree,
Had voices—and I thought of thee.

I thought of thee—I thought of thee,
   In Asia—on the Dardanelles;
Where swiftly as the waters flee,
   Each wave some sweet old story tells;
And, seated by the marble tank
   Which sleeps by Ilium's ruins old,
(The fount where peerless Helen drank,
   And Venus laved her locks of gold,)
I thrill'd such classic haunts to see,
Yet even here—I thought of thee

I thought of thee—I thought of thee,
   Where glide the Bosphor's lovely waters,
All palace-lined from sea to sea;
   And ever on its shores the daughters
Of the delicious East are seen,
   Printing the brink with slipper'd feet.
And oh, the snowy folds between,

What eyes of heaven your glances meet!
Peris of light no fairer be—
Yet—in Stamboul—I thought of thee.

I've thought of thee—I've thought of thee,
    Through change that teaches to forget;
Thy face looks up from every sea,
    In every star thine eyes are set,
Though roving beneath Orient skies,
    Whose golden beauty breathes of rest,
I envy every bird that flies
    Into the far and clouded West:
I think of thee—I think of thee!
Oh, dearest! hast thou thought of me?

MARGARET FULLER
1810–1850

The Dahlia, the Rose, and the Heliotrope

In a fair garden of a distant land,
    Where autumn skies the softest blue outspread,
    A lovely crimson dahlia reared her head,
To drink the lustre of the season's prime;
    And drink she did, until her cup o'erflowed
    With ruby redder than the sunset cloud.

Near to her root she saw the fairest rose
    That ever oped her soul to sun and wind,
And still the more her sweets she did disclose,
    The more her queenly heart of sweets did find,
    Not only for her worshipper the wind,
But for bee, nightingale, and butterfly,
Who would with ceaseless wing about her ply,
    Nor ever cease to seek what found they still would find
Upon the other side, nearer the ground,
    A paler floweret on a slender stem,

That cast so exquisite a fragrance round,
   As seemed the minute blossom to contemn,
Seeking an ampler urn to hold its sweetness,
And in a statelier shape to find completeness.

Who could refuse to hear that keenest voice,
Although it did not bid the heart rejoice,
And though the nightingale had just begun
His hymn; the evening breeze begun to woo,
When through the charming of the evening dew,
The floweret did its secret soul disclose?
By that revealing touched, the queenly rose
Forgot them both, a deeper joy to hope
And heed the love-note of the heliotrope.

Absence of Love

Though many at my feet have bowed,
   And asked my love through pain and pleasure,
Fate never yet the youth has showed
   Meet to receive so great a treasure.

Although sometimes my heart, deceived,
   Would love because it sighed *to feel*,
Yet soon I changed, and sometimes grieved
   Because my fancied wound would heal.

The One in All

There are who separate the eternal light
In forms of man and woman, day and night;
They cannot bear that God be essence quite.

Existence is as deep a verity:
Without the dual, where is unity?
And the "I am" cannot forbear to be;

But from its primal nature forced to frame
Mysteries, destinies of various name,
Is forced to give what it has taught to claim.

Thus love must answer to its own unrest;
The bad commands us to expect the best,
And hope of its own prospects is the test.

And dost thou seek to find the one in two?
Only upon the old can build the new;
The symbol which you seek is found in you.

The heart and mind, the wisdom and the will,
The man and woman, must be severed still,
And Christ must reconcile the good and ill.

There are to whom each symbol is a mask;
The life of love is a mysterious task;
They want no answer, for they would not ask.

A single thought transfuses every form;
The sunny day is changed into the storm,
For light is dark, hard soft, and cold is warm.

One presence fills and floods the whole serene;
Nothing can be, nothing has ever been,
Except the one truth that creates the scene.

Does the heart beat,—that is a seeming only;
You cannot be alone, though you are lonely;
The All is neutralized in the One only.

You ask *a* faith,—they are content with faith;
You ask to have,—but they reply, "It hath."
There is no end, and there need be no path.

The day wears heavily,—why, then, ignore it;
Peace is the soul's desire,—such thoughts restore it;
The truth thou art,—it needs not to implore it.

The Presence all thy fancies supersedes,
All that is done which thou wouldst seek in deeds,
The wealth obliterates all seeming needs.

Both these are true, and if they are at strife,
The mystery bears the one name of *Life*,
That, slowly spelled, will yet compose the strife.

The men of old say, "Live twelve thousand years,
And see the end of all that here appears,
And Moxen shall absorb thy smiles and tears."

These later men say, "Live this little day.
Believe that human nature is the way,
And know both Son and Father while you pray;

And one in two, in three, and none alone,
Letting you know even as you are known,
Shall make the you and me eternal parts of one."

To me, our destinies seem flower and fruit
Born of an ever-generating root;
The other statement I cannot dispute.

But say that Love and Life eternal seem,
And if eternal ties be but a dream,
What is the meaning of that self-same *seem*?

Your nature craves Eternity for Truth;
Eternity of Love is prayer of youth;
How, without love, would have gone forth your truth?

I do not think we are deceived to grow,
But that the crudest fancy, slightest show,
Covers some separate truth that we may know.

In the one Truth, each separate fact is true;
Eternally in one I many view,
And destinies through destiny pursue.

This is *my* tendency; out can I say
That this my thought leads the true, only way?
I only know it constant leads, and I obey.

I only know one prayer—"Give me the truth,
Give me that colored whiteness, ancient youth,
Complex and simple, seen in joy and ruth.

Let me not by vain wishes bar my claim,
Nor soothe my hunger by an empty name,
Nor crucify the Son of man by hasty blame.

But in the earth and fire, water and air,
Live earnestly by turns without despair,
Nor seek a home till home be every where !"

NOTE

Line 45: *Moxen,* Buddhist term for absorption into the divine mind.

HENRY DAVID THOREAU
1817–1862

Indeed indeed, I cannot tell

Indeed indeed, I cannot tell,
Though I ponder on it well,
Which were easier to state,
All my love or all my hate.
Surely, surely, thou wilt trust me
When I say thou dost disgust me.
O, I hate thee with a hate
That would fain annihilate;
Yet sometimes against my will,
My dear friend, I love thee still.
It were treason to our love,
And a sin to God above,
One iota to abate
Of a pure impartial hate.

I'm guided in the darkest night

I'm guided in the darkest night
By flashes of auroral light,
Which over dart thy eastern home
And teach me not in vain to roam.
Thy steady light on t'other side
Pales the sunset, makes day abide,
And after sunrise stays the dawn,
Forerunner of a brighter morn.

There is no being here to me
But staying here to be
When other laugh I am not glad,
When others cry I am not sad,
But be they grieved or be they merry
I'm supernumerary.
I am a miser without blame
Am conscience stricken without shame.

An idler am I without leisure,
A busy body without pleasure.
I did not think so bright a day
Would issue in so dark a night.
I did not think such sober play
Would leave me in so sad a plight,
And I should be most sorely spent
Where first I was most innocent.
I thought by loving all beside
To prove to you my love was wide,
And by the rites I soared above
To show you my peculiar love.

I knew a man by sight

I knew a man by sight,
    A blameless wight,
Who, for a year or more,
Had daily passed my door,
Yet converse none had had with him.

I met him in a lane,
    Him and his cane,
About three miles from home,
Where I had chanced to roam,
And volumes stared at him, and he at me.

In a more distant place
    I glimpsed his face,
And bowed instinctively;
Starting he bowed to me,
Bowed simultaneously, and passed along.

Next, in a foreign land
    I grasped his hand,
And had a social chat,
About this thing and that,
As I had known him well a thousand years.

Late in a wilderness
    I shared his mess,
For he had hardships seen,
And I a wanderer been;
He was my bosom friend, and I was his.

And as, methinks, shall all,
   Both great and small,
That ever lived on earth,
   Early or late their birth,
Stranger and foe, one day each other know.

HERMAN MELVILLE
1819–1891

Monody

To have known him, to have loved him
   After loneness long;
And then to be estranged in life,
   And neither in the wrong;
And now for death to set his seal—
   Ease me, a little ease, my song!

By wintry hills his hermit-mound
   The sheeted snow-drifts drape,
And houseless there the snow-bird flits
   Beneath the fir-trees' crape:
Glazed now with ice the cloistral vine
   That hid the shyest grape.

C—'s Lament

How lovely was the light of heaven,
What angels leaned from out the sky
In years when youth was more than wine
And man and nature seemed divine
Ere yet I felt that youth must die.

Ere yet I felt that youth must die
How insubstantial looked the earth,
Alladin-land! in each advance,

Or here or there, a new romance;
I never dreamed would come a dearth.

And nothing then but had its worth,
Even pain. Yes, pleasure still and pain
In quick reaction made of life
A lovers' quarrel, happy strife
In youth that never comes again.

But will youth never come again?
Even to his grave-bed has he gone,
And left me lone to wake by night
With heavy heart that erst was light?
O, lay it at his head—a stone!

After the Pleasure Party: Lines Traced Under an Image of Amor Threatening

> *Fear me, virgin whosoever*
> *Taking pride from love exempt,*
> *Fear me, slighted. Never, never*
> *Brave me, nor my fury tempt:*
> *Downy wings, but wroth they beat*
> *Tempest even in reason's seat.*

Behind the house the upland falls
With many an odorous tree—
White marbles gleaming through green halls,
Terrace by terrace, down and down,
And meets the starlit Mediterranean Sea.

'Tis Paradise. In such an hour
Some pangs that rend might take release.
Nor less perturbed who keeps this bower
Of balm, nor finds balsamic peace?
From whom the passionate words in vent
After long revery's discontent?

Tired of the homeless deep,
Look how their flight yon hurrying billows urge,
Hitherward but to reap
Passive repulse from the iron-bound verge!
Insensate, can they never know
'Tis mad to wreck the impulsion so?

An art of memory is, they tell:
But to forget! forget the glade
Wherein Fate sprung Love's ambuscade,
To flour pale years of cloistral life
And flush me in this sensuous strife.
'Tis Vesta struck with Sappho's smart.
No fable her delirious leap:
With more of cause in desperate heart,
Myself could take it—but to sleep!

Now first I feel, what all may ween,
That soon or late, if faded e'en,
One's sex asserts itself. Desire,
The dear desire through love to sway,
Is like the Geysers that aspire—
Through cold obstruction win their fervid way.
But baffled here—to take disdain,
To feel rule's instinct, yet not reign;
To dote, to come to this drear shame—
Hence the winged blaze that sweeps my soul
Like prairie fires that spurn control,
Where withering weeds incense the flame.

And kept I long heaven's watch for this,
Contemning love, for this, even this?
O terrace chill in Northern air,
O reaching ranging tube I placed
Against yon skies, and fable chased
Till, fool, I hailed for sister there
Starred Cassiopea in Golden Chair.
In dream I throned me, nor I saw
In cell the idiot crowned with straw.

And yet, ah yet scarce ill I reigned,
Through self-illusion self-sustained,
When now—enlightened, undeceived—
What gain I barrenly bereaved!
Than this can be yet lower decline—
Envy and spleen, can these be mine?

The pleasant girl demure that trod
Beside our wheels that climbed the way,
And bore along a blossoming rod
That looked the sceptre of May-day—
On her—to fire this petty hell,

His softened glance how moistly fell!
The cheat! on briars her buds were strung;
And wiles peeped forth from mien how meek.
The innocent bare-foot! young, so young!
To girls, strong man's a novice weak.
To tell such beads! And more remain,
Sad rosary of belittling pain.

When after lunch and sallies gay,
Like the Decameron folk we lay
In sylvan groups; and I—let be!
O, dreams he, can he dream that one
Because not roseate feels no sun?
The plain lone bramble thrills with Spring
As much as vines that grapes shall bring.

Me now fair studies charm no more.
Shall great thoughts writ, or high themes sung
Damask wan cheeks—unlock his arm
About some radiant ninny flung?
How glad with all my starry lore,
I'd buy the veriest wanton's rose
Would but my bee therein repose.

Could I remake me! or set free
This sexless bound in sex, then plunge
Deeper than Sappho, in a lunge
Piercing Pan's paramount mystery!
For, Nature, in no shallow surge
Against thee either sex may urge,
Why hast thou made us but in halves—
Co-relatives? This makes us slaves.
If these co-relatives never meet
Self-hood itself seems incomplete.
And such the dicing of blind fate
Few matching halves here meet and mate.
What Cosmic jest or Anarch blunder
The human integral clove asunder
And shied the fractions through life's gate?

Ye stars that long your votary knew
Rapt in her vigil, see me here!
Whither is gone the spell ye threw
When rose before me Cassiopea?
Usurped on by love's stronger reign—

But lo, your very selves do wane:
Light breaks—truth breaks! Silvered no more,
But chilled by dawn that brings the gale
Shivers yon bramble above the vale,
And disillusion opens all the shore.

    One knows not if Urania yet
The pleasure-party may forget;
Or whether she lived down the strain
Of turbulent heart and rebel brain;
For Amor so resents a slight,
And her's had been such haught disdain,
He long may wreak his boyish spite,
And boy-like, little reck the pain.

    One knows not, no. But late in Rome
(For queens discrowned a congruous home)
Entering Albani's porch she stood
Fixed by an antique pagan stone
Colossal carved. No anchorite seer,
Not Thomas a Kempis, monk austere,
Religious more are in their tone;
Yet far, how far from Christian heart
That form august of heathen Art.
Swayed by its influence, long she stood,
Till surged emotion seething down,
She rallied and this mood she won:

    Languid in frame for me,
To-day by Mary's convent shrine,
Touched by her picture's moving plea
In the poor nerveless hour of mine,
I mused—A wanderer still must grieve.
Half I resolved to kneel and believe,
Believe and submit, the veil take on.
But thee, armed Virgin! less benign,
Thee now I invoke, tough mightier one.
Helmeted woman—if such term
Befit thee, far from strife
Of that which makes the sexual feud
And clogs the aspirant life—
O self-reliant, strong and free,
Thou in whom power and peace unite,

Transcender! raise me up to thee,
Raise me and arm me!

                    Fond appeal.
For never passion peace shall bring,
Nor Art inanimate for long
Inspire. Nothing may help or heal
While Amor incensed remembers wrong.
Vindictive, not himself he'll spare;
For scope to give his vengenance play
Himself he'll blaspheme and betray.

    Then for Urania, virgins everywhere,
O pray! Example take too, and have care.

WALT WHITMAN
1819–1892

In Paths Untrodden

In paths untrodden,
In the growth by margins of pond-waters,
Escaped from the life that exhibits itself,
From all the standards hitherto publish'd, from the pleasures, profits,
    conformities,
Which too long I was offering to feed my soul,
Clear to me now standards not yet publish'd, clear to me that my
    soul,
That the soul of the man I speak for rejoices in comrades,
Here by myself away from the clank of the world,
Tallying and talk'd to here by tongues aromatic,
No longer abash'd, (for in this secluded spot I can respond as I
    would not dare elsewhere,)
Strong upon me the life that does not exhibit itself, yet contains all
    the rest,
Resolv'd to sing no songs to-day but those of manly attachment,

Projecting them along that substantial life,
Bequeathing hence types of athletic love,
Afternoon this delicious Ninth-month in my forty-first year,
I proceed for all who are or have been young men,
To tell the secret of my nights and days,
To celebrate the need of comrades.

City of Orgies

City of orgies, walks and joys,
City whom that I have lived and sung in your midst will one day
make you illustrious,
Not the pageants of you, not your shifting tableaus, your spectacles,
repay me,
Not the interminable rows of your houses, nor the ships at the
wharves,
Nor the processions in the streets, nor the bright windows with
goods in them,
Nor to converse with learn'd persons, or bear my share in the soiree
or feast;
Not those, but as I pass O Manhattan, your frequent and swift flash
of eyes offering me love,
Offering response to my own—these repay me,
Lovers, continual lovers, only repay me.

We Two Boys Together Clinging

We two boys together clinging,
One the other never leaving,
Up and down the roads going, North and South excursions making,
Power enjoying, elbows stretching, fingers clutching,
Arm'd and fearless, eating, drinking, sleeping, loving,
No law less than ourselves owning, sailing, soldiering, thieving,
threatening,
Misers, menials, priests alarming, air breathing, water drinking, on
the turf or the sea-beach dancing,
Cities wrenching, ease scorning, statutes mocking, feebleness
chasing,
Fulfilling our foray.

GEORGE HENRY BOKER
1823–1890

From *Sonnets: A Sequence on Profane Love*

XXXIII

As some new ghost, that wanders to and fro
By dreary Lethe, turns his vacant eyes,
Drowsy with recent death, to those dull skies,
And barren lands, and that black river's flow;
And finds, poor ghost, how strange and stranger grow
The wretched scene; till, stung with wild surprise,
His earthly memory lifts its piteous cries
For what it loved, but never more shall know.
Now thou art gone, so seems this empty place,
A darkness settles down o'er land and main,
A strangeness haunts the chambers of my brain;
Gone is the splendor of thy radiant face,
No prayer can summon back its tender grace;
So I lie down, and strive to die again.

LV

I strive to live my life in whitest truth,
Even in the face of this deceitful world;
And if in errors I am caught and whirled
From the fair courses of my candid youth,
I view my trespasses with thoughtful ruth;
And the poor mummer's scornful lip is curled,
And a low curse indignantly is hurled
At arts which others blindly take as sooth.
But when I enter thy pure presence, Sweet,
I come as one into a holy shrine.
I taste the mystic wafer and the wine,
And fraud and falsehood from my heart retreat.
Through thy divinity I grow divine,
And my world's mask lies empty at thy feet.

LXXIII

The satyr nature riots in my blood.
"Of the earth, earthly!" I in vain exclaim.
The text falls on me with its weight of blame,

Yet moves my stubborn feet no step towards good.
What is this fiend that cannot be withstood
By reason, pity, or consuming shame,
That makes my strongest purpose limping lame,
And melts to nought my manly hardihood?
Surely some mother of my buried race
Was caught by Pan, fast sleeping, in his grove,
And filled the hairy round of his embrace;
That I, their far descendant, blindly move
With the fierce frenzy of that ancient love,
And burn with fire whose source I cannot trace.

THOMAS WENTWORTH HIGGINSON
1823–1911

The Knock Alphabet

> Mr. Kennan tells us that Russian prisoners
> converse with each other in a complex alpha-
> bet, indicated by knocking on the walls of
> their cells.

Like prisoners, each within his own deep cell,
  We mortals talk together through a wall.
  "Was that low note indeed my brother's call?
  Or but a distant water-drop which fell?"
Yet to the straining ear each sound can tell
  Some woe that might the bravest heart appal,
  Or some high hope that triumphs over all:
  "Brother, I die to-morrow." "Peace!" "All's well!"
Oh, could we once see fully, face to face,
  But one of these our mates,—once speak aloud,
  Once meet him, heart to heart, in strong embrace,—
How would our days be glad, our hopes be proud!
  Perchance that wall is Life; and life being done,
  Death may unite these sundered cells in one.

Dwelling-Places

Where is thy home, O little fair head,
With thy sunny hair, on earth's clouded way?
"On my lover's breast; and I take my rest,
And I know no terror by night or day."

Where is thy home, O little fair heart,
With thy joyous hopes in life's shadows dim?
"In my lover's heart; and we never part,
For he carries me round the world with him."

Where is thy home, O little fair soul,
So brave 'mid the old world's sorrow and care?
"My home is in heaven. To me 't is given
To win my lover to meet me there."

To My Shadow

A mute companion at my side
Paces and plods, the whole day long,
Accepts the measure of my stride,
Yet gives no cheer by word or song.

More close than any doggish friend,
Not ranging far and wide, like him,
He goes where'er my footsteps tend,
Nor shrinks for fear of life or limb.

I do not know when first we met,
But till each day's bright hours are done
This grave and speechless silhouette
Keeps me betwixt him and the sun.

They say he knew me when a child;
Born with my birth, he dies with me;
Not once from his long task beguiled,
Though sin or shame bid others flee.

What if, when all this world of men
Shall melt and fade and pass away,
This deathless sprite should rise again
And be himself my Judgment Day?

RICHARD HENRY STODDARD
1825–1903

On the Town

The lamps are lighted, the streets are full,
   For coming and going like waves of the sea,
Thousands are out this beautiful night;
   They jostle each other, but shrink from me.
Men hurry by with a stealthy glance,
   Women pass with their eyes cast down;
Even the children seem to know
   The shameless girl of the town.

Hated and shunned I walk the street,
   Hunting—for what? For my prey, 'tis said;
I look at it, though, in a different light,
   For this nightly shame is my daily bread:
My food, my shelter, the clothes I wear,
   Only for this I might starve or drown;
The world has disowned me—what can I do
   But live and die on the town?

The world is cruel. It may be right
   To crush the harlot, but, grant it so,
What made her the guilty thing she is?
   For she was innocent once, you know.
'Twas Love! That terrible word tells all.
   She loved a man and blindly believed
His vows, his kisses, his crocodile tears;
   Of course the fool was deceived.

What had I to gain by a moment's sin
   To weigh in the scale with my innocent years,
My womanly shame, my ruined name,
   My father's curses, my mother's tears?
The love of a man! It was something to give,
   Was it worth it? The price was a soul paid down,
Did I get a soul, *his* soul in exchange?
   Behold me here on the town!

"Your guilt was heavy," the world will say,
   "And heavy, heavy your doom must be;

For to pity and pardon woman's fall
  Is to set no value on chastity.
You undervalue the virgin's crown,
  The spotless honor that makes her dear."
But I ought to know what the bauble is worth,
  When the loss of it brings me here!

But pity and pardon? Who are you
  To talk of pardon, pity, to me?
What I ask is justice, justice, sir,
  Let both be punished, or both go free.
If it be in woman a dreadful thing,
  What is it in man, now? Come, be just.
(Remember, she falls through her love for him,
  He through his selfish lust.)

Tell me what is done to the wretch
  Who tempts and riots in woman's fall?
His father curses, and casts him off?
  His friends forsake? He is scorned of all?
Not he. His judges are men like himself,
  Or thoughtless women who humor their whim.
"Young blood," "Wild oats," "Better hush it up."
  They soon forget it—in him!

Even his mother, who ought to know
  The woman-nature, and how it is won,
Frames a thousand excuses for him,
  Because, forsooth, the man is her son.
You have daughters, madam, (he told me so,)
  Fair, innocent daughters—"Woman, what then?"
Some mother may have a son like yours,
  Bid them beware of men!

I saw his coach in the street to-day,
  Dashing along on the sunny side,
With a liveried driver on the box:
  Lolling back in her listless pride
The wife of his bosom took the air.
  She was bought in the mart where hearts are sold:
I gave myself away for his love,
  She sold herself for his gold.

He lives, they say, in a princely way,
  Flattered and feasted. One dark night
Some devil led me to pass his house.

I saw the windows a blaze of light;
The music whirled in a maddening round,
 I heard the fall of the dancers' feet:
Bitter, bitter the thoughts I had,
 Standing there in the street.

Back to my gaudy den I went,
 Marched to my room in grim despair,
Dried my eyes, painted my cheeks,
 And fixed a flower or two in my hair.
Corks were popping, wine was flowing,
 I seized a bumper, and tossed it down:
One must do something to kill the time,
 And fit one's self for the town.

I meet his boy in the park sometimes,
 And my heart runs over towards the child;
A frank little fellow with fearless eyes,
 He smiles at me as his father smiled.
I hate the man, but I love the boy,
 For I think what my own, had he lived, would be:
Perhaps it is *he*, come back from the dead—
 To his father, alas, not me!

But I stand too long in the shadow here,
 Let me out in the light again.
Now for insult, blows, perhaps,
 And bitterer still my own disdain.
I take my place in the crowded street,
 Not like the simple women I see:
You may cheat them, men, as much as you please,
 You wear no masks with me.

I know ye! Under your honeyed words
 There lurks a serpent; your oaths are lies.
There's a lustful fire in your hungry hearts,
 I see it flaming up in your eyes!
Cling to them, ladies, and shrink from me,
 Or rail at my boldness. Well, have you done?
Madam, your husband knows me well,
 Mother, I know your son.

But go your ways, and I'll go mine:
 Call me opprobrious names if you will;
The truth is bitter, think I have lied:

"A harlot?" Yes, but a woman still.
God said of old to a woman like me,
    "Go, sin no more," or your Bibles lie.
But you, you mangle his merciful words
    To "Go, and sin till you die!"

Die! The word has a pleasant sound,
    The sweetest I've heard this many a year.
It seems to promise an end to pain,
    Anyway it will end it here.
Suppose I throw myself in the street?
    Before the horses could trample me down,
Some would-be friend might snatch me up,
    And thrust me back on the town.

But look—the river! From where I stand
    I see it, I almost hear it flow.
Down on the dark and lonely pier—
    It is but a step—I can end my woe.
A plunge, a splash, and all will be o'er,
    The death-black waters will drag me down;
God knows where! But no matter where,
    So I am off the town!

Beloved, since they watch us

Beloved, since they watch us,
    For all we meet are spies,
And we can have no messengers,
    Except our loving eyes,

I check my fiery feelings,
    The words I must not speak,
Content to see, I dare not pluck,
    The roses of thy cheek.

Give me a glance, belovèd,
    Now none are near to see:
My downcast eyes will read my palms,
    I will not look at thee.

It is not resignation,
    It is the deepest art:

Be wary, then, and doubt no more,
   But trust my loving heart.

The Messenger at Night

A face at the window,
   A tap on the pane;
Who is it that wants me
   To-night in the rain?

I have lighted my chamber,
   And brought out my wine,
For a score of good fellows
   Were coming to dine.

The dastards have failed me,
   And sent in the rain
The man at the window,
   To tap on the pane.

I hear the rain patter,
   I hear the wind blow;
I hate the wild weather,
   And yet I must go.

I could moan like the night wind,
   And weep like the rain,
But the Thing at the window
   Is tapping again.

It beckons, I follow.
   Good-by to the light.
I am going, O whither?
   Out into the Night!

BAYARD TAYLOR
1825–1878

The Torso

I.

In clay the statue stood complete,
  As beautiful a form, and fair,
As ever walked a Roman street
  Or breathed the blue Athenian air:
  The perfect limbs, divinely bare,
Their old heroic freedom kept,
  And in the features, fine and rare,
A calm, immortal sweetness slept.

II.

O'er common men it towered, a god,
  And smote their meaner life with shame,
For while its feet the highway trod,
  Its lifted brow was crowned with flame
  And purified from touch of blame:
Yet wholly human was the face,
  And over them who saw it came
The knowledge of their own disgrace.

III.

It stood, regardless of the crowd,
  And simply showed what men might be:
Its solemn beauty disavowed
  The curse of lost humanity.
  Erect and proud, and pure and free,
It overlooked each loathsome law
  Whereunto others bend the knee,
And only what was noble saw.

IV.

The patience and the hope of years
  Their final hour of triumph caught;
The clay was tempered with my tears,
  The forces of my spirit wrought
  With hands of fire to shape my thought,

That when, complete, the statue stood,
  To marble resurrection brought,
The Master might pronounce it good.

V.
But in the night an enemy,
  Who could not bear the wreath should grace
My ready forehead, stole the key
  And hurled my statue from its base;
  And now its fragments strew the place
Where I had dreamed its shrine might be:
  The stains of common earth deface
Its beauty and its majesty.

VI.
The torso prone before me lies;
  The cloven brow is knit with pain:
Mute lips, and blank, reproachful eyes
  Unto my hands appeal in vain.
  My hands shall never work again:
My hope is dead, my strength is spent:
  This fatal wreck shall now remain
The ruined sculptor's monument.

L'Envoi

Unto the Desert and the Desert steed
  Farewell! The journey is completed now:
Struck are the tents of Ishmael's wandering breed,
  And I unwind the turban from my brow.

The sun has ceased to shine; the palms that bent,
  Inebriate with light, have disappeared;
And naught is left me of the Orient
  But the tanned bosom and the unshorn beard.

Yet from that life my blood a glow retains,
  As the red sunshine in the ruby glows;
These songs are echoes of its fiercer strains,—
  Dreams, that recall its passion and repose.

I found, among those Children of the Sun,
  The cipher of my nature,—the release

Of baffled powers, which else had never won
   That free fulfilment, whose reward is peace.

For not to any race or any clime
   Is the completed sphere of life revealed;
He who would make his own that round sublime,
   Must pitch his tent on many a distant field.

Upon his home a dawning luster beams,
   But through the world he walks to open day,
Gathering from every land the prismal gleams,
   Which, when united, form the perfect ray.

Go, therefore, Songs!—which in the East were born
   And drew your nurture—from your sire's control:
Haply to wander through the West forlorn,
   Or find a shelter in some Orient soul.

And if the temper of our colder sky
   Less warmth of passion and of speech demands,
They are the blossoms of my life,—and I
   Have ripened in the suns of many lands.

To a Persian Boy

In the bazaar at Smyrna

The gorgeous blossoms of that magic tree
Beneath whose shade I sat a thousand nights,
Breathed from their opening petals all delights
Embalmed in spice of Orient Poesy,
When first, young Persian, I beheld thine eyes,
And felt the wonder of thy beauty grow
Within my brain, as some fair planet's glow
Deepens, and fills the summer evening skies.
From under thy dark lashes shone on me
The rich, voluptuous soul of Eastern land,
Impassioned, tender, calm, serenely sad,—
Such as immortal Hafiz felt when he
Sang by the fountain-streams of Rocnabad,
Or in the bowers of blissful Samarcand.

EMILY DICKINSON
1830–1886

Her breast is fit for pearls

Her breast is fit for pearls,
But I was not a "Diver"—
Her brow is fit for thrones
But I have not a crest.
Her heart is fit for *home*—
I—a Sparrow—build there
Sweet of twigs and twine
My perennial nest.

Going—to—Her!

Going—to—Her!
Happy—Letter! Tell Her—
Tell Her—the page I never wrote!
Tell Her, I only said—the Syntax—
And left the Verb and the Pronoun—out!
Tell Her just how the fingers—hurried—
Then—how they—stammered—slow—slow—
And then—you wished you had eyes—in your pages—
So you cold see—what moved—them—so—

Tell Her—it wasn't a practised writer—
You guessed—
From the way the sentence—toiled—
You could hear the Bodice—tug—behind you—
As if it held but the might of a child!
You almost pitied—it—you—it worked so—
Tell her—No—you may quibble—there—
For it would split Her Heart—to know it—
And then—you and I—were silenter!

Tell Her—Day—finished—before we—finished—
And the old Clock kept neighing—"Day!"
And you—got sleepy—and begged to be ended—
What could—it hinder so—to say?

Tell her—just how she sealed—you—Cautious!
But—if she ask "where you are hid"—until the evening—
Ah! Be bashful!
Gesture Coquette—
And shake your Head!

Precious to Me—She still shall be

Precious to Me—She still shall be—
Though She forget the name I bear—
The fashion of the Gown I wear—
The very Color of My Hair—

So like the Meadows—now—
I dared to show a Tress of Theirs
If haply—She might not despise
A Buttercup's Array—

I know the Whole—obscures the Part—
The fraction—that appeased the Heart
Till Number's Empery—
Remembered—as the Milliner's flower

When Summer's Everlasting Dower—
Confronts the dazzled Bee.

HORATIO ALGER, JR.
1832–1899

Friar Anselmo

Friar Anselmo (God's grace may he win!)
Committed one sad day a deadly sin;

Which being done he drew back, self-abhorred,
From the rebuking presence of the Lord,

And, kneeling down, besought, with bitter cry,
Since life was worthless grown, that he might die.

All night he knelt, and, when the morning broke,
In patience still he waits death's fatal stroke.

When all at once a cry of sharp distress
Aroused Anselmo from his wretchedness;

And, looking from the convent window high,
He saw a wounded traveller gasping lie

Just underneath, who, bruised and stricken sore,
Had crawled for aid unto the convent door.

The friar's heart with deep compassion stirred,
When the poor wretch's groans for help were heard

With gentle hands, and touched with love divine,
He bathed his wounds, and poured in oil and wine.

With tender foresight cared for all his needs,—
A blessed ministry of noble deeds.

In such devotion passed seven days. At length
The poor wayfarer gained his wonted strength.

With grateful thanks he left the convent walls,
And once again on death Anselmo calls.

When, lo! his cell was filled with sudden light,
And on the wall he saw an angel write,

(An angel in whose likeness he could trace,
More noble grown, the traveller's form and face),

"Courage, Anselmo, though thy sin be great,
God grants thee life that thou may'st expiate.

"Thy guilty stains shall be washed white again,
By noble service done thy fellow-men.

"His soul draws nearest unto God above,
Who to his brother ministers in love."

Meekly Anselmo rose, and, after prayer,
His soul was lighted of its past despair.

Henceforth he strove, obeying God's high will,
His heaven-appointed mission to fulfil.

And many a soul, oppressed with pain and grief,
Owed to the friar solace and relief.

The Whipporwill and I

In the hushed hours of night, when the air is quite still,
I hear the strange cry of the lone whippoorwill,
Who chants, without ceasing, that wonderful trill,
Of which the sole burden is still, "Whip-poor-Will."

And why should I whip him? Strange visitant, say,
Has he been playing truant this long summer day?
I listened a moment; more clear and more shrill
Rang the voice of the bird, as he cried, "Whip-poor-Will."

But what has poor Will done? I ask you once more;
I'll whip him, don't fear, if you'll tell me what for.
I paused for an answer; o'er valley and hill
Rang the voice of the bird, as he cried, "Whip-poor-Will."

Has he come to your dwelling, by night or by day,
And snatched the young birds from their warm nest away?
I paused for an answer; o'er valley and hill
Rang tile voice of the bird, as he cried, "Whip-poor-Will."

Well, well, I can hear you, don't have any fears,
I can hear what is constantly dinned in my ears.
The obstinate bird, with his wonderful trill,
Still made but one answer, and that, "Whip-poor-Will."

But what *has* poor Will done? I prithee explain;
I'm out of all patience, don't mock me again.
The obstinate bird, with his wonderful trill,
Still made the same answer, and that, "Whip-poor-Will."

Well, have your own way, then; but if you won't tell,
I'll shut down the window, and bid you farewell;
But of one thing be sure, *I won't whip him until*
You give me some reason for whipping poor Will.

I listened a moment, as if for reply,
But nothing was heard but the bird's mocking cry.
I caught the faint echo from valley and hill;
It breathed the same burden, that strange "Whip-poor-Will."

The Fountain of Youth

"There sleeps beneath some favored sky,
  Beyond the desert's track,
A fountain fraught with magic power
  To bring our lost youth back.

"Who quaffs from it a plenteous draught,
  Shall shed time's envious stains,
And feel the ruddy wine of youth
  Go bounding through his veins."

So sang the poets long ago,
  And many a pilgrim, worn with age,
Went forth in unavailing search—
  A weary pilgrimage.

They could not read the hidden sense
  Of this fair fount the poets sung,
The springs of kindness in the heart
  Keep it forever young.

For age comes not with time alone—
  Our wrinkles and gray hairs
Are but the creased and faded robes
  The youthful spirit wears.

EDMUND CLARENCE STEDMAN
1833–1908

Anonyma: Her Confession

If I had been a rich man's girl,
  With my tawny hair, and this wanton art
Of lifting my eyes in the evening whirl
  And looking into another's heart;
Had love been mine at birth, and friends
  Caressing and guarding me night and day,

With doctors to watch my finger-ends,
   And a parson to teach me how to pray;

If I had been reared as others have,—
   With but a tithe of these looks, which came
From my reckless mother, now in her grave,
   And the father who grudged me even his name,—
Why, I should have station and tender care,
   Should ruin men in the high-bred way,
Passionless, smiling at their despair,
   And marrying where my vantage lay.

As it is, I must have love and dress,
   Jewelled trinkets, and costly food,
For I was born for plenteousness,
   Music and flowers, and all things good.
To that same father I owe some thanks,
   Seeing, at least, that blood will tell,
And keep me ever above the ranks
   Of those who wallow where they fell.

True, there are weary, weary days
   In the great hotel where I make my lair,
Where I meet the men with their brutal praise,
   Or answer the women, stare for stare.
'T is an even fight, and I'll carry it through,—
   Pit them against me, great and small:
I grant no quarter, nor would I sue
   For grace to the softest of them all.

I cannot remember half the men
   Whose sin has tangled them in my toils,—
All are alike before me then,
   Part of my easily conquered spoils:
Tall or short, and dark or fair,
   Rich or famous, haughty or fond,
There are few, I find, who will not forswear
   The lover's oath and the wedding bond.

Fools! What is it that drives them on
   With their perjured lips on poison fed;
Vain of themselves, and cruel as stone,
   How should they be so cheaply led?
Surely they know me as I am,—
   Only a cuckoo, at the best,

Watching, careless of hate and shame,
   To crouch myself in another's nest.

But the women,—How they flutter and flout,
   The stupid, terribly virtuous wives,
If I but chance to move about
   Or enter within their bustling hives!
Buz! Buz! In the scandalous gatherings,
   When a strange queen lights amid their throng,
And their tongues have a thousand angry stings
   To send her traveling, right or wrong.

Well, the earth is wide and open to all,
   And money and men are everywhere,
And, as I roam, 't will ill befall
   If I do not gain my lawful share:
One drops off, but another will come
   With as light a head and heavy a purse;
So long as I have the world for a home,
   I'll take my fortune, better or worse!

Holyoke Valley

                       "Something sweet
             Followed youth, with flying feet,
             And will never come again."

How many years have made their flights,
   Northampton, over thee and me,
Since last I scaled those purple heights
   That guard the pathway to the sea;

Or climbed, as now, the topmost crown
   Of western ridges, whence again
I see, for miles beyond the town,
   That sunlit stream divide the plain?

There still the giant warders stand
   And watch the current's downward flow,
And northward still, with threatening hand,
   The river bends his ancient bow.

I see the hazy lowlands meet
   The sky, and count each shining spire,

From those which sparkle at my feet
  To distant steeples tipt with fire.

For still, old town, thou art the same:
  The redbreasts sing their choral tune,
Within thy mantling elms aflame,
  As in that other, dearer June,

When here my footsteps entered first,
  And summer perfect beauty wore,
And all thy charms upon me burst,
  While Life's whole journey lay before.

Here every fragrant walk remains,
  Where happy maidens come and go,
And students saunter in the lanes
  And hum the songs I used to know.

I gaze, yet find myself alone,
  And walk with solitary feet:
How strange these wonted ways have grown!
  Where are the friends I used to meet?

In yonder shaded Academe
  The rippling metres flow to-day,
But other boys at sunset dream
  Of love, and laurels far away;

And ah! From yonder trellised home,
  Less sweet the faces are that peer
Than those of old, and voices come
  Less musically to my ear.

Sigh not, ye breezy elms, but give
  The murmur of my sweetheart's vows,
When Life was something worth to live,
  And Love was young beneath your boughs!

Fade beauty, smiling everywhere,
  That can from year to year outlast
Those charms a thousand times more fair,
  And, O, our joys so quickly past!

Or smile to gladden fresher hearts
  Henceforth: but they shall yet be led,
Revisiting these ancient parts,
  Like me to mourn their glory fled.

To Bayard Taylor, with a Copy of *The Iliad*

Bayard, awaken not this music strong,
While round thy home the indolent sweet breeze
Floats lightly as the summer breath of seas
O'er which Ulysses heard the Sirens' song.
Dreams of low-lying isles to June belong,
And Circe holds us in her haunts of ease;
But later, when these high ancestral trees
Are sere, and such melodious languors wrong
The reddening strength of the autumnal year,
Yield to heroic words thy ear and eye;—
Intent on these broad pages thou shalt hear
The trumpets' blare, the Argive battle-cry,
And see Achilles hurl his hurtling spear,
And mark the Trojan arrows make reply!

ADAH ISAACS MENKEN
1835–1868

My Heritage

"My heritage!" It is to live within
The marts of Pleasure and of Gain, yet be
No willing worshiper at either shrine;
To think, and speak, and act, not for my pleasure,
But others'. The veriest slave of time
And circumstances. Fortune's toy!
To hear of fraud, injustice, and oppression,
And feel who is the unshielded victim.
     Cold friends and causeless foes!
     Proud thoughts that rise to fall.
Bright stars that set in seas of blood;
Affections, which are passions, lava-like
Destroying what they rest upon. Love's
Fond and fervid tide preparing icebergs

That fragile bark, this loving human heart.
    O'ermastering Pride!
    Ruler of the Soul!
Life, with all its changes, cannot bow ye.
    Soul-subduing Poverty!
That lays his iron, cold grasp upon the high
Free spirit: strength, sorrow-born, that bends
But breaks not in his clasp—all, all
These are "my heritage!"
And mine to know a reckless human love, all passion and intensity,
    and see a mist come o'er the scene, a dimness steal o'er the soul!
Mine to dream, of joy and wake to wretchedness!
Mine to stand on the brink of life
One little moment where the fresh'ning breeze
Steals o'er the languid lip and brow, telling
Of forest leaf, and ocean wave, and happy
Homes, and cheerful toil; and bringing gently
To this wearied heart its long-forgotten
Dreams of gladness.
But turning the fevered cheek to meet the soft kiss of the winds, my
    eyes look to the sky, where I send up my soul in thanks. The sky
    is clouded—no stars—no music—the heavens are hushed.
My poor soul comes back to me, weary and disappointed.
The very breath of heaven, that comes to all, comes not to me.
Bound in iron gyves of unremitting toil, my vital air is wretchedness—
    what need I any other?
"My heritage!" The shrouded eye, the trampled leaf, wind-driven
    and soiled with dust—these tell the tale.
Mine to watch
The glorious light of intellect
Burn dimly, and expire; and mark the soul,
Though born in Heaven, pause in its high career,
Wave in its course, and fall to grovel in
The darkness of earth's contamination, till
Even Death shall scorn to give a thing
So low his welcome greeting!
Who would be that pale,
Blue mist, that hangs so low in air, like Hope
That has abandoned earth, yet reacheth
Not the stars in their proud homes?
A dying eagle, striving to reach the sun?
A little child talking to the gay clouds as they flaunt past in their
    purple and crimson robes?

A timid little flower singing to the grand old trees?
Foolish waves, leaping up and trying to kiss the moon?
A little bird mocking the stars?
Yet this is what men call Genius.

A Memory

I see her yet, that dark-eyed one,
  Whose bounding heart God folded up
In His, as shuts when day is done,
  Upon the elf the blossom's cup.
On many an hour like this we met,
  And as my lips did fondly greet her,
I blessed her as love's amulet:
  Earth hath no treasure, dearer, sweeter.

The stars that look upon the hill,
  And beckon from their homes at night,
Are soft and beautiful, yet still
  Not equal to her eyes of light.
They have the liquid glow of earth,
  The sweetness of a summer even,
As if some Angel at their birth
  Had dipped them in the hues of Heaven.

They may not seem to others sweet,
  Nor radiant with the beams above,
When first their soft, sad glances meet
  The eyes of those not born for love;
Yet when on me their tender beams
  Are turned, beneath love's wide control,
Each soft, sad orb of beauty seems
  To look through mine into my soul.

I see her now that dark-eyed one,
  Whose bounding heart God folded up
In His, as shuts when day is done,
  Upon the elf the blossom's cup.
Too late we met, the burning brain,
  The aching heart alone can tell,
How filled our souls of death and pain
  When came the last, sad word, *Farewell!*

Infelix

Where is the promise of my years;
   Once written on my brow?
Ere errors, agonies and fears
Brought with them all that speaks in tears,
Ere I had sunk beneath my peers;
   Where sleeps that promise now?

Naught lingers to redeem those hours,
   Still, still to memory sweet!
The flowers that bloomed in sunny bowers
Are withered all; and Evil towers
Supreme above her sister powers
   Of Sorrow and Deceit.

I look along the columned years,
   And see Life's riven fane,
Just where it fell, amid the jeers
Of scornful lips, whose mocking sneers,
For ever hiss within mine ears
   To break the sleep of pain.

I can but own my life is vain
   A desert void of peace;
I missed the goal I sought to gain,
I missed the measure of the strain
That lulls Fame's fever in the brain,
   And bids Earth's tumult cease.

Myself! Alas for theme so poor
   A theme but rich in Fear;
I stand a wreck on Error's shore,
A spectre not within the door,
A houseless shadow evermore,
   An exile lingering here.

CHARLES WARREN STODDARD
1843–1909

Expectation

What news, I wonder, from the South!
  I saw a sail blow past the Head.
I wonder if my lovers still
Are watching for me from the hill,
Whereon the palms are dry with drouth,
  And ferns are crisp and dead.

I wonder if my lovers yet
Are all beginning to forget
How dear that day was when we sat
Upon our Island Ararat,
  While floods were beating at its base,
And winds in anger seemed to fret
  Our new-found dwelling place!

The bark was driving on the beach;
How far life seemed beyond our reach!
The shore was thronged with savage men;
They plunged into the surf, and then,
  Above the breakers' deafening roar,
They gave us each some cheering speech,
  And helped us to the shore.

What sweet, unprofitable hours
  We passed within the silent land:
Calm, or impatient, sadly mute,
Or merry in a mild dispute;
Long days of summer, ripe and hale,
Horizons all hemmed in with flowers,
Till, rescued by a passing sail,
  We gave each dusky friend a hand,
  And parted on the sand.

I wonder how my lovers are!
  I wonder if the lime has shed
The name I cut upon its bark!
I wonder if they speared the shark

We chased one night by torch and star—
   He had our pet kid in his mouth!
The sea rolls in with easy swell;
   I saw a sail blow past the Head;
   "She's from the Line," I heard it said—
And there is where my lovers dwell,
   Along the burning South.

Utopia

> Scene: Moku, in the South Sea.
> The poet under his vine and fig-tree.
> Piolani, his "Man Friday," in attendance.

   The Poet speaks:
A cottage on a cliff,
And a vine beside the door;
While the wind with fragrant whiff,
Wakes the parrot in a tiff,
Puffs the matting from the floor,
Swings the window open wide.
   —Piolani, please to slide
Wine-jar or a calabash
Close against the window-sash.
Drops a spider from the thatch
Down upon my writing table;
Splendid specimen to catch,
I'll secure him with dispatch,
Pin him up and write his label.

   With her song so bland,
By the cocoas in the sand,
Singing with her siren's voice,
The sea leans on the land.
I listen and rejoice,
For I like this tawny hour;
When the stars begin to flower,
As it were; and day is pleading,
With those heavy drooping lids,
And a glance of love exceeding,
For one moment more of power.
Thrumming crickets, katydids,
Clouds of giddy butterflies;
Oddest fowls of every feather

Hail me with their plaintive cries.
Moths and insects of all breeding
Upon one another feeding,
Huddle here together.
—Piolani, take the broom,
Chase that lizard from the room.
There's another on the wall!
How the slimy creatures crawl
Over everything and all.

After hours of heat,
And leagues of burning dust,
How soft and passing sweet
Is the turf beneath my feet.
See this wondrous blossom thrust
From its dusky tent of green,
In its splendid pride and lust,
Like a painted savage queen.

—Piolani, do you know
Of the nature of this shrub?
Why the waters ebb and flow?
Where the butterflies all go,
Or the future of the grub?
You have never thought of these,
Yet are happier than I,
Who am trying to descry
What my brother watcher sees
In a very distant sky.
Do you ever question fate?
Do you hate with burning hate
One who cannot think with you?
Do you send us white-faced men
To a hot perdition, when
You have found our faith untrue?
That is what we Christians do.
Do you pity when you hear
How we turn about and dread
Being numbered with the dead,
And the only God we know
Is a God to scorn or fear?
Do not tell me that your foe
Meets you with unflinching gaze,
Certain that the weaker dies!

That you let the life-blood flow,
For a coward you despise!
So your soul through endless days
Walks the valley of its youth;
Goes the old familiar ways;
And shall sleep no more, forsooth!
Do not say we cannot touch
The one God we fear so much!
Do not say we cannot prove
The one volume that we love!
Do not scorn us when you see
How we never can agree—
How we never have agreed!
—Kill that scudding centipede
In the corner on the floor!
Would you land upon our shore
And destroy our too frail hopes?
Better is the mind that gropes
Toward some divine ideal
Than the mind that sleeps in sloth!
Hopeless, aimless, hating both;
Doubting what the years reveal.
Let us worship each his way,
Though some saints would doubtless say
That this very liberal view,
And the plan in question, too,
Can't, of course, apply to you.

Piolani, if you like,
Having brought my coffee in,
Strip your body to the skin,
Don't imagine you will strike
Consternation to this breast.
Thus it was we found you drest,
Nature in this case knew best.
Take your little Idol down;
Cold and stony, rude and brown,
Eyeless, earless, noseless too,
But it's all the same to you.
Nor foot, nor hand in any part,
Utterly devoid of art,
But a comfort to your heart.
Fall before it as of old,

Sing your *melis* manifold.
Burn the boughs of resinous trees,
Solemn incantations blending
With the savory smoke ascending.
Prone upon your hands and knees,
Care not that a stranger sees;
Be a savage as you please.
Be not watchful nor alert,
Nor regard with eye suspicious
Any matter I assert.
Do not try with surreptitious
Spell my spirit to convert.
Union we can scarce expect—
Let our hearts our ways direct—
I will call you some new sect.

Piolani, I can hear
Your sweet voice rise strong and clear.
Is it god or goddess now
Whom you flatter with a vow?
Under deepest tropic skies
Let our two-fold prayer arise.
Question not but in the end
It will reach the self-same friend,
Who will judge us well indeed—
Each according to his meed.

Piolani, this is all,
Swing the hammock in the hall,
Roll your mat out at my feet,
Day is weary, night is sweet.
Day with toil and trouble teems,
Night is hallowéd with dreams.
Asleep already, at the start!
Piolani, bless your heart!
If peace of spirit rest insures
What a conscience must be yours.

So I swing, and think of this;
Saying as I shut my eyes,
This is ignorance and bliss.
If it isn't, then what is,
  And who of us is wise?

The Secret Well

I know a well so deep and cool
And hid, the crystal-hearted pool
Hath never thrilled a swallow's throat
   Or sweetened one lark's note.

No fainting stag, though perishing,
Hath ventured to disturb this spring:
No leopard with its fiery breast
   This fountain dares molest.

No cunning, silver-caséd trout
The sheltered source can e'er find out—
No tongue but mine may ever tell
   The secret of this well.

I build about its guarded rim
With added stones; I know the dim,
Still twilight of its mossy cell
   Where the sweet waters dwell.

For spirits go between us two
With flasks; they brim with softest dew.
I drink and am refreshed, and seem
   As living in a dream.

This well, that is alone for me,
Is but a fount of memory:
And every year that I have known
   Is but an added stone.

My willing thoughts, as spirits, haste
To draw the draught I love to taste.
There is an ever full supply,
   Yet who may drink but I?

SARAH ORNE JEWETT
1849–1909

A Caged Bird

High at the window in her cage,
  The old canary sits and sings,
Nor sees across the curtain pass
  The shadow of a swallow's wings.

A poor deceit and copy this
  Of larger lives that count their span,
Unreckoning of wider worlds,
  Or gifts that Heaven keeps for man!

She gathers piteous bits and shreds,
  This solitary mateless thing,
Patient to build again the nest
  So rudely scattered spring by spring;

And sings her brief, unheeded songs,
  Her dreams of bird-life wild and free,
Yet never beats her prison bars
  At sound of song from bush or tree.

Yet in my busiest hours I pause,
  Held by a sense of urgent speech,
Bewildered by that spark-like soul
  Able my very soul to reach.

She will be heard; she chirps me loud
  When I forget those gravest cares,
Her small provision to supply—
  Clear water or the seedsman's wares.

She begs me now for that chief joy
  The round great world is made to grow—
Her wisp of greenness. Hear her chide
  Because my answering thought is slow!

What can my life seem like to her?
  A dull, unpunctual service mine,

Stupid before her eager speech,
　　Her flitting steps, her insight fine!

To open wide thy prison door,
　　Poor friend, would give thee to thy foes;
And yet a plaintive note I hear,
　　As if to tell how slowly goes

The time of thy long prisoning.
　　Bird! does some promise keep thee sane?
Will there be better days for thee?
　　Will thy soul too know life again?

Ah, none of us have more than this—
　　If one true friend green leaves can reach
From out some fairer, wider place,
　　And understand our wistful speech!

Together

I wonder if you really send
　　These dreams of you that come and go!
I like to say, "She thought of me,
　　And I have known it." Is it so?

Though other friends are by your side,
　　Yet sometimes it must surely be
They wonder where your thoughts have gone—
　　Because I have you here with me.

And when the busy day is done,
　　When work is ended, voices cease,
And everyone has said good-night
　　In fading twilight, then, in peace,

Idly I rest; you come to me,
　　Your dear love holds me close to you.
If I could see you face to face,
　　It would not be more sweet and true.

And now across the weary miles
　　Light from my star shines. Is it, dear,
You never really went away—
　　I said farewell, and—kept you here?

Flowers in the Dark

Late in the evening, when the room had grown
Too hot and tiresome with its flaring light
And noise of voices, I stole out alone
Into the darkness of the summer night.
Down the long garden walk I slowly went;
A little wind was stirring in the trees;
I only saw the whitest of the flowers,
And I was sorry that the earlier hours
Of that fair evening had been so ill spent,
Because, I said, I am content with these
Dear friends of mine who only speak to me
With their delicious fragrance, and who tell
To me their gracious welcome silently.
The leaves that touch my hand with dew are wet;
I find the tall white lilies I love well.
I linger as I pass the mignonette,
And what surprise could dearer be than this:
To find my sweet rose waiting with a kiss!

WE'WHA
1849–1896

Legend

The gods of Chi'pia were hungry.[1] They had no meat, and they were
hungry for meat. There had been no rains for a long time, but there
had been a little lightning. Shits'ukïa said to Kwe'lele: "I think I will
go to-morrow to look for deer." The ancestral gods of the A'shiwi were
also hungry, but the gods of Chi'pia did not know this. Shits'ukïa and
Kwe'lele were so hungry that they ate their moccasins, and Shits'ukïa
ate his earrings of deer tails; and so in the morning he started after
deer. There was no game in his country, and he considered: "Which
route shall I take? I think I will go to the west, whence the lightning
came; the deer, I guess, live there." He was barefoot and poorly clad,

for he had eaten everything; he had only a little meal of sweet corn and a few seeds of the same. The afternoon of the fourth day he came to tall green grass, and sitting in the grass were two sisters washing a buckskin. When they discovered the stranger they turned a large pottery bowl over the buckskin. Shits'ukĭa, approaching them, inquired: "What are you doing?" "I have been washing." "What have you been washing?" "I have been washing myself." "No," said Shits'ukĭa, "I know what you have been washing; you have been washing buckskin." "Did you see?" "Yes; I saw you a long time. I have been watching you." The girls then removed the bowl and showed the buckskin, and then continued their washing. When it was done, one said, addressing her sister: "Now we will go home." The girl then invited Shits'ukĭa to accompany her home. These people were the Kwal'ashi kwin'na (Black raven). These raven people then lived in a high mountain. On reaching the house the father exclaimed: "Who is that boy who has come?" The mother also asked the question. The daughter replied: "I don't know; he has been traveling four days and nights." The father said to the elder girl: "Well, he will be good for your husband." The parents were eating and had much meat before them. They invited Shits'ukĭa to eat. The father had just returned from the cornfield. After he had finished his meal he said to the stranger: "I will take you for my son. You are poor. You will live with me. Look at both my children. You shall have one as your wife. Look at both and tell me the one you choose." Shits'ukĭa replied: "I wish the elder daughter for my wife." "It is well," said the father. At bedtime the father said: "I guess you are very tired. You will sleep alone with your wife in the upper room." On reaching his room Shits'ukĭa found his bed made of deerskins. He slept all night with his wife. When they arose in the morning the father said: "Now I will show you all our game—elk, deer, antelope, rabbits, and rats." Going a short distance away, he exclaimed: "Ah, ha, my children, I am glad to see you; good day." The game answered: "Kets'anishi (all good come to you)." Shits'ukĭa said to the game: "I am hungry and want meat. Which of you shall I kill?" An elk replied, "Kill me;" and Shits'ukĭa killed the elk, flayed him, and then returned to the house. For four days he killed deer and dried the meat. The fifth day he asked the father: "Where is a good place to plant my corn? I have a few seeds." "A little way off there is a good place." "Well, I have lots of meat. I will take it with me and stay two nights at the field." He went off and planted the corn; he did not intend to sleep in the field. That night he wrapped the meat up in a skin and went to Ko'thluwala'wa. Pau'tiwa was delighted to see the meat. He asked: "My child, where did you find the deer?" "I sat outside my house after sundown and saw a little lightning. I thought I would look for my children in the direction whence it came, and I found them." He told the story of meeting with the Kwal'ashi people. He remained all night at Ko'thluwala'wa. Shits'ukĭa said: "Pretty soon I will steal all the game." He also told of his planting the corn. "Well," said Pau'tiwa, "your corn will be ripe in four days and I shall be contented to have you steal all the game; my people are very hungry for meat." All night they talked. Pau'tiwa went out and brought in a beautiful girl and said: "When you bring the deer, then this girl shall be your wife. I sent the eagle for game and he returned without having seen it. I also sent the hawk, and he returned without having seen any. But you are wiser than the others; you are my child." Shits'ukĭa returned early in the morning to where he had planted the corn. The corn was already quite high—over a foot. He hoed the ground and sang till sunset, and then returned to the Kwal'ashi people and slept that night with his wife. He said to the father: "My corn is good; it is already quite high." He remained four nights with these people, going each day to his corn-field. He also killed many deer, and dried the meat. The fourth day he said to the Kwal ashi man: "Now I am going to my cornfield. My corn I think is ripe. Now I will roast some corn."

Shits'ukĭa went to the field, and made a great fire at night and threw the corn in, and all the gods came from Ko'thluwala'wa and ate the corn and meat. After all had gathered, Shits'ukĭa said to the cougar: "Father, I wish you to come to me." And in a little while the cougar appeared. He then called the bear, then the lynx, and then the coyote. Shits'ukĭa said to the cougar: "Father, what will you have to eat? Will you have the rabbit?" "No." "Will you have the antelope?" "No; I wish the deer." Then he said to the bear: "My father, warrior, what will you have to eat?" "I will have the same as the cougar—the deer." He then said to the lynx: "My warrior, what will you have? Will you have the deer?" "No." "Will you have antelope?" "No; I want the rabbit. I do not run about much; I will eat the rabbit." Then he asked the coyote: "What will you have? Will you have the rabbit?" "No." "The antelope?" "No; I will have the deer." "Well, let us go." And they all went to the deer house. When they came close to the great stone fence which surrounded the game he said to all: "We must not speak loud." And on reaching the gate he spoke to the deer, saying: "Deer, my children, come hither; my father and warriors wish to eat; whom shall I kill?" A deer replied: "Kill me." "Come outside, my child," said Shits'ukĭa. "Where shall I go? It is dark, I can not see." "Here; come out." The deer passed out the door. The cougar made a second attempt before he caught the deer. Then Shits'ukĭa called the bear. The hair was so heavy over his small eyes that he could hardly see. "Stand here," said

Shits'ukĭa. A second deer was called. When the deer passed out of the gate the bear walked about, but could not see the deer; the deer went far away, and the bear failed to catch him.[2] Shits'ukĭa said: "Now you have failed to catch the deer; no longer shall you eat deer. You will be my warrior still, but you shall eat only medicine."[3] Then Shits'ukĭa called the lynx, who has eyes like the cougar, and he caught the rabbit and ate it. Then the coyote was called up, and the deer came, as for the cougar. "Pass out," said Shits'ukĭa. The coyote had fallen asleep, and awoke after the deer had passed, exclaiming: "Where is the deer?" "He has gone," Shits'ukĭa said, "go after him." But with all the coyote's running he could not catch the deer. When he returned Shits'ukĭa asked him if he had caught the deer. The coyote replying in the negative, Shits'ukĭa said: "Well, hereafter you shall not eat the meat of any animal. You shall eat only blood. In the past the coyote ate only blood, and therefore the fetish sus'ki (coyote) is dipped into the blood of the deer. The cougar and bear fetishes also eat blood of the deer.

Then Pau'tiwa and Shits'ukĭa both said to the game: "My children, you shall no longer stay here. We will open the gates that you may pass over the earth and eat the grass of the earth." The game had but little to eat in their stone house. Pau'tiwa said: "You will find good places where you can have your young, and when we want food we will kill and eat you, and your otherselves will come and live in my house." And all the game passed out of the gates. One of the Kwal'ashi, hearing, ran to tell the others, and all left the house to see, and they cried: "Who has let out our game?" Shits'ukĭa at once spat out the medicine[4] Pau'tiwa had given him over the Kwal'ashi people, and they all turned into ravens and, croaking, flew away, to return no more to their homes.

NOTES

1. *Chi'pia* is the abiding place of certain gods who preceded the Zuñis to this world. It is located, according to Zuñi history, near Shi'papolima, the home of the Zuñi prey gods.

2. "The cougar has eyes like fire and sees all things. The bear only walks about slowly, continually dropping chips."

3. This medicine is found in the earth by the bear. Whenever the Zuñis see him, he is still walking around, dropping chips and hunting in the earth for his medicine. In the old time Shits'ukĭa gave the bear the medicine, which he still eats.

4. This medicine was given to Shits'ukĭa by Pau'tiwa when he first visited Ko'thluwala'wa after Pau'tiwa told him he wished him to steal all the game. Shits'ukĭa replied that perhaps the Kwal'ashi people had good heads and would find out and kill him. Then Pau'tiwa gave him the medicine and said it would destroy the people. Shits'ukĭa returned to Ko'thluwala'wa with Pau'tiwa, and lived there a long time, and

had the girl as his wife. He did not take his Kwal'ashi wife with him when he returned to his home. On his return he passed south of I'twanna (Zuñi). Shits'ukĭa and Kwe'lele still visit Ko'thluwala'wa.

EDGAR SALTUS
1855–1921

Infidelity

In dreams released from memory's oubliette,
   I leave the echoing corridors of care—
   And now with Manon, now with La Valliere,
Move to the measure of the minuet.
Sappho's astounding eyes and mine have met
   And I have lunged in storied gardens, where
   To greet me came Yseult and Guinevere,
Francesca, Marguerite and Juliet.
I too have wandered with Calirrohoë
   Along the laurel reaches of the stream
   That pulses through the blue nymph-haunted seas,—
And back again through all of Arcady.
Yet ever in the pauses of the dream
   'Twas You I sought, and only you,—not these.

Imeros

Beautiful as an uncommitted sin,
   You stood before me, as that winter day
   Sank precipate into the dusk away.
Ah Love! I cannot now again begin
To tell how earnestly I strove to win
   Some hope, nor how I urged to hear you say
   The word that turns December into May,
And makes the heart throb riotous within.

And yet you would not, and so I went away—
  And wandered through the giant avenues
When suddenly beneath the wan lamplight
  I thought I saw your face and heard you say
In that dull sing-song that the harlots use,
  "Come, sir! and let us taste of love tonight."

Hope

Rich in the dreams that youth can scarce outlast,
  I strolled beneath Venetian stars, and thought
  Of all the pleasant things that life had brought—
And planned a future fairer than the past.
And while I mused this wise in scenes forecast—
  A man with haggard eyes as one distraught
  Approached me suddenly, and when I sought
To distance him, he caught and held me fast.
In vain I struggled. To his face had pressed
  Whole chronicles of grief and crime and hate,
But still his eyes shone out familiarly.
  "What is it that you would with me?" I gasped.
"I am thyself," he cried, "O Insensate!
  The image that the future holds of thee!"

HENRY BLAKE FULLER
1857–1929

Tobias Holt, Bachelor

At twenty
Holt seemed like other chaps
In his own set and circle:
He waltzed and redowa'd,
Was handy-brisk at picnics,

Took all the girls on buggy-rides,
Ushered at weddings—
In short, was generally popular.

At twenty-eight,
Though long regarded as a "catch,"
He was still single;
Had ushered all his chums and pals
Into the married state,
But stopped outside himself.
Some said he had no enterprise, no spunk;
Others thought he could see no individual girl
Among the crowd,—the forest hid the trees;
And others still declared
That what he really preferred to be
Was Little Brother to the Whole Wide World.

This last guess was nearest of the three;
Holt was simply—kind.
His little "life ideal" was just this:
To be in pleasant, comfortable circumstances himself
(No scansion whatsoever, there!);
To "go" with others similarly placed;
To do these others various little favors,
Kindnesses, obliging turns,
And to make life, within such narrowed limits,
A "nice" and friendly thing.
No passion; no vicissitudes;
Good-will all round.
Does such a spirit
Help move the real world on?
Well, perhaps not.

Now, as a bachelor in his thirties,
Holt made the rounds:
Dined with married friends,
Brought presents for their children,
And in the case of couples six months wed,
And facing their first sag,
Jumped in the threatening breach and pulled them through.
He had the run of several pleasant homes,
And Mrs. C.H. Mack,
Whom he had often taken
To parties and on buggy-rides,

Always invited him to dinner
On Thanksgiving Day.

As he neared fifty,
The various welcomes
Grew more sedate;
Some, even cool.
Folks had their own concerns, perhaps;
And then, again,
His youthful charm—this is just possible—
Had become impaired.
And one November
The invitation for Thanksgiving
Did not come.
Panic!—no less.
But it turned out
Alicia Mack had not forgotten:
Sickness in the house.
Heaven be blessed!—
Henceforward a new lease of life,
With doubled works of friendliness and zeal,
And yet—what might the future bring from others?
So, a high resolve to gird him,
To hold the slipping ground,
And last through to the end.

Daily Holt became
More strenuous, more assiduous:
The sliding clutch must stick.
More calls, more flowers, more loans of books,
More friendly offices,
More theater-parties for married pairs,
More jokes and funny stories
Laboriously rehearsed and sprung.
He learned the two-step:
Young girls would dance with him
When younger partners failed,
And, if the daughters of his early friends,
Would call him "Uncle Toby."
And gay young dogs,
Who'd not yet learned the latest step,
But meant to,
Would snicker on the outskirts:
Tail-Holt, they'd say, was better Holt than none!

He kept the run of birthdays,
And of anniversaries
Husbands themselves forgot.
And one December,
When fate had been adverse,
He set aside all notion
Of a new business-suit
And put the money saved
Into a round of presents.
"Not much," people might say,
On opening their parcels;
"But, anyway, he's not forgotten us
Completely." Thus he'd arrange
A welcome, not too chill,
For one year more.

Holt, at sixty-five,
Was finding life still busy
But rather bleak;
And one day he lay down in bed,
A bachelor in a boarding-house,
To think about it.
Next day the doctor came. . . .
Well, now,
Shall I be brusque, or sentimental?
Communicative, or quite mute,
Leaving it all to you?
Did he get well, or die?
Did people rally, or remain away?
Dear reader, you shall have it as you choose.

Did fellows at the clubs say, "H'm!"
And keep their chairs?
Did a wide circle read about his death
Only to say, "Well! well!";
And did the office satisfy itself
With a ten-dollar wreath?

Or did a wave of general kindliness—
Equivalent for all the little waves
Himself had set in motion—
Gather impetus
And waft him out
On the Great Sea?

Did Alicia Mack,
Or others of that early coterie,
Come to his doleful room
With sympathy and flowers
(And even, mayhap,

A favorite grandchild
To clamber on his bed),
Showing a friendly tear in worldly eyes?
Did far-back chums sit down beside his pillow,
Sucking their cane-heads, saying:
"Cheer up, old chap; you're coming through all right!"?

Yes, perhaps he did
Come through all right—
With much or little sympathy—
To take up, with what zest he could,
The frantic rôle
Of buying favors from a cooling world.
Spend as you will,
It's sad to be old, and alone.
(Fudge! that's the very thing
I tried hard not to say!)

KATHARINE LEE BATES
1859–1929

To One Who Waits

I count the years by Junes that flush our laurel,
Our clustered bushes at the corner-wall,
And coax the crinkled buds to spread their small,
White chalices pricked out with rose and coral.
Slow are the seasons, yet I may not quarrel
With beauty. Dawns and stars, blossoms that foam
Enchanted orchards, where the orioles call,
Green leaves that flutter, golden leaves that fall,

Cloud caravans of snow will bring me home.
I count the years by Junes that flush our laurel.

What changes chronicle the life eternal?
Beyond the starry archipelagoes,
How do you calendar the stream that flows,
Forever singing, from the Throne supernal?
For as in wheat the sweetness of the kernel
Is ripened with the sunshine more and more,
Let sorrow trust, where mortal wisdom knows
Nothing, ah nothing, that the love of those
Who made earth heaven is greater than before
And watches for us in the life eternal.

If human love be but the soul's rehearsal
For that high harmony so piercing sweet
Its rhythm is pulsing in the wildest beat
Of passion, in the quietest dispersal
Of household blessings, Love the universal
Music of being, must not, Dear and True,
Our love that longs in me still yearn in you,
New-christened at the wide-winged Mercy seat
To a redeeming grace, my Paraclete,
For the divine accord my soul's rehearsal?

I count the years by Junes that flush our laurel,
And you, perchance, in some shy interspace
Of Paradise, have found a woodsy place,
A bit of wild that welcomes fern and sorrel,
Where mystery of moss and prickly moral
Of briar-rose may spring in finer bloom,
And Time's old witchery so far presume
That you, impatient for the glad embrace,
May now and then a dewy footpath trace
To see if June again has flushed the laurel.

A Mountain Soul

A mountain soul, she shines in crystal air
    Above the smokes and clamors of the town.
Her pure, majestic brows serenely wear
    The stars for crown.

The buzzing wings of folly, slander, spite,
    Fall frozen in her alien atmosphere.
Her heart's at home with sunrise and with night
        As neighbors dear

Who tell her ancient tales of time and law,
    The miracle of love breathed into dust,
Until her sweet gray eyes are brimmed with awe
        And steadfast trust.

Remote she dwells 'mid her celestial kin,
    Rainbow and Moon and Cloud, yet none the less
Full many a weak earth-creature shelters in
        Her friendliness.

She comrades with the child, the bird, the fern,
    Poet and sage and rustic chimney-nook,
But Pomp must be a pilgrim ere he earn
        Her mountain look,—

Her mountain look, the candor of the snow,
    The strength of folded granite, and the calm
Of choiring pines, whose swayed green branches strow
        A healing balm.

Oft as the psalmist lifted up his eyes
    Unto the hills about Jerusalem,
Did not God's glory with a new surprise
        Transfigure them?

That royal harper, passionate for rest,
    Held one still summit dearest to his dream,
And only to the golden chords confessed
        Its hour supreme;

For lovely is a mountain rosy-lit
    With dawn, or steeped in sunshine, azure-hot,
But loveliest when shadows traverse it
        And stain it not.

The Victory

The blue sky at its deepest was pricked by one keen star
That flashed a signal to the moon's uplifted scimitar,

And like a quarrel in a dream we spake with angry breath,
Till in that place of shadows our Love was done to death.

God hung the dawn with carmine and pillared it with gold
To welcome in our new Love, the angel of the old.
With lips still pale from requiems and litanies she came,
But home-sweet lights were in her eyes,—the same, and not the
    same.

All that was mortal of her, the passion, the caprice,
We had wrapt in cloud-white linen and laid away at peace;
But the living Spirit stood within the temple of the sun,
Her agony accomplished, her consecration won.

GEORGE SANTAYANA
1863–1952

To W.P.

I.

Calm was the sea to which your course you kept,
Oh, how much calmer than all southern seas!
Many your nameless mates, whom the keen breeze
Wafted from mothers that of old have wept.
All souls of children taken as they slept
Are your companions, partners of your ease,
And the green souls of all these autumn trees
Are with you through the silent spaces swept.
Your virgin body gave its gentle breath
Untainted to the gods. Why should we grieve,
      But that we merit not your holy death?
We shall not loiter long, your friends and I;
Living you made it goodlier to live,
Dead you will make it easier to die.

II.

With you a part of me hath passed away;

For in the peopled forest of my mind
A tree made leafless by this wintry wind
Shall never don again its green array.
Chapel and fireside, country road and bay,
Have something of their friendliness resigned;
Another, if I would, I could not find,
And I am grown much older in a day.
But yet I treasure in my memory
Your gift of charity, and young heart's ease,
And the dear honour of your amity;
For these once mine, my life is rich with these.
And I scarce know which part may greater be,—
What I keep of you, or you rob from me.

III.

Your ship lies anchored in the peaceful bight
Until a kinder wind unfurl her sail;
Your docile spirit, wingèd by this gale,
Hath at the dawning fled into the light.
And I half know why heaven deemed it right
Your youth, and this my joy in youth, should fail;
God hath them still, for ever they avail,
Eternity hath borrowed that delight.
For long ago I taught my thoughts to run
Where all the great things live that lived of yore,
And in eternal quiet float and soar;
There all my loves are gathered into one,
Where change is not, nor parting any more,
Nor revolution of the moon and sun.

IV.

In my deep heart these chimes would still have rung
To toll your passing, had you not been dead;
For time a sadder mask than death may spread
Over the face that ever should be young.
The bough that falls with all its trophies hung
Falls not too soon, but lays its flower-crowned head
Most royal in the dust, with no leaf shed
Unhallowed or unchiselled or unsung.
And though the after word will never hear
The happy name of one so gently true,
Nor chronicles write large this fatal year,
Yet we who loved you, though we be but few,

Keep you in whatsoe'er things are good, and rear
In our weak virtues monuments to you.

Apollo in Love or the Poet Lost in the Platonist

The stern palestra moulded well my youth,
That I might wring from the taut-corded lyre
      Music and truth
To lighten souls, and move to holy ruth.

Much did I wander through the Delphic glen
Where the rapt sibyl strained to catch my song
      Through field and fen
Eurotas watered, nurse of perfect men.

And through all lovely lands, where beauty fed
The eyes with joy, and left the heart secure,
      Which only bled
When my sweet boy, my Hyacinth, was dead.

Till, goddess, seeing thee, my soul was fired
With might of all the beauties ever seen,
      For all conspired
In thy one form, divine and all-desired.

In thee I found all friends, all gifts, all power
Of music, and all harmonies—in thee,
      With richer dower,
My Hyacinth came back, immortal flower.

But that, alas, which should my psalm inspire
Confounds me quite, and leaves me dumb, abashed;
      So great desire
Chokes my faint voice, and snaps the pulsing lyre.

Dedication of the Later Sonnets to Urania

How shall I give thee what was never mine?
I have no voice, no hope beneath the sky;
All sound and silence are a melody
Played on my heartstrings by some touch of thine.
Thine is the glory of my brave design,
The ardour, the compulsion, and the cry;

Mine but the hoarseness and the unbidden sigh
Muffling the silver music of the line.
If aught of rapture from the feeble string
Escape and swell and tremble as I sing,
Think what the might of loveliness must be,
That from the dust could raise a living thing,
And from the cold heart of a doubter wring
This book of verses, writ in love of thee.

LOGAN PEARSALL SMITH
1865–1946

Two Loves

Two loves are lords of life, each Nature's child;
One haunts the valleys and to men draws near
By stream and farm and orchard, where the clear
Soft voices echo through the evening mild.
His are the gifts of earth, the fruit up-piled,
All harvests of the golden, mellowing year;
Warm-housed, with wife, with children, he can hear
The gossip of the fire in winter wild.

The other love is barren as the sea,
The wandering sea, that knows nor rest nor home,
Washing against earth's shores with vain desire.
Yet heroes sail those highways, bold and free;
And to that bosom the stars of heaven come,
And glitter there, bright firmaments of fire.

The Magic Streets

Within an ancient wood, where far from heat,
Far mid blue shadows all the summer day
Dawn's twilight lingers, there I love to stray

On paths o'er-arched by trees, and worn by feet
Of secret forest folk I never meet;
Outlaws, I wonder, clad in green array,
Or Fauns who down the glimmering alleys play
And scare the Dryads to their cool retreat?

Thus could I ever live; yet oft I change
That whispering roof of leaves for smoky skies,
Those silent paths for multitudes of men.
The magic streets allure me, faces strange
That pass and pass, and haunting human eyes,
Eyes that I love, and never see again.

Fulfilment

I built my house to my desire.
One day, without the garden wall,
I heard an unknown voice enquire
    "And is this all?"

"It is my dream," I said, "come true.
Happy I am whate'er befall."
"Alas," that voice whispered anew,
    "So this is all?"

"Hast thou ne'er dreamed of other bliss?
Thy youth, that dream, canst thou recall?
Have all thy hopes but come to this?
    Can this be all?"

"I lead my life to my desire,
Farewell." I heard his faint footfall.
And then I fell to weeping dire
    That this was all.

HASTEEN KLAH
1867–1937

Song of the Sun

Song of how the Sun was made.

They emerged; they say He is planning it:[1]
They emerged; they say He is planning it;
They emerged; they say He is planning it;
   Right on the edge of the Emergence Pit,
      they say He is planning it;
   In the center of the first man's hogahn,
      they say He is planning it;
   In the center of a hogahn of soft goods;
      they say He is planning it;
   On top of a pile of soft goods;
      they say He is planning it;
The sun will be created, they say He is planning it;
Its face will be blue, they say He is planning it;
Its eyes[2] will be black, they say He is planning it;
Its chin will be yellow, they say He is planning it;
Its horns will be blue, they say He is planning it.
   The (space) around it being black;
      they say He is planning it;
   The (space) around it being white;
      they say He is planning it;
   The (space) around it being yellow;
      they say He is planning it;
   Its strength is dangerous;[3] they say He is planning it;
   The sacred words will be (created),
      they say He is planning it;
They emerged; they say He is planning it;
They emerged; they say He is planning it;
They emerged; they say He is planning it.
   Right on the edge of the Emergence Pit,
      they say He is planning it;
   In the center of the first woman's hogahn,
      they say He is planning it;

In the center of a hogahn of hard things,
    they say He is planning it;
On top of a pile of hard things;
    they say He is planning it;
The moon will be created; they say He is planning it;
Its face will be white, they say He is planning it;
Its pupils will be black, they say He is planning it;
Its chin will be yellow, they say He is planning it;
Its horns will be white, they say He is planning it;
    The (space) around it being black;
        they say He is planning it;
    The (space) around it being yellow;
        they say He is planning it;
    The (space) around it being blue;
        they say He is planning it;
    The (space) around it being red;
        they say He is planning it;
    Its strength is dangerous; they say he is planning it;
    The sacred words will be (created),
        they say He is planning it.
They emerged; they say He is planning it;
They emerged; they say He is planning it;
They emerged; they say He is planning it.

NOTES

    1. That is, the Creator is planning the creation of the sun.
    2. Literally: "his eye interior" that in his eyes.
    3. Literally: "his body has danger on it"; this refers, according to Klah, to the intense heat of the sun.

The Song of the Earth Spirit

> The purpose of this song is the identification of the person for whom the ceremony is given with the earth in every aspect.

It is lovely indeed, it is lovely indeed, it is lovely indeed,
It is lovely indeed, it is lovely indeed.
    I, I am the spirit within the earth;
    It is lovely indeed, it is lovely indeed,
    It is lovely indeed, it is lovely indeed,

The feet of the earth are my feet;
It is lovely indeed, it is lovely indeed,
It is lovely indeed, it is lovely indeed,
The legs of the earth are my legs;
It is lovely indeed, it is lovely indeed,
It is lovely indeed, it is lovely indeed,
The bodily strength of the earth is my bodily strength;
It is lovely indeed, it is lovely indeed,
It is lovely indeed, it is lovely indeed,
The thoughts of the earth are my thoughts;
It is lovely indeed, it is lovely indeed,
It is lovely indeed, it is lovely indeed,
The voice of the earth is my voice,
It is lovely indeed, it is lovely indeed,
It is lovely indeed, it is lovely indeed,
The feather of the earth is my feather;
It is lovely indeed, it is lovely indeed,
It is lovely indeed, it is lovely indeed,
All that belongs to the earth belongs to me;
It is lovely indeed, it is lovely indeed,
It is lovely indeed, it is lovely indeed,
All that surrounds the earth surrounds me;
It is lovely indeed, it is lovely indeed,
It is lovely indeed, it is lovely indeed,
I, I am the sacred words of the earth;
It is lovely indeed, it is lovely indeed,
It is lovely indeed, it is lovely indeed;
It is lovely indeed, it is lovely indeed, it is lovely indeed,
It is lovely indeed, it is lovely indeed.

Old Age Song

> To the Navajos, "old age" means
> long life and to be desired, and this song
> shows the universe full of long duration.

Old age, old age, moves about on its surface;
Old age, old age, moves about on its surface;

The earth, old age moves about on its surface;
Sahanabray Bekay Hozhon, old age moves about on its surface;

Old age, old age moves about under it;
Old age, old age moves about under it;

The black sky, old age moves about under it;
Shahanabray Bekay Hozhon, old age moves about under it;

Old age, old age, moves about on its surface;
Old age, old age, moves about on its surface;

The mountain spirit, old age moves about on its surface;
Sahanabray Bekay rozhon, old age moves about on its surface;

Old age, old age moves about under it;
Old age, old age moves about under it;

The sun, old age moves about under it;
Sahanahray Bekay Hozhon, old age moves about under it;

Old age, old age moves about among them;
Old age, old age moves about among them;

All sorts of waters, old age moves about among them;
The sacred words, old age moves about among them;

Old age, old age moves about among them;
Old age, old age moves about among them.

JESSIE B. RITTENHOUSE
1869–1949

The Secret

I go in vesture spun by hands
Upon no loom of earth,
I dwell within a shining house
That has no walls nor hearth;

I live on food more exquisite
Than honey of the bee,
More delicate than manna
It falls to nourish me;

But none may see my shining house
Nor taste my food so rare,
And none may see my moon-spun robe
Nor my star-powdered hair.

Myself

They look at me as if they knew me,
   All these people whom I meet,
But to myself I am a stranger
   Passing in the street.

I meet the stranger's eyes with question
   Looking into mine,
And with a sudden recognition
   We give a sign.

Then we are lost again, we mingle
   In the effacing crowd,
And I forget those eyes that called me
   As though one spoke aloud,—

Until another signal moment
   Flashes identity,
And in the maze of life, arrested,
   My soul looks out at me.

The Door

There was a door stood long ajar
That one had left for me,
While I went trying other doors
To which I had no key;

And when at length I turned to seek
The refuge and the light,
A gust of wind had shut the door
And left me in the night.

WILLBUR D. NESBIT
1871–1927

An Artificial Tragedy

There was an artificial man—
  His hair was not his own;
One eye was glass; one ear was wax;
  His nose was carved from bone;
His legs were manufactured ones; .
  His teeth were deftly made;
Six ribs of rubber also were
  Within his form arrayed.

He wooed a maid of paint and puff,
  Whose face and form were art,
And found she had, when they were wed,
  An artificial heart.
However, they did not indulge
  In petty stress and strife—
They hired their fussing done, and led
  An artificial life.

They read by artificial light;
  Ate artificial rice;
Drank artificial water, cooled
  By artificial ice;
An artificial organ played
  Them artificial tunes;
A phonograph would soothe their babe
  With artificial croons.

Alas! At last there came a day
  To harrow up the soul!
The artificial man could not
  Buy artificial coal,
And with no artificial heat
  To warm their chilly breath,
They imitated other folks
  In artificial death.

The Trail to Boyland

Where the maple leaves are yellow
And the apples plump and mellow,
And the purple grapes are bursting with their rich autumnal wine,
And the oak leaves redly flaming—
All the blaze of sunset shaming—
Is a trail that wanders idly to a land of yours and mine.

It goes through the grassy hollows
And across the hills; it follows
All the playful turns and curvings of the ever-singing streams;
Overgrown with tangled grasses,
All the olden haunts it passes
Till it fades into a vista that is cherished in our dreams.

Past the pokeweeds and their berries
And the dance-halls of the fairies,
Over field and through the forest it goes ever on and on,
With the thrush and killdee singing;
And the redbird madly winging
Far ahead of us to somewhere, where the sunset meets the dawn.

Up and down, the hillside hugging,
With the hazel bushes tugging
At our arms, and blushing sumach holding spicy berries out;
And the haw-trees and the beeches,
Hickories and plums and peaches—
Just as young and just as plenty—all our thoughts of age to flout!

So it stretches and it glistens,
Far away—and he who listens
Hears the echo of the hailing and the murmur of a song
That comes through the silence throbbing—
Half with laughter, half with sobbing—
Till it clutches at the heart-strings and would hold them overlong.

'Tis the trail—the Trail to Boyland—
How it spans the miles to joyland!
Passing leafy lane and blossom-tangled vine, and bush and tree,
Coaxing bees till they, in coming,
Fill the hush of noon with humming—
And the wondrous way to Boyland stretches fair for you and me!

The Four Guests

A knock at the door—but he
  Was dreaming a dream of fame,
And the one who knocked drew softly back,
  And never again he came.
A knock at the door—as soft,
  As soft, as shy, as a dove.
But the dreamer dreamed till the guest was gone—
  And the guest was Love.

A knock at the door—again
  The dreamer dreamed away,
Unheeding, deaf to the gentle call
  Of the one who came that day.
A knock at the door—no more
  The guest to that door came.
Yet the dreamer dreamed of the one who called,
  For the guest was Fame.

A knock at the door—but still
  He gave it no reply;
And the waiting guest gave a cheery hail
  Ere he slowly wandered by.
A knock at the door—in dreams
  The dreamer fain would grope
Till the guest stole on, with a humbled sigh—
  And the guest was Hope.

A knock at the door—'twas loud,
  With might in every stroke;
And the dreamer stopped in his dreaming thought,
  And suddenly awoke.
A knock at the door! He ran
  With the swiftness of a breath;
And the door swung wide, and the guest came in—
  And the guest was Death.

WILLA CATHER
1873–1947

Sonnet

Alas, that June should come when thou didst go;
I think you passed each other on the way;
And seeing thee, the Summer loved thee so
That all her loveliness she gave away;
Her rare perfumes, in hawthorn boughs distilled,
Blushing, she in thy sweeter bosom left,
Thine arms with all her virgin roses filled,
Yet felt herself the richer for thy theft;
Beggared herself of morning for thine eyes,
Hung on the lips of every bird the tune,
Breathed on thy cheek her soft vermilion dyes,
And in thee set the singing heart of June.
And so, not only do I mourn thy flight,
But Summer comes despoiled of her delight.

Antinous

With attributes of gods they sculptured him,
    Hermes, Osiris, but were never wise
To lift the level, frowning brow of him
    Or dull the mortal misery in his eyes;
The scornful weariness of every limb,
    The dust begotten doubt that never dies,
Antinous, beneath thy lids, though dim,
The curling smoke of altars rose to thee,
Conjuring thee to comfort and content.
    An emperor sent his galleys wide and far
To seek thy healing for thee. Yea, and spent
    Honor and treasure and red fruits of war
    To lift thy heaviness, lest thou should'st mar
The head that was an empire's glory, bent
A little, as the heavy poppies are.
    Did the perfection of thy beauty pain
Thy limbs to bear it? Did it ache to be,

As song hath ached in men, or passion vain?
Or lay it like some heavy robe on thee?
    Was thy sick soul drawn from thee like the rain,
Or drunk up as the dead are drunk, each hour
To feed the color of some tulip flower?

Asphodel

As some pale shade in glorious battle slain,
    On beds of rue, beside the silent streams,
    Recalls outworn delights in happy dreams;
The play of oars upon the flashing main,
The speed of runners, and the swelling vein,
    And toil in pleasant upland field that teems
    With vine and gadding gourd—until he seems
To feel wan memories of the sun again
    And scent the vineyard slopes when dawn is wet,
But feels no ache within his loosened knees
    To join the runners where the course is set,
Nor smite the billows of the fruitless seas,—
    So I recall our day of passion yet,
    With sighs and tenderness, but no regret.

AMY LOWELL
1874–1925

Orientation

When the young ladies of the boarding-school take the air,
They walk in pairs, each holding a blush-red parasol against the
    sun.
From my window they look like an ambulating parterre
Of roses, I cannot tell one from one.

There is a certain young person I dream of by night,
And paint by day on little two-by-three inch squares

Of ivory. Which is she? Which of all the parasols in sight
Covers the blithe, mocking face which stares
At me from twenty miniatures, confusing the singleness of my
   delight?

You know my window well enough—the fourth from the corner.
   Oh, you know.
Slant your parasol a bit this way, if you please,
And take for yourself the very correct bow
I make toward the line of demure young ladies
Perambulating the street in a neat row.
It is true I have never seen beneath your parasol,
Therefore my miniatures resemble one another not at all.

You must pick yourself like a button-hole bouquet,
And lift the parasol to my face one day,
And let me see you laughing at the sun—
Or at me. Then I will choose the one
Of my twenty miniatures most like you
And destroy the others, with which I shall have nothing more to
   do.

Crepuscule du Matin

All night I wrestled with a memory
   Which knocked insurgent at the gates of thought.
   The crumbled wreck of years behind has wrought
Its disillusion; now I only cry
For peace, for power to forget the lie
   Which hope too long has whispered. So I sought
   The sleep which would not come, and night was fraught
With old emotions weeping silently.
I heard your voice again, and knew the things
   Which you had promised proved an empty vaunt.
I felt your clinging hands while night's broad wings
Cherished our love in darkness. From the lawn
   A sudden, quivering birdnote, like a taunt.
My arms held nothing but the empty dawn.

The Letter

Little cramped words scrawling all over the paper
Like draggled fly's legs,

What can you tell of the flaring moon
Through the oak leaves?
Or of my uncurtained window and the bare floor
Spattered with moonlight?
Your silly quirks and twists have nothing in them
Of blossoming hawthorns,
And this paper is dull, crisp, smooth, virgin of loveliness
Beneath my hand.

I am tired, Beloved, of chafing my heart against
The want of you;
Of squeezing it into little inkdrops,
And posting it,
And I scald alone, here, under the fire
Of the great moon.

DAVID O'NEIL
1874–1947

The Beach

The chill clung to the water;
A bevy of boys,
In naked beauty,
Venturesome,
Shivering,
Shy with wonderment,
Huddled into themselves,
Like street sparrows,
On snowy mornings.

A Character

His life was well ordered,
And monotonously clean

As an orchard with white-washed trees;
But he felt not the cool
Of the sun-splotched wood,
Nor the mad blue brilliance
Of the sea.

The Explorer

"Will you go home with me
By the light of my lantern?
The night is dark
And the way is rough."

"I do not fear the ruts
Of the traveled road,
And your lantern blinds my sight
When I would see
The darkness clearer."

ROSE O'NEILL
1874–1944

She wrote it

To Kallista

She wrote, "only your own words
could tell you how I am loving you."

She wrote it, "Only your own words."
She, who called like bulls and birds,
She, who throbbed a thrushes throat
And bayed the wind back as he cried,
She, who moaned the pigeon's note
And shook the pinetree when she sighed:
Mistress of all words and wails,
Giving tongue with nightingales!

She, whose pea-cock coloured cries
Woke the dead man in his bed,
And fooled him back from Paradise,
With his pale heart turned to red:
She, the horn that warriors led,
Clamour of the larks that rise,
And viol of the swan that dies!

She wrote it! She, my lyric you!
You beat of drum, you lull of lute!
You voice of cataract and dew,
You verse, you violin, you flute!
You roar! You sound of loves that sue!
Tongue of the world, who pierce and coo!

The Master-Mistress

All in the drowse of life I saw a shape,
A lovely monster reared up from the restless rock,
More secret and more loud than other beasts.
It, seeming two in one,
With dreadful beauty doomed
Folded itself, in chanting like a flood.
I said, "Your name, O Master-mistress?"
But it, answering not,
Folded itself, in chanting like a flood.

The Sonnet Begs Me

The Sonnet begs me like a bridegroom,
    "Come within."
    "This palace! Not for me, the desert-born!"
I turn me, as from some too lordly sin,
    And like a singing Hagar, pause and pass—
To lift for night's sweet thieves my houseless horn
    In broken rhythms of the windy grass.
I will not be the measure-pacing bride,
    But where the flutes come faintly,
        Sing outside.
Like drifting sand my love doth drift and change—
I strangely sing because my love is strange.

GERTRUDE STEIN
1874–1946

From "Lifting Belly"

Nothing pleases me except dinner.

I have done as I wished and I do not feel any responsibility
to you.

Are you there.

Lifting belly.

What do I say.

Pussy how pretty you are.

That goes very quickly unless you have been there too long.

I told him I would send him Mildred's book. He seemed
very pleased at the prospect.

Lifting belly is so strong.

Lifting belly together.

Lifting belly oh yes.

Lifting belly.

Oh yes.

Remember what I say.

I have no occasion to deliberate.

He has not heart but that you can supply.

The fan goes alright.

Lifting belly what is earnest. Expecting an arena to be
monumental.

Lifting belly is recognised to be the only spectacle present.
Do you mean that.

Lifting belly is a language. It says island. Island a strata.
Lifting belly is a repetition.

Lifting belly means me.

America

Once in English they said America. Was it english to them.
Once they said. Belgian.
We like a fog.
Do you for weather.
Are we brave.
Are we true.
Have we the national color.
Can we stand ditches.
Can we mean well.
Do we talk together.
Have we red cross.
A great many people speak of feet.
And socks.

Your Own

Complain to me.
I like it better just that much better.
You are sure of that.
I think it's too wet.
Now how do you feel about summer.

Sunny isn't hot.
I prefer painted wood.
I am right about wood.
I prefer knitting to crochet.
Because it is pleasant and because it is a third part of an art.
What do you feel about windows.
I prefer windows french and long and open.
And what is your idea of resistance.
And fruit.
And sweet.
And what do you think about leaks.
Leeks are the asparagus of the poor.

ALICE DUNBAR-NELSON
1875–1935

You! Inez!

Orange gleams athwart a crimson soul
Lambent flames; purple passion lurks
In your dusk eyes.
Red mouth; flower soft,
Your soul leaps up—and flashes
Star-like, white, flame-hot.
Curving arms, encircling a world of love.
You! Stirring the depths of passionate desire!

The Gift

Like wine, your kisses touch my lips,
Like wine, the blood thrills through my veins;
The honey that the gold bee sips,
The purple draught that foams and stains
Are in your tender, sweet caress;
My heart is yours, I could give less—

I could give less, but all my life
Lies at your feet, to take or no.
  I crave your clasp that shields from strife,
The kiss you gave me, loving so.
I love your breath upon my hair,
  Myself I love—you think me fair.

I Sit and Sew

I sit and sew—a useless task it seems,
My hands grown tired, my head weighed down with dreams—
The panoply of war, the martial tred of men,
Grim-faced, stern-eyed, gazing beyond the ken
Of lesser souls, whose eyes have not seen Death,
Nor learned to hold their lives but as a breath—
But—I must sit and sew.

I sit and sew—my heart aches with desire—
That pageant terrible, that fiercely pouring fire
On wasted fields, and writhing grotesque things
Once men. My soul in pity flings
Appealing cries, yearning only to go
There in that holocaust of hell, those fields of woe—
But—I must sit and sew.

The little useless seam, the idle patch;
Why dream I here beneath my homely thatch,
When there they lie in sodden mud and rain,
Pitifully calling me, the quick ones and the slain?
You need me, Christ! It is no roseate dream
That beckons me—this pretty futile seam,
It stifles me—God, must I sit and sew?

HELEN HAY WHITNEY
1876–1944

Love and Death

I can believe that my Beloved dies,
    That all her virtue, all her youth shall fail,
    And life, her rosy life, grow cold and pale,
To bloom again in braver Paradise.
I must believe that death shall close her eyes,
    And hold her heart beyond a heavy veil,
    Where silences surround her spirit frail
And waste the form where all my loving lies.

Ah, God! but no. And is my love so weak?
    Her heart may pause, may falter and grow still,
But not her laugh, the color in her cheek—
        That may not fade; the catch that lifts her breath,
    Sobbing against my heart. Essay your will—
        These are too dear to fill *your* grave, O Death!

Lyric Love

The world deserves its wisdom. You and I,
  Serene within the shadow, crowned with hours,
Cinctured with solitude, the bended sky
  Folds us in hues of tulip twilight flowers.

Knowledge is chill; your hair is warm with gold,
  A lock lies heavily across your cheek.
I somewhere heard of darkness, pain, and cold—
  Keep your own, world. Ah, Love, stir not nor speak.

To a Woman

Take all of me, pour out my life as wine,
  To dye your soul's sweet shallows. Violent sin
  Blazed me a path, and I have walked therein,
Strong, unashamed. Your timorous hands need mine,
As the white stars their sky, your lips' pale line
  Shall blush to roses where my lips have been.
  I ask no more. I do not hope to win—
Only to add myself to your design.

Take all of me. I know your little lies,
Your light dishonor, gentle treacheries.
  I know, I lie in torment at your feet,
Shadow to all your sun. Take me and go,
  Use my adoring to your honor, sweet,
Strength for your weakness—it is better so.

NATALIE CLIFFORD BARNEY
1876–1972

The Love of Judas

Love, take me back to you, and make me whole,
Who am divided and in unbelief:
An infidel in thought and word and grief,
A double heart and a promiscuous soul!

And what if Judas offered Christ that bowl
Of greatest bitterness without relief.
Revenge, not silver, tempted such a thief:
Betrayed betrayer of the kiss he stole.

He loved the most: those others loved but well,
They drowsed: in dreadful paths his anguish trod,
Not thrice denied the love that sold his God.

No pity for his throbbing jealous side,
No pity for his false obscure farewell;
Yet he alone for his lost master died!

Double Being

A northern mind, a face from Italy,
A double fate lived all too fatally,
A look fresh as a child's, both soft and sharp,
A clarion-voice, the liquid as a harp!
A natural being, yet from nature freed,
Like a Shakespearean boy of fairy breed—
A sex perplexed into attractive seeming
—Both sex at best, the strangeness so redeeming!—
Hands hard to loosen if for once they cling,
Yet frail as Leicester's wearing a queen's ring.
A page-clothed Rosalind to play a part,
A brow of genius and a lonely heart.

Love's Comrades

You say I've lived too long in France
And wearied of the senses' dance?

Like fresh air in an opium den
You'll lead me out—to when? and when?

. . . I fear no country's ready yet
For our complexities: forget
The best of flesh and food to go
A'roaming o'er the world, and know
Discomfort's great surprises few—?
No, let me travel just to you!

ESTHER M. CLARK
1876-?

The Pictured Eyes

She that hath sorrowful eyes
    Haunteth me early and late.
Was she too proud, or too wise,
    For passionate railings at Fate?
Was she of lofty estate?
    Was she as haughty as fair?
Is it all writ in these great,
    Luminous eyes of despair?

Ah, were she living! But now
    Heavy the churchyard dust lies
Thick on the beautiful brow,
    Thick on the sorrowful eyes.
Dead! With her sorrow unwept!
    Dead! Yet how mockingly fair
That which the canvas hath kept,
    Picturing forth her despair.

Her Mouth

She has eyes that can be steely,—
They would make you shiver, really;
She's an eminently practical young miss
    And my faint heart goes a-flutter
    At the wisdom she can utter;
But the corners of her mouth turn up like this ⌣

    She's unearthly fond of learning,
    But her journalistic yearning
Those of masculine persuasion take amiss.
    They're a precious lot of stupids
    Not to see that bow of Cupid's,
Where the corners of her mouth turn up like this ⌣

    She's distractingly specific
    On all matters scientific;
She's a living, breathing, moving sacrifice
    On the altar of her calling;
    And her firmness is appalling,
But the corners of her mouth turn up like this ⌣

    She's cold-blooded—and we know it—
    Independent—and she'll show it—
And her style is far from being hit or miss.
    She's the essence of precision,
    She has plenty of decision,
But the corners of her mouth turn up like this ⌣

    She's the dearest little woman,
    Could I just be sure she's human,
(Heaven grant she doesn't take the doubt amiss!)
    I've a mind to tell her, nearly,
    That I love her, dearly, dearly,
When the corners of her mouth turn up like this ⌣

The Heart's Desire

My heart and I, we sit alone
    Beside the embers of a fire;
We make no cry, we make no moan,
    But we have lost the heart's desire.

Love lightly came and lightly went,
   And came not back this way again;
And left us with our goods all spent,
   Yet we are richer now than then.

Because a gracious sense is here,
   Of peace that can not be denied;
Since on that day Love passed so near,
   A voice within us woke and cried.

A shameless voice it was, and bold;
   It cried aloud and spoke Love's name.
Love turned and smiled, and all was told,
   But we were mute for very shame.

Love lightly came and lightly went,
   As comes and goes the summer rain;
And though he left us well content,
   Our only recompense is pain.

My heart and I, we sit alone
   Beside the embers of a fire;
And naught have we to call our own,
   Nor have we yet the heart's desire.

MARSDEN HARTLEY
1877–1943

Un Recuerdo—Hermano—Hart Crane R.I.P.

"Death thou has left behind,
the center of life is here;
no wounding needst thou fear
nothing can hurt thee more,
nothing can force thee or bind
thy self is no longer near;
no hostile voice canst thou hear,
upon this infinite shore."

JACOPONE DA TODI

"For when Urizen shrunk away
From Eternals he sat on a rock
Barren: a rock which himself
From redounding fancies had petrified.
Many tears fell on the rock,
Many sparks of vegetation.
Soon shot the pained root
Of Mystery under his heel:
It grew a thick tree: he wrote
In silence his book of iron."

WM. BLAKE, *THE BOOK OF AHANIA*
CHAP. III, V.III

And, should it be left like this,
dear Hart, like this,
too much of fulfillment, no more promise,
given over petulantly, fevered,
you the severing, we the severed,
to wind-wash,
wave-flow, wave-toss and thrash,
beating forward, backward, to and fro,
in the unremitting high and low
in the never ending torment of today,
yesterday, so redolent of geniality—
never again to know tomorrow,
Atonatiuh crying loudly, augmenting our sorrow,
"what is life worth, if in the moment
it can be destroyed"—ancient Aztec lament
come over to us,
never a respite of tomorrow.

Wave is wave, Hart, wave is wave,
can it comfort to be wind-slave,
blow with the silence of the quasi-brave
upon a wide, unsensing mead,
heeding not death, or being dead?
Are they dearer for being nearer
to this bronzed outspoken earth
with its sandalled, molten mirth,
loved, cared for richly, this loud-lunged earth
so perpetually antiphonal, majestically antiphonal
to the crowded ear and shrouded soul?
Has it sense or double meaning
to be hushed, equivocally still,
seized and kept from sacred quiver

of delicious, sunlit earth-fever,
to be forever and forever
keepsake of so listless a lover?
Is it, is it, Hart, you find
it easier to give in to wave-din
freed of the harsh travailing of mind
fierce beating of the burning heart
and its veiled, surging smart,
seeking respite from the day and night
night and day refrain?

Loved you were, Hart,
surely you had well surmised—
you must have known, and prized;
It is not work to love
when the curved, rhythmic trace thereof
shines through, as bright light beams
through clipped obsidian blade
in warming, crenelated shade
white with unhindered orchestrating gleams
of morning with no obfuscating shadow laid
upon its never too promising brow, for the hue
and measure of love is not in cry and shout
but in sure-spoken unspoken certitude
without cheap subterfuge of bargain-hunting nonsense
never blurred with roistering word,
goodfellow-like, procrastinatingly inferred.
Love is love, Hart, and you were loved—
How could useless more be proved
in the round and round about,
and from us yourself have taken,
left us withered, worn, torn, shaken,
broken with the thought, we might have won
and you too have won, if you had sworn
the sane, same faithfulness to the sun.
Crash of noon, Hart. How could you see
it through with the gongs of midnoon clashing,
clanging welcome of renown
from azul-vistas and previstas down
huge blasts from the bellows
of the sun.
You knew them, yet could mistake
them once for dark insinuations toward

an everlasting dark, ineffable intake
from which no glib protest can glide
or childishly, or even manfully hide.
Earth wanted you, because she knew,
she always knows who has his cue
in place to be dictioned perfectly in space,
true inflection never falters, never alters
when the tone comes booming from the breast,
life discerns the rest, she knows and hears
above the monotone of roar and grind
each moment she herself be found
forsaken and foregone, she herself is pained
at losses never to be regained.
You had this lover, what more to be desired?
Earth hears the rumble of our thronged and sandalled feet
and finds their music sweet,
she craves
the tender, lustrous worship of her slaves.
In ebony and oxbone whitened in the sun
are you housed and harboured now,
symbolled of profusioned hours and what came—
white for a blanched and listless one,
black for the blankness, black for blame
of them that took you down, and kept you
wish or no wish, to drown.
Why should we be driven therefore, to condone,
left to condone a lecherous, treacherous prank
with none but instabilities to thank?
Oxbone and ebony and a vision neath a film
of cellophane, this was he, to say,
before he went away, and only yesterday
we had the genial bulk and blood and all
its amiable hardihood.
You Hart, had the bright front of the fall,
but we have the dull thud, and the pall
of it, all of it—you have at least the calm
of soul, rest in bosom, and we
no one or nothing to praise, no way to phrase
the shock of this strategy.

K. von F.—1914—Arras-Bouquoi

"by the haste of a cruel stop, ill-placed"
—Robert Crashaw

Man in perfect bloom
of sixfoot splendour
lusty manhood time—all made of youthful fire
and simplest desire,
voiceless now these many years—
what music in the voice that was,
beyond all calumny of tears.

What makes it seem
as if you never went away
what gentle gleam from out
the perfidy of wars
gives hint of immortality?

In dream I saw you once
all made of living fire—
clothed in lightning's wondrousness
there to cherish, there to bless—
the light flew up my willing side
and filled me with fraternal pride,
all made of pristine fire
you were,
symbol of your natural attire;
Yourself the moment that I saw
and took into my heart
is still an image that I worship—
not death but love inspire
to keep this everlasting fellowship.

He Too Wore a Butterfly

He wore a butterfly upon his flanks,
upsetting the woman and the ship in their angles,
and down his midrib the image of Christ, the feet
and the nails, touching his navel.
He wore a butterfly upon his shoulder blade and
one above his knee, as if—like the indian in the
race, whose thighs are brushed with eagle feathers to

give him speed in the run.
He wore a butterfly upon his flanks as though he
felt the fear of being musclebound,
or, saying to himself—"I must have the breath of
spring upon my beam"—that smiling morning of a man
and—as if the sea had crowded all its waves
within his eyes, making him think of numberless
casual afternoons, the lashes curling up to let the
floods of evening in,
staving off for later years the pale textures of
immitigable distance.

DOUGLAS MALLOCH
1877–1938

The Bachelor

He walked the way of life alone,
No wife, no child, no house his own;
A quiet man, he did not dare
To think a maiden anywhere
For such a one would ever care.

Nor did I think a woman would—
For men are always understood
The way themselves they understand;
Yes, so ourselves we often brand,
And mould our lives with our own hand.

I know he worshipped women, yes
With strange detachment, tenderness—
With something now that seems to me
Much sweeter, holier, to be
Than loudly shouted chivalry.

And I remember now, at last,
That oftentimes, when he had passed,
The eyes of many women turned

And followed him, as if they yearned
To tell him what he never learned.

So slipped away the days of youth,
And John wed Mary, William Ruth.
The road of life is fair and wide,
And none is happiness denied;
And yet he always stepped aside.

The lovely girls of younger days
He saw take up their wedded ways;
Alone he faced the storm, the strife,
And ever lonelier his life
As friendship turned from friend to wife.

And yet I know what hurt the most:
As years rolled on, a happy host
Of little children he would meet,
Of little children fair and sweet,
Each morning in the village street.

He always something had for each:
A scarlet apple, velvet peach,
Perhaps in wintertime a toy,
A word of counsel for the boy,
Some little help, some little joy.

I used to pity him; and then
One day he did not wake again.
And yet he did not lie alone,
The one who wife had never known,
Nor house nor children of his own.

I thought he knew no woman's love;
I think he learned at last above,
From tears that womanhood let fall,
From sobbing of the children small,
He was the one most loved of all.

The Love of a Man

The love of a woman is sweet;
   In life I have fondled a few,
Have felt the red blood as it beat
   The uttermost arteries through.

Yet God in His wisdom divine,
  Yet God in His infinite plan,
Made nothing as holy and fine
  As the love of a man for a man.

There was one with the dark in her hair,
  There was one with the dawn in her eyes,
There was one who had kisses to spare—
  For never a memory dies.
But, maids, you were nothing but maids;
  You passed, as the waters that ran.
For what are the angels or jades
  By love of a man for a man?

The love of a woman is warm;
  Her kisses as hot as the South,
And glorious battle to storm
  The road to her amorous mouth.
But what is the nectar you drink,
  The fragile and beautiful span,
By one indestructible link,
  The love of a man for a man?

For when she has thrown you aside,
  Has passed from embraces and sight,
And all of the noonday has died
  And left but the stars and the night,
You feel on your shoulder a hand,
  For comfort you come where you can,
And deep in your heart understand
  The love of a man for a man.

He'll go with you over the trail,
  The trail that is lonesome and long;
His faith will not falter nor fail,
  Nor falter the lilt of his song.
He knows both your soul and your sins,
  And does not too carefully scan.
The highway to Heaven begins
  With the love of a man for a man.

One

There runs a pathway by the hedge
  And up across the clearing,

A ribbon through the woodland's edge,
  Appearing, disappearing,
That fades beyond the hills of gray
  Where red the west is burning;
And many men have passed this way,
  And few who came returning.

Full many men have followed it,
  The path beside the shanty;
And some there were with wealth or wit,
  And some who sang a chanty;
And some were sad and some were gay,
  And there were some who flattered;
Yes, many men have passed this way—
  But only one who mattered.

PERSIS M. OWEN
?–?

The Dead have mourners plenty

The Dead have mourners plenty
And honor to their name
But who wreaths tenderly the living dead
Those broken ones who soon as peace has come
So soon must feel the old familiar bag
Creep 'round the knees
Who soon must know once more
The meagerness of life
Those broken ones whose souls deep wakened in war's hell
Cry blindly out for some release
For some new better mode their glory to proclaim
Only to find that living fibre
Grimly holds to meager fare
And binds its rightful master hopeless, captive
Through long dead barren years
Oh, God! some pity show

For those who wonderingly come back from hell
And face reality
For man remembers not the living
But the Dead
It is so easy to sit quietly and mourn.

Dawn at Abbazia

A pearling road along a rock gray shore
A tawny beach, man made, a mile or more
A sea, blue Hyacinth, cupped close against that shore
And stretching far away till in a pale uncertainty
It mingles with the dawn and is the sky
And brooding over all a listening hush
Which hears but faintly in the rising light
The call of winging gull of lapping wave
A dream crushed by reality
When on the sand a beach-man flings a red umbrella wide
To cut a bleeding wound in Nature's quivering side.

[Poem: I–VII]

I.
I watched today a lone brown leaf
Which quivered in a sharp November's gale
Until all fearful of its lingering
It broke from off the maple tree
And drifted far away
Then quite unbidden
A tear sprang to my eye
The last tear for our love
Now it is gone
And I am stripped and barren
Barren as the maple tree.

II.
I would that I could rest
And quietly forget
And shed my clinging memories
Like autumn trees
Who shed their golden leaves

And for a little while
Know no quick surge of life
No running sap
But just a quietness a peaceful hush
I would that I could rest
And quietly forget.

III.
My heart to you is always calling
An aching throb which only I can hear
Oh call more loudly lonely heart
Else stop your beating
And let me have repose in quiet death
But wait I am afraid that even death
This longing would not ease
And I should go on ever calling
Calling through eternity.

IV.
I was done with life
The pain you brought me
Stopped my ears and dimmed my eyes
I neither saw nor felt
But finally after bitter years
My soul has broken through
This little outward me
I am not done with life
But only thee.

V.
Why should you call it perfidy
That now I lie in other arms
To see the dawn
Break in the east
Why blame you me
For often did I call to you
A little knowledge I would gain
But in the bitter strife of life
You gave no heed
Another came
And told me that which I would know
And so I rested satisfied
But not by you
Or pleadingly I begged a drink

My parched and thirsty soul to ease
But gaming in the market place
You did not hear
He heard and gave to me a cup
And quenched my thirst
And then again I begged of you
To hold me close
While night bloomed forth
A velvet pansy field
But worn from toil
You slept nor woke
He answered me
And starred my night
Why should your eyes accuse and shame
That now I have no need of you
Nor will accept your condemnation
Nor your blame.

VI.
My heart cries out to rest
My weary head upon your breast
To ease my fevered brain
Of this world weary pain
But since it may not be
I try to smile and see
That just to love is good
Which only God has understood.

VII.
Love lies dying in my garden
And autumn creeps into my heart
Dead memories cling to every bush
And rattle menacingly
Yet still a little warmth of summer lingers
A fading warmth that chills me even now
And foretells when love dies completely
How bitter winter winds will be.

CHARLES HANSON TOWNE
1877–1949

Haunted

There came a whisper in the night,
  A little cry across the years;
And I who heard, in deep affright,
  Awakened with unnumbered fears.

"It is some deed that I have done,
  Some sin I wrought long, long ago;
But hush! Am I the only one?
  Wherefore am I then troubled so?

"For all men do some evil deed,
  And some men falter, some men fall;
Do ghosts of Selfishness and Greed
  Come back, O God, to haunt them all?"

Then came a whisper in the night,
  A little cry across the years;
And I who heard, in deep affright,
  Listened with wild, unnumbered fears.

"I am the ghost of that pure deed
  You might have done, but did not do;
I am the ghost of that good seed
  You might have sown when Life was new.

"And this it is that haunts you now,
  That deed undone, that seed unsown;
Too late, too late to take the plough,
  The Spring is fled, the May is flown!"

And this I heard amid the night,
  This voice that called across the years,
And when the dawn came, silver-white,
  I was companioned with my tears.

Vision

Sometimes, in a crowded street I see
The faces of those that love, and those that are loved.

And in the rush of the traffic,
The thundering sounds of the city, I pause,
Wondering about their loves—which are their lives.

I know them by their eyes, and by their glances;
I know them in a way I may not name,
And I know those that have won and those that have lost
In the eternal battle of the world.
But they that have lost have not always a sad countenance;
Sometimes their lips smile,
As if with an old comprehension,
And one might be deceived, save for the tragic eyes—
The smiling, yet unsmiling eyes above the mouth.
Those eyes have read in the great Book of Love,
And they are changed, they are changed forever.
And those lips have kissed the pages of the book,
And they too are changed forever.
Only, lips can lie—but eyes can never deceive.

And those that have won—not always do they smile.
Often they seem to be secretly weeping,
As if with a joy too terrible to bear. . . .
Strange, strange are the countenances of those that love.

I know them all—brother and sisters of Love.
I know them, and they know me too.
I can tell by their eyes—
Their eyes that follow me with knowledge,
With pity, with solemn understanding.

A World of Windows

Behind my house are windows,
  Each lit with yellow flame,
And each one is a little world
  Set in a little frame.

A shop-girl, through her mirror,
  Looks at her ashen face.
Below her, in a peignoir
  Of shabby, dirty lace,

A woman, stout and lazy,
  Sits playing solitaire;

Disheveled is her ill-lit room,
  And tumbled is her hair.

There is one little window
  Set high above the rest;
I see the edge of an iron bed,
  And a young girl thinly dressed.

Her face is full of sorrow—
  One seldom sees her laugh;
Each night she bends above an old
  And faded photograph.

She takes it from the bureau
  In that small, stuffy place;
One evening, I could almost see
  The tears upon her face,

When the wild gas-jet flickered
  Above her heavy hair.
That whole long night I saw her,
  An image of despair,

Beside her tiny window
  Gazing at the white moon.
I wondered what her life must be—
  Had Love gone by so soon?

A week dragged on; her shutters
  Were drawn, as if to hide
The little drama of her world;
  And then—one night—she died.

She killed herself. I read the truth,
  Hidden among the news—
A little item, stale enough:
  How many love—and lose!

Three days—and then another girl
  Took up her story there.
Two flights below, a woman still
  Sat playing solitaire,

In the same shabby peignoir
  Of yellow, dirty lace,
And the poor shop-girl, in her glass,
  Looked at her pallid face.

Behind my house are windows,
  Each lit with yellow flame;
Each is a world for some one
  Who plays the old, old game.

And when one world is emptied,
  Through terror or disgrace,
How soon another brave one comes
  To fill the vacant place!

JOHN ERSKINE
1879–1951

Beneath this beauty

Beneath this beauty when my spirit swayeth
  And with the praise of it my soul is stirred,
Love on my lips a wary finger layeth
  And bindeth in my heart the eager word!
My heart, that for love's sake these long years holdeth
  One dear desire to win all ways of speech,
Whose secret, love himself, I dreamed, unfoldeth—
  O, is it silence, Love, that thou wouldst teach?
I have desired to suffer thy sweet burning
  And prayed thy fiercest blow should on me fall;
I have grown scarred and wise in bitter learning,
  But not to love I never learned at all.
Now to thy mischief, Love, add not this choice—
To know not love, or never use love's voice.

Love That Never Told Can Be

No bird hath ever lifted note so clear,
  Or poured so prodigal his lyric breast,
  But carried still some music from the nest,

When Winter laid the seal of silence there.
No sea hath ever woo'd the shore so fair
  But turn of tide left something half expressed;
  Nor true love every burned so strangely blest
That words could hold it all or heart could hear.

And yet the tide will turn again, and tell
  Its sweet persistent story o'er and o'er—
The bird take up the cadence where it fell,
  And pipe it towards the ending more and more—
And only love be inexpressible,
  The endless song, the sea that hath no shore.

Parting

Music's meaning first is known,
  Though the bird sing all day long,
When the last faint-falling tone
  Divides the silence from the song.

Not in absence, nor when face
  To face, thy love means most to me,
But in the narrow parting-space,
  The cadence of felicity.

ANGELINA WELD GRIMKÉ
1880–1958

A Mona Lisa

1.
I should like to creep
Through the long brown grasses
  That are your lashes;
I should like to poise
  On the very brink

Of the leaf-brown pools
  That are your shadowed eyes;
I should like to cleave
  Without sound,
Their glimmering waters,
  Their unrippled waters,
I should like to sink down
  And down
    And down . . .
      And deeply drown.

2.
Would I be more than a bubble breaking?
  Or an ever-widening circle
  Ceasing at the marge?
Would my white bones
  Be the only white bones
Wavering back and forth, back and forth
  In their depths?

For the Candle Light

The sky was blue, so blue that day
  And each daisy white, so white,
Oh, I knew that no more could rains fall gray—
  And night again be night.

I knew, I knew. Well, if night is night,
  And the gray skies grayly cry,
I have in a book for the candle light
  A daisy dead and dry.

El Beso

Twilight—and you
Quiet—the stars;
Snare of the shine of your teeth,
Your provocative laughter,
The gloom of your hair;
Lure of you, eye and lip;
Yearning, yearning,
Languor, surrender;

Your mouth,
And madness, madness,
Tremulous, breathless, flaming,
The space of a sigh;
Then awakening—remembrance,
Pain, regret—your sobbing;
And again, quiet—the stars,
Twilight—and you.

WITTER BYNNER
1881–1968

The Ballad of a Dancer

He was born among the dragon-flowers
Under a shooting star,
And had, as a boy, for paramours
As many as there are.

He was always loving somebody—
But mostly birds and apples
And little twigs of ebony
And baby pigs with dapples.

He would catch at the fingers of a girl
But never wait for an answer:
Skipping along, while men would curl
Their nostrils at a dancer.

Tradition he would set at naught
And never shed a tear:
No scripture we were ever taught
Accords with his career.

Persons who conserve the race
With families and fatigue
He would encounter face to face
And never care a fig.

He would snap his fingers at the young
And thumb his nose at the old,
Believing in some of the things that are sung
But in none of the things that are told. . . .

Lit by the moon from chin to hair,
Looking a little Asian,
He would go to bed without a prayer,
Being of no persuasion.

And then he would sing to the Milky Way—
"The night is milk and honey,
And that's a better coin to pay
Than ordinary money."

"While other men have married well
And then as well repented,
All my affairs are asphodel
And all my heirs contented."

Yesterday, because of a pain,
An unmistakable warning,
He ran out naked in the rain,
And he was worse this morning. . . .

He whispered, "Please, no funeral!
Only the dragon-flowers!"
But we shall dress in black and all
And bury him for hours.

The Earth-Clasp

Whether you fled from me, not to have less
Of love, but to have all without a night
Too much, like one who moves a cup which might
Brim over with the mounting of excess;
Or whether you had felt in my caress
The finger-tips of surfeit and of blight
Attempting love; or whether your quick flight
Was to another love; I will not guess.

I touch the pillow that has touched your head;
And the brief candle that has lighted you
Sheds bleak and ashen light upon a face
As absent as the moon,—till to replace

Those arms, earth's body beckons me anew,
And in her clasp something of you is dead.

Ghost

He rises from his guests, abruptly leaves,
Because of memory that long moons ago
Others now dead had dined with him, and grieves
Because these newer persons he must know
Might not have loved his ghosts, his unknown dead.
There are new smiles, new answers to his quips;
But there are intervals when, having said
His dinner-table say, he hears dead lips. . . .
The dead have ways of mingling in the uses
Of life they leave behind, the dead can rise
When dinner's done. But one of them refuses
To go away and gazes with dead eyes
Piercing him deeper than a rain can reach,
Leaving him only motion, only speech.

WALTER DE CASSERES
1881–1900

The Battle of the Passions

From out of the depths of the night,
A blood-red battalion they come,
They laugh, for with them lies the might,
And they know we shall have to succumb.

Heart-eating, venomous worms,
Brain-burning, horrible things,
That make the heart shudder and pale
And shatter the soul with their stings.

Silently onward they press,
And, writhing around and beneath,

They sting and they pierce with their fangs
And bite with their terrible teeth.

Soon—soon the dread battle is over,
But the conquerors never retire,
And ever are watchful and wakeful
And ever are scourging with fire.

But now draweth near the avengers,
The invincible Army of Death—
They charge with the rush of a whirlwind
And scatter the worms with their breath.

And the sound of the wearisome struggle
And the thought of that terrible fight
Pass on as a dream that the devils
Have whispered to us in the night.

Phantoms

A group of phantoms in the Halls of Death
That hand in hand amid the wastes of night
In trembling terror stand with bated breath,
Each compassed by a pale, reflective light
That seems forever on the wane.
And some there are who murmur, "It is Fate,"
And some cry out in fear, while others wait
In faith and trust that God will lead aright,
But ever wait in vain.
For dimmer grow the lights as years pass on,
Until at last they fade and die away.
And why this happens none may say.
And none may know whereto his friend has gone.

The Suicide

He sought for things he could not find,
He hunted through the weary years,
The path was watered by his tears,
And Life was cold, though Death was kind.

He sought for love in a woman's heart,
For truth within a woman's eyes—

He sought for truth where falsehood lies
And looked for love where love is not.

He cried to God, but He was dead;
To her, but she did not reply;
He thought perhaps 'twere best to die,
His dreams forever left unsaid.

MINA LOY
1882–1966

Songs to Joannes: XIII

Come to me   There is something
I have got to tell you   and I can't tell
Something taking shape
Something that has a new name
A new dimension

A new use
A new illusion

It is ambient   And it is in your eyes
Something shiny   Something only for you
                       Something that I must not see

It is in my ears   Something very resonant
Something that you must not hear
                       Something only for me

Let us be very jealous
Very suspicious
Very conservative
Very cruel
Or we might make an end of the jostling of aspirations
Disorb inviolate egos

Where two or three are welded together
They shall become god

— — — — — —
Oh that's right
Keep away from me   Please give me a push
Don't let me understand you   Don't realise me
Or we might tumble together
Depersonalized
Identical
Into the terrific Nirvana
Me you—you—me

Lunar Baedeker

A silver Lucifer
serves
cocaine in cornucopia

To some somnambulists
of adolescent thighs

draped
in satirical draperies

Peris in livery
prepare
Lethe
for posthumous parvenues

Delirious Avenues
lit
with the chandelier souls
of infusoria
from Pharoah's tombstones

lead
to mercurial doomsdays
Odious oasis
in furrowed phosphorous— — —

the eye-white sky-light
white-light district
of lunar lusts

— — —Stellectric signs
"Wing shows on Starway"
"Zodiac carrousel"

Cyclones
of ecstatic dust
and ashes whirl
crusaders
from hallucinatory citadels
of shattered glass
into evacuate craters

A flock of dreams
browse on Necropolis

From the shores
of oval oceans
in the oxidized Orient

Onyx-eyed Odalisques
and ornithologists
observe
the flight
of Eros obsolete

And "Immortality"
mildews . . .
in the museums of the moon

"Nocturnal cyclops"
"Crystal concubine"
— — — — — —

Pocked with personification
the fossil virgin of the skies
waxes and wanes— — — —

Faun Fare

Surreptitious fanfare
of unadams
amingle with ouradams

a seemingly uniform guesthood
met in unsolemn sociability

the amiable scuffle
of cocktail party.

Hooveless fauns
their goat-haunch

discard to antiquity
their hairiness
woven to our worsted.

Most smiles are similes
some
almost imperceptibly
simper to mystery—

As were the tail of the eye
lidded with unlisted likings
on ocular trail
of invitation
to untypical trysts

As were the tail of the eye
feeling for fallacious Foci
a Flitting tongue
licking its luminous chops
o'er tit-bits of other tastes
undue

to the apple
the devil
delivered to Eve.

Neo-Fauns

Whom no forestal feminae
need flee

Altered is the prey.
Of priceless use to civilization

You faun
are balm

to night-club addict
undercover-virgin

for whom
Adonis as escort
—obliging her prestige
as cosmetics her cheek—
is a must.

Faun in you
may she trust

to stage no thrust
of Sabine rape
behind the chauffeur's back

O unisex
Black marketing Amor

with your intermuscular caress
of wrestling entry
to Felicity's
unsentinelled
Arcana.

Your something-for-nothing
Variance
to infertile "Sin."

You
dual yet single
Votaries of Venuseros

As in Athens
So in Manhattan
Erosvenus evoes
his-her worshipper

or whispers

Eros is ours
for is not
Eros
forever overall
a male?

Or implores
for fauns' ease.

Quiet please!
As mondial calliopes
Blaring the bisexual norm
foment the Fauns'
allergy to diapers.

EDWARD SLOCUM
1882–1946

The Garden

Sometimes I come to my secret dreams
To a garden rich and fair
Where a lad so debonair
With white limbs in Love's own glory gleams.

How can I mourn, who have drunk delight
From that Tree in that Garden rare,
Have kissed its blossoms fair,
Have seen Love himself in his full might?

Some men from cup of the crescent moon
Have drunk a strange, wild amaze,
But I in the Sun's full blaze
Have kissed the lips of a lad in June.

Sumer Is Icumen In

When you are standing thus 'mid the tall grass
Pan might shrill his pipes with old time might,
So that these modern days should fade and pass,—
That we again should live in Phoebos' light.
Press we with gladness back to ancient ways
Where we shall find full peace and comfortings,—
Not even Paradise could promise days
More fair than these, lived 'mid familiar things.

Sweet, let us kiss so long we shall not hear
Over our heads the whisper of the leaves,
Or glancing flight of swallow, very near,
Winging his way to his own love-nest's eaves,—
Lingering so long we shall not be aware
How love-mad June weaves blossoms for her hair.

The Dark Mirror

In the dark mirror of the quiet stream
Where Herakles might think that Hylas stood

I see reflected back the glorious dream
Of thine own self in Nature's plenitude.

Is there no nymph nearby to drag thee down
To silent watery depths,—no Salmacis,
As in the olden tale that Beaumont told,—
To crush thy protests with a loving kiss?

No mirror e'er in ancient goddess' hands
Sent back to eyes so fair, so true a sight!
Ah, let me now, like nymph, taste of thy sweets,
Send on poor me the gladness of thy light!

BADGER CLARK
1883–1957

The Lost Pardner

I ride alone and hate the boys I meet.
    Today, some way, their laughin' hurts me so.
I hate the mockin'-birds in the mesquite—
    And yet I liked 'em just a week ago.
I hate the steady sun that glares, and glares!
    The bird songs make me sore.
I seem the only thing on earth that cares
    'Cause Al ain't here no more!

'Twas just a stumblin' hawse, a tangled spur—
    And, when I raised him up so limp and weak,
One look before his eyes begun to blur
    And then—the blood that wouldn't let 'im speak!
And him so strong, and yet so quick he died,
    And after year on year
When we had always trailed it side by side,
    He went—and left me here!

We loved each other in the way men do
    And never spoke about it, Al and me,
But we both *knowed*, and knowin' it so true

Was more than any woman's kiss could be.
We knowed—and if the way was smooth or rough,
   The weather shine or pour,
While I had him the rest seemed good enough—
   But he ain't here no more!

What is there out beyond the last divide?
   Seems like that country must be cold and dim.
He'd miss the sunny range he used to ride,
   And he'd miss me, the same as I do him.
It's no use thinkin'—all I'd think or say
   Could never make it clear.
Out that dim trail that only leads one way
   He's gone—and left me here!

The range is empty and the trails are blind,
   And I don't seem but half myself today.
I wait to hear him ridin' up behind
   And feel his knee rub mine the good old way.
He's dead—and what that means no man kin tell.
   Some call it "gone before."
Where? I don't know, but God! I know so well
   That he ain't here no more!

My Enemy

   All mornin' in the mesa's glare
After his crouchin' back I clattered,
   And quick shots cut the heavy air
And on the rocks the hot lead spattered.
   A dollar crimped, a word too free—
   My enemy! My enemy!

   He reined beside a rattlers' den
And faced me there to fix the winnin'.
   And I wished that he would turn again,
For it was hard to kill him grinnin'.
   His hands were empty, I could see.
   My enemy! My enemy!

   He pointed up; he pointed back.
I looked, and half forgot my hatin'.
   A coyote sneaked along our track,
A buzzard hung above us, waitin'.

"Are us four all akin?" says he.
  My enemy! My enemy!

The coyote crossed the desert's rim,
The buzzard circled up and faded.
  I halved my only smoke with him
And when dark found us limp and jaded,
  He sat and kep' the fire for me,
    My enemy! My enemy!!

The Smoke-Blue Plains

Kissed me from the saddle and I still can feel it burning,
  But he must have felt it cold, for ice was in my veins.
I shall always see him as he waved above the turning,
  Riding down the canyon to the smoke-blue plains.
Oh, the smoke-blue plains! how I used to watch them sleeping,
  Thinking peace had dimmed them with the shadow of her wings;
Now their gentle haze will seem a smoke of death a-creeping,
  Drifted from the battles in the country of the kings.

Joked me to the last, and in a voice without a quaver—
  Man o' mine!—but underneath the tan his cheek was pale.
Never did the nation breed a kinder or a braver
  Since our fathers landed from the long sea trail.
Oh, the long sea trail he must leave me here and follow—
  He that never saw a ship—to dare its chances blind,
Out the deadly reaches where the sinking steamers wallow.
  Back to trampled countries that his fathers left behind.

Down beyond the plains among the fighting and the dying,
  God must watch his reckless foot and follow where it lights;
Guard the places where his blessed tousled head is lying—
  Head my shoulder pillowed through the warm, safe nights!
Oh, the warm, safe nights, and the pines above the shingles!
  Can I stand their crooning and the patter of the rains?
Oh, the sunny quiet, and a bridle bit that jingles,
  Coming up the canyon from the smoke-blue plains!

SARA TEASDALE
1884–1933

To a Picture of Elenora Duse in *The Dead City*

Your face is set against a fervent sky,
Before the thirsty hills that sevenfold
Return the sun's hot glory, gold on gold,
Where Agamemnon and Cassandra lie.
Your eyes are blind whose light shall never die,
And all the tears the closèd eyelids hold,
And all the longing that the eyes have told,
Is gathered in the lips that make no cry.
Yea, like a flower within a desert place,
Whose petals fold and fade for lack of rain,
Are these, your eyes, where joy of sight was slain,
And in the silence of your lifted face,
The cloud is rent that hides a sleeping race,
And vanished Grecian beauty lives again.

Song

You bound strong sandals on my feet,
   You gave me bread and wine,
And sent me under sun and stars,
   For all the world was mine.

Oh, take the sandals off my feet,
   You know not what you do;
For all my world is in your arms,
   My sun and stars are you.

What do I care

What do I care, in the dreams and the languor of spring,
   That my songs do not show me at all?
For they are a fragrance, and I am a flint and a fire,
   I am an answer, they are only a call.

But what do I care, for love will be over so soon,
  Let my heart have its say and my mind stand idly by,
For my mind is proud and strong enough to be silent,
  It is my heart that makes my songs, not I.

GEORGE SYLVESTER VIERECK
1884–1962

2. Samuel, I. 26

To T.E.H.

God's iron finger wrote the law
  Upon an adamantine scroll
That thrilled my life with tender awe
  When first I met you soul to soul.

Thence springs the great flame heaven-lit,
  Predestined when the world began,
Whereby my heart to yours is knit
  As David's was to Jonathan.

The Master Key

To William Shakespeare

Two loves have I, both children of delight:
    One is a youth, like Eros' self, to whom
    My heart unfolds, as lotus blossoms bloom
When her mysterious service chants the Night;
And one is like a poppy burning bright.
    Her strong black tresses bind the hands of doom,
    She is a wraith from some imperial tomb,
Of love enhungered, in the grave's despite.

Lord, though thou be, O Shakespeare, of all rhyme,
  Life is more strong than any song of thine.

For thou wast thrall to circumstance, and Care
With rankling poison marred thy singing time:
  From hell's own lees I still crush goodly wine,
    And like a Greek, and smiling, flout despair!

Children of Lilith

To François Villon

Now tell me, Villon, where is he,
  Young Sporus, lord of Nero's lyre,
Who marked with languid ecstasy
  The seven hills grow red with fire?
And he whose madness choked the hall
  With roses and made night of day?
Rome's rulers for an interval,
  Its boyish Caesars, where are they?

Where is that city by the Nile,
  Reared by an emperor's bronze distress
When the enamoured crocodile
  Clawed the Bithynian's loveliness?
The argent pool whose listening trees
  Heard Echo's voice die far away?
Narcissus, Hylas, Charmides,
  O brother Villon, where are they?

Say where the Young Disciple roved
  When the Messiah's blood was spilt?
None knows: for he whom Jesus loved
  Was not the rock on which He built.
And tell me where is Gaveston,
  The second Edward's dear dismay?
And Shakespeare's love, and Jonathan,
  O brother Villon, where are they?

Made—for what end?—by God's great hand,
  Frail enigmatic shapes, they dwell
In some phantastic borderland,
  But on the hitherside of hell!
Children of Lilith, each a sprite,
  Yet wrought like us of Adam's clay,
And when they haunt us in the night
  What, brother Villon, shall we say?

WILLIAM ALEXANDER PERCY
1885-1942

Safe Secrets

I will carry terrible things to the grave with me:
   So much must never be told.
My eyes will be ready for sleep and my heart for dust
   With all the secrets they hold.
The piteous things alive in my memory
   Will be safe in that soundless dwelling:
In the clean loam, in the dark where the dumb roots rust
   I can sleep without fear of telling.

Prologue

Whose blood runs gay as summer's,
Whose heart is sure and proud,
Whose days are all newcomers,
Whose nights are dream-endowed,—
Pass on, lest you should hear
Speech neither sweet nor clear.

Whose blood is slowly spilling,
Whose heart has crimson scars,
Whose days have lost their thrilling,
Whose nights have lost their stars—
Pause here and you will find
One of your kith and kind.

In New York

1. *On Sunday Morning*
Far, far from here the church bells ring,
   As when I was a child,
And there is one I dearly love
   Walks in the sunlight mild.
To church she goes, and with her once
   I went, a little child.

The church bells ring far, far away,
  The village streets are bright,
The sunlight falls in slanting bars
  And fills the church with light.
And I remember when I knelt
  Beside her, in delight.

There's something lost, there's something lost,
  Some wisdom has beguiled!
My heart has flown a thousand miles
  And in the sunlight mild
I kneel and weep beside her there
  As she prays for her child.

2. *The Song You Love*
When I have sung the sweet songs and the sad,
The songs of magic drifting from above,
The trumpet songs that shout across men's souls,
The sleep-song, breasted softer than the dove,
Still there will be one song I have not sung—
  The song you love, the song you love.

What are the torches of the world to you,
The words that comfort men and calm their fears?
What are the stars with their strange harmonies,
Or fate that shadows all, or death that jeers?
There must be laughter in the song you love
  And at the end there must be tears.

When I have come to that green place we know
Where cedars stand that have no faith in spring,
Where through the utter peace of afternoon
The mocking-birds their heartless raptures fling,
Long after it is dust, one heart there'll be
  Restless with words it could not sing.

3. *Weariness*
I sometimes think Thou art my secret love;
But not to-night. . . . To-night I have the need
Of human tenderness; not hovering wings,
But one warm breast where I may lay my head
And close my eyes. For I am tired to-night. . . .
The park was full of lovers,
And such a slender moon looked down on them. . . .

For one kiss of one mouth, free-given, I
Would give—what's left of me to-night
To the last dream!
Art Thou a jealous god?
Dost think to force by loneliness
Unwilling love to Thee?
Beware, beware! The winds of madness blow
Strong, strong on nights like these! . . .
Thou dost deny me what's of life most sweet,
The bending head and lovely eyes of love—
Then give, beseech Thee, give me sleep.

4. *In the Night*
Drifting, groping
For delight;
Longing, hoping
All the night.
Perfume of
Blossomed hair—
Where is love?
Ah, no, not there! . . .
Not there.

Turning, turning,
Sleepless-eyed,
Something burning
At my side—
Winds that sweep
Poppied hair,
Where is sleep?
Ah, no, not there! . . .
Not there?

5. *Home*
I have a need of silence and of stars;
Too much is said too loudly; I am dazed.
The silken sound of whirled infinity
Is lost in voices shouting to be heard.
I once knew men as earnest and less shrill.
An undermeaning that I caught I miss
Among these ears that hear all sounds save silence,
These eyes that see so much but not the sky,
These minds that gain all knowledge but no calm.
If suddenly the desperate music ceased,

Could they return to life? or would they stand
In dancers' attitudes, puzzled, polite,
And striking vaguely hand on tired hand
For an encore, to fill the ghastly pause?
I do not know. Some rhythm there may be
I cannot hear. But I—oh, I must go
Back where the breakers of deep sunlight roll
Across flat fields that love and touch the sky;
Back to the more of earth, the less of man,
Where there is still a plain simplicity,
And friendship, poor in everything but love,
And faith, unwise, unquestioned, but a star.
Soon now the peace of summer will be there
With cloudy fire of myrtles in full bloom;
And, when the marvelous wide evenings come,
Across the molten river one can see
The misty willow-green of Arcady.
And then—the summer stars. . . . I will go home.

H. D.
1886–1961

Toward the Piraeus

Slay with your eyes, Greek,
men over the face of the earth,
slay with your eyes, the host,
puny, passionless, weak.

Break as the ranks of steel
broke when the Persian lost:
craven, we hated them then:
now we would count them Gods
beside these, spawn of the earth.

Grant us your mantle, Greek!
grant us but one

to fright (as your eyes) with a sword,
men, craven and weak,
grant us but one to strike
one blow for you, passionate Greek.

1.
You would have broken my wings,
but the very fact that you knew
I had wings, set some seal
on my bitter heart, my heart
broke and fluttered and sang.

You would have snared me,
and scattered the strands of my nest;
but the very fact that you saw,
sheltered me, claimed me,
set me apart from the rest

Of men—of *men*, made you a god,
and me, claimed me, set me apart
and the song in my breast,
yours, yours forever—
if I escape your evil heart.

2.
I loved you:
men have writ and women have said
they loved,
but as the Pythoness stands by the altar,
intense and may not move,

till the fumes pass over;
and may not falter or break,
till the priest has caught the words
that mar or make
a deme or a ravaged town;

so I, though my knees tremble,
my heart break,
must note the rumbling,
heed only the shuddering
down in the fissure beneath the rock
of the temple floor;

must wait and watch
and may not turn nor move,

nor break from my trance to speak
so slight, so sweet,
so simple a word as love.

3.
What had you done
had you been true,
I can not think,
I may not know.

What could we do
were I not wise,
what play invent,
what joy devise?

What could we do
if you were great?

(Yet were you lost,
who were there then,
to circumvent
the tricks of men?)

What can we do,
for curious lies
have filled your heart,
and in my eyes
sorrow has writ
that I am wise.

4.
If I had been a boy,
I would have worshipped your grace,
I would have flung my worship
before your feet,
I would have followed apart,
glad, rent with an ecstasy
to watch you turn
your great head, set on the throat,
thick, dark with its sinews,
burned and wrought
like the olive stalk,
and the noble chin
and the throat.

I would have stood,
and watched and watched

and burned,
and when in the night,
from the many hosts, your slaves,
and warriors and serving men
you had turned
to the purple couch and the flame
of the woman, tall like the cypress tree
that flames sudden and swift and free
as with crackle of golden resin
and cones and the locks flung free
like the cypress limbs,
bound, caught and shaken and loosed,
bound, caught and riven and bound
and loosened again,
as in rain of a kingly storm
or wind full from a desert plain.

So, when you had risen
from all the lethargy of love and its heat,
you would have summoned me,
me alone,
and found my hands,
beyond all the hands in the world,
cold, cold, cold,
intolerably cold and sweet.

5.
It was not chastity that made me cold nor fear,
only I knew that you, like myself, were sick
of the puny race that crawls and quibbles and lisps
of love and love and lovers and love's deceit.

It was not chastity that made me wild, but fear
that my weapon, tempered in different heat,
was over-matched by yours, and your hand
skilled to yield death-blows, might break

With the slightest turn—no ill will meant—
my own lesser, yet still somewhat fine-wrought,
fiery-tempered, delicate, over-passionate steel.

For Bryher and Perdita

They said:
she is high and far and blind

in her high pride,
but now that my head is bowed
in sorrow, I find
she is most kind.

We have taken life, they said,
blithely, not groped in a mist
for things that are not—
are if you will, but bloodless—
why ask happiness of the dead?
and my heart bled.

Ah, could they know
how violets throw strange fire,
red and purple and gold,
how they glow
gold and purple and red
where her feet tread.

At Baia

I should have thought
in a dream you would have brought
some lovely, perilous thing,
orchids piled in a great sheath,
as who would say (in a dream)
I send you this,
who left the blue veins
of your throat unkissed.

Why was it that your hands
(that never took mine)
your hands that I could see
drift over the orchid heads
so carefully,
your hands, so fragile, sure to lift
so gently, the fragile flower stuff—
ah, ah, how was it

You never sent (in a dream)
the very form, the very scent,
not heavy, not sensuous,
but perilous—perilous—
of orchids, piled in a great sheath,

and folded underneath on a bright scroll
some word:

Flower sent to flower;
for white hands, the lesser white,
less lovely of flower leaf,

or

Lover to lover, no kiss,
no touch, but forever and ever this.

LEONARD BACON
1887–1954

Sonnet on a Portuguese

> Eu sou aquelle occulto e grande Cabo.
> —CAMOENS, "LUSIADS"

The swarthy fellow, with a Latin smile
And perfect courtesy, led me to the road,
Which I had lost, and other virtue showed
New England has forgotten this long while.
He managed too my fancy to beguile.
In his dark eyes an ancient demon glowed.
Another logic in another mode
Revealed itself in an exotic style.

Henry the Navigator brought him here.
No doubt in dreams he had seen the awful shape
Of the strange spirit of another Cape,
That troubled Diaz with a dubious speech.
That's why he walked with a rose behind his ear
To dig "quahaugs" on a white South Shore beach.

The Eyes

The eyes are watching you, sharp and shifty,
And you have pondered and you have tried.

And what have you gained as you drift past fifty
That you did not have on the sunny side

Of thirty? Have you yet learned to be wise,
Discovered a cordial way to act,
Or how to look in the watching eyes,
Or how to maintain the spirit intact,

That came to you troubled and divided
Against itself, between living and dead,
Simple yet dreadfully many-sided,
A trivial riddle unfit to be read?

The noble dream, the divine intention,
Look small on the edge of the black abyss.
But to humble themselves before convention!—
There must be something wrong about this.

Why should I not walk more gaily, erectly?
Really, you know, I think that I may
Wander hereafter less circumspectly.
And whatever Apolyon may straddle the way

Breathing out fire, I shall cut my caper.
Retro me Satana! Fiend, avaunt!
What are you? A phantom of paper and vapor.
Infernal ghost of a maiden aunt.

Mnemonic System for Psycho-analysts

A. is for anima playing a role
A trifle obscure in the masculine soul.
B. is for brain. And at first glance it's plain
That C. must be chaos which rules in the brain.
D. is for dream, I will say in effect,
Whose meaning you never are led to expect.
E. is for extrovert, finest that lives,
Whom the introvert neither forgets nor forgives.
F. is for Freud who invented analysis,
So also for fantasy, feeling, and fallacies.
G.'s Greta Garbo. It's plainer than day.
She's an anima-figure in quite a big way.
H. is hypothesis, daring as Hell,
Which no one but Jung understands very well.

I. is for introvert taking a ride
In a squirrel-cage hung in his little inside.
J. is for Jung who perpetually plots
New methods for tying the soul into knots.
K. is for Keyserling, playing around
This subject and others in dullness profound.
L. is libido which surges and rolls
In furious streams through remarkable souls.
M. is for mana. It's one of my curses
That somehow I can't get it into my verses.
N. is for neurot. I'll mention to you
That the rot is quite rotten, and the new isn't new.
O. is for opposites yoked in a pair.
P. is psychology, not that I care.
Q. is the quibble which starts up the clacking
When reasonable themes for discussion are lacking.
R. is for Rivers who tied without fail
Anthropology's can to Psychology's tail.
S. is for sex which makes Freudians gay.
T. is taboos and the devil to pay.
U. is the unbewusst under us all
Where animae whimper and animi brawl.
V. is Vienna where Freud once upset
The box of Pandora, I think, on a bet.
W.'s wind. You had better not sow
Too heavy a crop or the whirlwind will blow.
X. is the things that your analyst knows
But for reasons of state can't be brought to disclose.
Y. is for Yan. It is also for Yin,
Meaning masculine virtue and feminine sin.
Z. is for Zürich, where it is well known
That the far wandering nut has come into his own.

SAMUEL LOVEMAN
1887–1976

Belated Love

That fool am I to whom love came,
　　Not as the soft wind comes at last,
But something terrible with flame,
　　Lighted and stricken in the blast.

With all the universe in bliss,
　　Close and yet closer grew despair;
Till I, before the dim abyss,
　　Found emptiness and ruin there.

Understanding

You knew this thing as we two sat together,
　　Friends without friends and alien as your doom,
'Scaped from the leash that held us both in tether,
　　Exquisite souls but broken on fate's loom;
Till I, who whispered guardedly at first,
　　Of refluent water's flow and shining sun,
Of youngsters, bathing where a great wave burst,
　　And of the gulls returning one by one—

Heard your close, tremulous heart-beat at my side,
　　And saw your lips made passionate and wise,
As in your gaze beneficent and deep,
　　A light that caught my speech ere the word died,
Kindled immortally with mortal eyes,
　　The pagan heart of me that woke from sleep.

Remonstrance

I that am Beauty's slave,
　　Drunk as a moth with light,
How shall I bear to have
　　These eyelids filled with night?

The heart of me a sun,
   The soul of me a star—
O cheap oblivion,
   To make and then to mar!

T. S. ELIOT
1888–1965

The Love Song of St. Sebastian

I would come in a shirt of hair
I would come with a lamp in the night
And sit at the foot of your stair;
I would flog myself until I bled,
And after hour on hour of prayer
And torture and delight
Until my blood should ring the lamp
And glisten in the light;
I should arise your neophyte
And then put out the light
To follow where you lead,
To follow where your feet are white
In the darkness toward your bed
And where your gown is white
And against your gown your braided hair.
Then you would take me in
Because I was hideous in your sight
You would take me in without shame
Because I should be dead
And when the morning came
Between your breasts should lie my head.

I would come with a towel in my hand
And bend your head beneath my knees;
Your ears curl back in a certain way
Like no one's else in all the world.
When all the world shall melt in the sun,

Melt or freeze,
I shall remember how your ears were curled.
I should for a moment linger
And follow the curve with my finger
And your head beneath my knees—
I think that at last you would understand.
There would be nothing more to say.
You would love me because I should have strangled you
And because of my infamy;
And I should love you the more because I had mangled you
And because you were no longer beautiful
To anyone but me.

Hysteria

As she laughed I was aware of becoming involved in her laughter and being part of it, until her teeth were only accidental stars with a talent for squad-drill. I was drawn in by short gasps, inhaled at each momentary recovery, lost finally in the dark caverns of her throat, bruised by the ripple of unseen muscles. An elderly waiter with trembling hands was hurriedly spreading a pink and white checked cloth over the rusty green iron table, saying: "If the lady and gentleman wish to take their tea in the garden, if the lady and gentleman wish to take their tea in the garden. . . ." I decided that if the shaking of her breasts could be stopped, some of the fragments of the afternoon might be collected, and I concentrated my attention with careful subtlety to this end.

Eyes that last I saw in tears

Eyes that last I saw in tears
Through division
Here in death's dream kingdom
The golden vision reappears
I see the eyes but not the tears
This is my affliction

This is my affliction
Eyes I shall not see again
Eyes of decision
Eyes I shall not see unless

At the door of death's other kingdom
Where, as in this,
The eyes outlast a little while
A little while outlast the tears
And hold us in derision.

HANIEL LONG
1888–1956

The Masker

I fell in love with you
　　(Guessing that you were truth),
For you were masked and strange,
　　And you were Youth.

And then when I was sure
　　That love and youth were true,
I took the mask away
　　And you were You.

But gazing on you still
　　As hungry lovers do,
I saw that you were more
　　Than Youth, or You;

You had a third Shape, too,
　　Hidden for my surprise—
I looked, and saw it masked
　　Within your eyes.

Song of Young Burbage

The goat that rubbed my knees last night
　　And left his ancient smell
Maddened my heart that I was what
　　A hornéd goat could tell.

For if his favour singled me
    Out of the passing crowd,
It's plain I'm not too well disguised,
    Nor yet too worldly proud.

Most difficult it is to-day
    Beneath a coat and vest;
I feared my old identity
    Might fade with all the rest.

But I'll go back to hill and sky
    And hold a colloquy;
I need those ancient presences
    Whose tumult still is—*me*.

Ordeal by Fire

And so she was condemned to pass the night
    Above, beneath, beside, within a flame;
And everywhere she looked the sky was bright,
    And everywhere she turned the burning came.

Tongues licked her body, and a blaze
    Piled up as though her April skin were pitch;
And yet she rose unharmed, and went her ways,
    And the grey monks intoned, She was no witch,
        She was no witch!

SCUDDER MIDDLETON
1888–1959

Friends

These acres now belong to me,
His land is over there.
We worked these fields together once,
And each have even share.

In other days, my hand and his
Were closer linked than now,
And by that doubled strength of ours,
These fields were light to plow.

Now weak my hands, for lack of his,
Upon the coulter press,
And though no earth I share with him,
These fields now yield me less.

Pilots

The horns of the boats on the river
Speak to one another through the fog,
Articulate in the night.
You and I on a darker stream
Call to each other,
Exchanging words for words.

Well do the pilots of the river ships
Know the significant horns.
But we must guess at the meaning of speech,
While our craft are drawn by tides,
Stronger than our throbbing engines,
Across the invisible water.
No matter what we say,
We shall be warped to the same black wharf in the end. . . .

Yet my call and your answer
Create the illusion of decision,
Give us the dream of direction,
Strengthen our hands on the wheel.

Rebellion

Come, let us for to-night forget
That we were ever lovers!
Let us be two people born to die,
Mice in an old house, or sheaves of wheat,
Or little casks of burgundy
Rolled up and down the world—
I'm sick of love!

My heart is in rebellion
Against the mucilaginous,
Against all hope of being something else,
Against the whole androgynous
Conceit of modern lovers. . . .
Come, let us sit beside black water
And watch the sea-hawk fish.

ANTOINETTE SCUDDER
1888–1958

The Lesbians

They had been here a fortnight, maybe more,
In the cottage oddly named "The Peony;"
The stout and blowsy blonde who always wore
A sweater none too clean and knickerbockers
That slipped and bagged above her coarse yarn stockings,
And the other one, the slim and wistful one—
Eyes of a mermaid, green and azure blending
To a silvery remoteness. Lithe and small,
She always made me think of a lonely bird,
Straining its tenuous wings against the wind.

They were both artists—the stout one modelled queer
Symbolic things in clay, all feet and stomach;
And the other painted landscapes with a soft
Vague sweep of brush that puzzled and eluded.
There was talk about them from the very first.
They would work apart—one of them in the house
And the other down on the beach—but they would drop
Their tools and brushes twenty times a day
To wander and seek each other, and on finding,
Would hug and fondle in a mawkish fashion.
And sometimes the fat one would go prowling off
And leave the other under lock and key.

I was passing once with Brita Sorenson,
And we heard the captive whimpering in the house
Like a hurt animal. Then, Brita said,
Biting her lip—she is a champion swimmer,
As clean and wholesome as a northern wind—
"There are some things I can't stand or understand."
Then, three weeks later, on an August evening,
Some four or five of us were playing cards
At the Sunflower Cottage just across the way,
When we heard a sound of running and a splash
And stifled shrieks. We all rushed out and found
The grotesque couple struggling in the water.
There were men in our group, but Brita was the first
To drag the fragile one, half-drowned and choking,
On the beach where she lay helpless on the sand.
It was Brita who knelt beside her, grasped her wrists
And labored till the faint and broken gasps
Grew to a steady breath. Meanwhile, the fat one
Was blundering around and blubbering out:
"She tried to drown herself; she tried to drown—"
Wringing her hands, the tears on her gross cheeks—
It made me ill. And when the frail one roused
And opened wide, wet eyes, she turned and clung
To Brita. The stout creature hurried up,
But Brita snapped out, "Keep away from her,"
With blue eyes flashing like a young Valkyrie's.
I thought to see the swing of a naked sword
Between the two. Then Brita put her arm
Around the frail one's waist. "She'll go with me"—
And go she did—a trail of rain-drenched ivy
Or clematis around a staunch young oak.
And the fat one stayed there on the moonlit beach,
Awkward and helpless, with distorted teardrops
Dangling 'round mouth and chin. The rest of us
Had no more heart for cards. I was near hysterics
Till someone shook me roughly. Then I went
With Sara Howland—She's a grave and quiet
Person of fifty years and teaches Greek
In a girls' college. She took me to her room
And gave me spirits of ammonia,
For she's a strict teetotaler. But when
I muttered, "I agree with Brita. This

Was merely nasty," Sara smiled a little,
Then went to her bookcase, took down a copy
Of Sappho and read from that divine brief note
That floats forever between the sea and stars. . . .
I could not wholly grasp her fluent Greek
But I remember still the swift, wry look
That Sara gave me as she thrust the volume
In her bookcase—right beside her Thomas a Kempis—
And said: "My friend, can any of us judge?"

The Swimming Pool

On my back, both arms extended,
I lie and watch the light
As it quivers and breaks above me
On the thick, ribbed glass of the ceiling.
In spots like peacock eyes,
Goblin eyes, serpent eyes.

I like to come here early,
Before three o'clock, when the chattering mob
Of schoolgirls spoil it all
With their splashing and giggling and snorting
And chasing each other around.
I am not very much of a swimmer,
But I like coming down the steps
There at the shallow end
And feeling the slow green water mount
From ankle to knee like the clasp
Of coaxing, naiad fingers.
And I love floating here at the deeper end
Not far from the marble rim,
And feeling myself quite daring
With eight feet of water below me.
It seems I have to wear
A shapeless, one-piece bathing suit
Of faded blue and a cap.
And the rules typed plainly there
On a yellow card say I must take
A shower before going in
And another on coming out.
But all this cannot hinder me

From thinking of supple polished limbs
In the spray—the sudden lift
Of tawny golden hair
On the surge of a lifting wave—
Of darting shapes that gleam
Through the green like bits of pearl
Set in veinless onyx.

Now, it's the Amazon
Hyppolita swimming a bowshot out
From the shore to the Ship of Theseus,
Feeling the long, cool swell
Of a billow lift her up and up
Toward the purple and rosy drift
Of the low rushing clouds.
She laughs to see the bright drops run
Along her sunburned arm,
To taste the salt on her lips and know
That she is as bold and lithe
And enduring as any lad.

Then I think of Phryne the fair,
Of her who bathed in the sea
Near Athens before a wondering crowd.
I think she must have teased them all,
Laughing and splashing about
While they waited and stared and wondered,
Not letting them see too often
Her bosom like hawthorn flowers
And either moony shoulder.

There's a dark girl must have been handsome once
Though lame and twisted now.
She walks with a cane—comes limping in
Two or three times a week
And sits and watches. I've learned
A deal from her about different strokes.
She told me her story once,
For she was a splendid swimmer—
Won races, was photographed
As a "glorious example
Of feminine beauty and vigor."
Then—she struck her head while diving,
Was paralyzed for months

And afterwards always a cripple.
"And my best fellow," she said,
Went back on her—married someone else.
I remember the low, sad monotone
Of her voice and how it blended
With the faint drip drip of the shower bath.
But I liked the steady glow
In her ruddy hazel eyes.
They can't keep romance out
With neat brass railings and printed cards
And one-piece bathing suits—
For some of us will have it.

Tea Making

My lady love
Is making tea—she strikes
A match and the shrill blue flame leaps up
While the kettle's polished round
Reflects her smiling face.

And then she dips
By such a slender chain
A silver ball in the steaming draught
That slowly turns from crystal pure
To amber golden brown.

Just so, my heart
These many moons has swung
From her finger tip and bubbled and brewed
Such a strong, such a seething hot
Witch's drink of desire.

And last of all,
She drops into the cup
A cube of sugar moon-white that melts
And crumbles away like my heart
Whenever she looks at me.

WILLARD AUSTIN WATTLES
1888–1950

John

John, my beloved, come with me apart
In this dim garden for a little space.
I cannot rest me though the others sleep;
There is a time to wake them, but not now.

Is it not good to climb this hill to-night
After the glad hosannas in the streets,
The crowding faces, life and men and love,
Here on the slope of the eternal stars
To watch the lights that shine through Kedron's Vale
And 'neath the olives walk alone with God?

'Tis not the first time that we two have walked
Shoulder to shoulder underneath the stars;
Nor yet the last, John, though to-morrow's sun
Should dawn upon you, and on you alone.

Nay, my good brother, loose your fingers' grip.
You could not keep me if I willed to go:
Your heart enfolds me, not your fearful arm—
The lights shine clearer through the dusky vale,
And with their coming, John, we say good-by.

We say good-by, for every road must end,
All pleasant journeys underneath the sun;
Claspt hands are severed, hungry lips must part,
The long night comes at close of every day,
And men must slumber when their work is done.

Nay, it is better,—light is not light alone;
Were there no shadows, even suns were blind;
Only by parting do men meet again.

And we have met, John, met in a holy land
Alone with God in his great silences
Where never men have ventured—you and I.
And we have looked beyond the gates of heaven,

Beyond the stars, beyond the flaming sun,
Beyond all time, and known that God is love.

Was it not worth it, just to dare to be
One's simple self, to think, to love, to do,
And not to be ashamed? To live one life
Fearless and pure and strong, true to one's self,
Though the false world were full of lies and hate,
Where blind men lead each other through the dark,
Too weak to sin, ashamed of what is good,
Unable to do evil, thinking it.

But we have dared. David and Jonathan
Drank no divinelier in courts of Saul
Than we together in Gethsemane.
And though to-night I drain the cup of death
Down to the stinging dregs of Judas' kiss,
The wine of love lies sweeter on my lips—
I see the lanterns gleaming. Kiss me, John.

Only a Cloud Dissolving

I do not remember whether as man or woman
I heard the crashing of thickets and rose from Thessalian grass
As he burst with his gold-bronze shoulders the clutching tangle of
     olives
And over the dusky violets I saw his four feet pass.

I do not remember except that I was not frightened,
Only I stopped in wonder that such a thing could be
Though the fireside whispers warned me of a horse with a man's
     great body
Whose clasp was fire and thunder, whose breast like a crag at sea.

I do not remember, only a cloud dissolving
And the leap of his hooves behind him and the curl of the waves
     below,
Only the curve of his shoulder and his arms of iron round me
And the brown drift of sea-weed in green water is all I know.

How Little Knows the Caliph

Above a street in Bagdad set in the solid wall
There is a latticed window where the checkered sunbeams fall,

A little latticed window that looks upon the street—
And down between the houses comes a lad on sun-browned feet.

Oh, is he from the mountains high, or is he from the sea,
For never caliph trod in state on step so light as he,

Or is he only shepherd boy come in with goats to town,
With lips of the pomegranate flower and pillared throat of brown?

Oh, quick and drop it at his feet, the spicy cassia bud,
And I shall know if ghost he be, or vintaged warm with blood.

Oh, quick and swing the little door that is so straight and small. . . .
I weary of my lattices set in a solid wall.

Oh, he has climbed the musty stair, and passed the darkened door,
And kissed the aching from my lips that were numb before.

I did not know that love could be so merciful as this,
Or that a slender shepherd boy could hold so close a kiss,

For now I lie in jeweled arms and marvel hour by hour
How little knows the caliph of my red pomegranate flower.

CLAUDE McKAY
1889–1948

Absence

Your words dropped into my heart like pebbles into a pool,
Rippling around my breast and leaving it melting cool.

Your kisses fell sharp on my flesh like dawn-dews from the limb,
Of a fruit-filled lemon tree when the day is young and dim.

Like soft rain-christened sunshine, as fragile as rare gold lace,
Your breath, sweet-scented and warm, has kindled my tranquil face.

But a silence vasty-deep, oh deeper than all these ties
Now, through the menacing miles, brooding between us lies.

And more than the songs I sing, I await your written word,
To stir my fluent blood as never your presence stirred.

The Barrier

I must not gaze at them although
Your eyes are dawning day;
I must not watch you as you go
Your sun-illumined way.

I hear but I must never heed
The fascinating note,
Which, fluting like a river reed,
Comes from your trembling throat.

I must not see upon your face
Love's softly glowing spark;
For there's the barrier of race,
You're fair and I am dark.

Adolescence

There was a time when in late afternoon
    The four-o'clocks would fold up at day's close,
Pink-white in prayer. Under the floating moon
    I lay with them in calm and sweet repose.

And in the open spaces I could sleep,
    Half-naked to the shining worlds above;
Peace came with sleep and sleep was long and deep,
    Gained without effort, sweet like early love.

But now no balm—nor drug nor weed nor wine—
    Can bring true rest to cool my body's fever,
Nor sweeten in my mouth the acrid brine,
    That salts my choicest drink and will forever.

DJUNA BARNES
1892–1982

Six Songs of Khalidine

To the Memory of Mary Pyne

The flame of your red hair does crawl and creep
Upon your body that denies the gloom
And feeds upon your flesh as 't would consume
The cold precision of your austere sleep—
And all night long I beat it back, and weep.

It is not gentleness but mad despair
That sets us kissing mouths, O Khalidine,
Your mouth and mine, and one sweet mouth unseen
We call our soul. Yet thick within our hair
The dusty ashes that our days prepare.

The dark comes up, my little love, and dyes
Your fallen lids with stain of ebony,
And draws a thread of fear 'tween you and me
Pulling thin blindness down across our eyes—
And far within the vale a lost bird cries.

Does not the wind moan round your painted towers
Like rats within an empty granary?
The clapper lost, and long blown out to sea
Your windy doves. And here the black bat cowers
Against your clock that never strikes the hours.

And now I say, has not the mountain's base
Here trembled long ago unto the cry
"I love you, ah, I love you!" Now we die
And lay, all silent, to the earth our face.
Shall that cast out the echo of this place?

Has not one in the dark funereal
Heard foot-fall fearful, born of no man's tread,
And felt the wings of death, though no wing spread,
And on his cheek a tear, though no tear fell—
And a voice saying without breath "Farewell!"

Lullaby

When I was a young child I slept with a dog,
I lived without trouble and I thought no harm;
I ran with the boys and I played leap-frog;
Now it is a girl's head that lies on my arm.

Then I grew a little, picked plantain in the yard;
Now I dwell in Greenwich, and the people do not call;
Then I planted pepper-seed and stamped on them hard.
Now I am very quiet and I hardly plan at all.

Then I pricked my finger on a thorn, or a thistle,
Put the finger in my mouth, and ran to my mother.
Now I lie here, with my eyes on a pistol.
There will be a morrow, and another, and another.

First Communion

The mortal fruit upon the bough
Hangs above the nuptial bed.
The cat-bird in the tree returns
The forfeit of his mutual vow.

The hard, untimely apple of
The branch that feeds on watered rain
Takes the place upon her lips
Of her late lamented love.

Many hands together press
Shaped within a static prayer
Recall to one the chorister
Docile in his sexless dress.

The temperate winds reclaim the iced
Remorseless vapors of the snow.
The only pattern in the mind
Is the cross behind the Christ.

JAMES FENIMORE COOPER, JR.
1892–1918

Isolation

Eternally apart are we,
And as the planets glide
Their narrow ways unchangingly
'Mid all the starry tide,
So must we live
And fitful light to others give.

Eternally apart are we
Beyond the keenest sight:
I have my own adversity
To guide my course aright,
Nor canst thou know
The things I seek, nor where I go.

Then do thou treasure jealously
The flash that comes and dies,
Engrave it on thy memory—
Make it thy dearest prize:
Lest it be true
That I can never live in you!

The Tryst

Impatient one—why can you not wait?
Your lover will come.

When day is over and the scents of evening arise from the grass,
When the last tint is dwelling in the west
And one star shines—
Then will thine image arise before him
Then will his steps infallibly turn hither,

Be not impatient,
He will come.

To a Friend

Thy voice, as tender as the light
That shivers low at eve—
Thy hair, where myriad flashes bright
Do in and outward weave—
Thy charms in their diversity
Half frighten and astonish me.

Thy hands, that move above the keys
With eager touch and swift—
Whereby thy mind, with magic ease
Doth into music drift—
They fill me with a strange delight
That doth defy expression quite.

Thine eyes, that hold a mirth subdued—
Like deep pools scattering fire—
Mine dare not meet them in their mood,
For fear of my desire,
Lest thou that secret do descry
Which evermore I must deny.

Thy very quiet dignity
Thy silence, too, I love—
Nay—thy light word is destiny
Decreed in spheres above—
My mind, my heart is bowed to thee,
And hard it is that I must flee.

Hard is a world that dare not give
For every love a place:
Hard is a power that bids us live
A life bereft of grace—
Hard, hard to lose thy figure dear,
My star and my religion here!

EDNA ST. VINCENT MILLAY
1892–1950

I, being born a woman and distressed

I, being born a woman and distressed
By all the needs and notions of my kind,
Am urged by your propinquity to find
Your person fair, and feel a certain zest
To bear your body's weight upon my breast:
So subtly is the fume of life designed,
To clarify the pulse and cloud the mind,
And leave me once again undone, possessed.
Think not for this, however, the poor treason
Of my stout blood against my staggering brain,
I shall remember you with love, or season
My scorn with pity,—let me make it plain:
I find this frenzy insufficient reason
For conversation when we meet again.

Night is my sister, and how deep in love

Night is my sister, and how deep in love,
How drowned in love and weedily washed ashore,
There to be fretted by the drag and shove
At the tide's edge, I lie—these things and more:
Whose arm alone between me and the sand,
Whose voice alone, whose pitiful breath brought near,
Could thaw these nostrils and unlock this hand,
She could advise you, should you care to hear.
Small chance, however, in a storm so black,
A man will leave his friendly fire and snug
For a drowned woman's sake, and bring her back
To drip and scatter shells upon the rug.
No one but Night, with tears on her dark face,
Watches beside me in this windy place.

I too beneath your moon almighty Sex

I too beneath your moon, almighty Sex,
Go forth at nightfall crying like a cat,
Leaving the lofty tower I laboured at
For birds to foul and boys and girls to vex
With tittering chalk; and you, and the long necks
Of neighbours sitting where their mothers sat
Are well aware of shadowy this and that
In me, that's neither noble nor complex.
Such as I am, however, I have brought
To what it is, this tower; it is my own;
Though it was reared To Beauty, it was wrought
From what I had to build with: honest bone
Is there, and anguish; pride; and burning thought;
And lust is there, and nights not spent alone.

MERCEDES DE ACOSTA
1893–1968

Infatuation

It is not that I shall ever forget
The charm of your face, this I do not fear,
Or the rhythmic sway of your form, nor yet
The melody of the voice I loved to hear.
These things I shall remember.
I shall remember, too, the beauty of your eyes
And the stirring curves of your crimson mouth,
Like lightning storms and wind-swept flaming skies
Set on fire by the hot sun of the South.
I can recall all the words you promised and said,
Your seductive caressing ways, and the false kisses you gave to me;
Remembering these I cannot help harboring the dread
That some day I will return, remembering no longer your cruelty.

Soiled Hands

After everyone had left,
It was always so wonderful sitting in the dark theatre with you.
There was a mystery about it,
As though the echo of many plays
Still lingered in the folds of the curtain,
While phantom figures crouched low in the chairs,
Beating suppressed applause with vapor hands.
Do you remember how we always sat silently?
I would shut my eyes to feel your closeness nearer.
Then slowly and like a ritual
I would take your hand,
And you would laugh a little and say,
"My hands are awfully sticky"—or
"I can't seem to keep my hands clean in this theatre,"
As if that mattered . . . as if that mattered. . . .

We Three

There is something that from between us has slipped away and left
     me chill,
Something that by its loss has made the world less warm
And made me feel as though the sun rising o'er the purple dew-
     touched hill,
Finds its rays cold as it touches the face of dawn.

Although we kiss and meet the same each day,
You speak my name and I yours and we clasp hands,
Yet from somewhere, I do not know which way,
Stealing between us a lurking figure stands.

A figure clad in gray. . . .
To me a dream, a phantom come to steal
My starlight quite away.
To you a gay figure, not strange but real.

And all the while it lurks and turns,
And from every cell and corner of my brain
I feel its presence and the burns
Even of your kisses cannot make me sane.

Why should this figure strange and sinister
Keep on coming? Why should she in the night
Breathe words of comfort and administer
Balm to my soul, pointing the way to light?

While when we meet in the day a dread silence lingers,
A silence chill which with no kindness blends
A word of cheer, or kind touch for my trembling fingers;
No look to prove that we are even friends.

Sometimes when you call my name I hear a tone
Of her voice within yours, and you say
Things which she will say at night and when alone,
Or what she's said before just that way.
They say we dream in sleep, but I must dream by day,
Because on waking she is a dream child, nor seems less fair,
Though more cruel than when I left her in my sleep sitting there.

If I could brush away this vision and start once again,
If I could see sunlight and feel less sad,
If I could only steady the confusion of my brain,
Somewhere, somehow I might again be glad.
And by a laugh or carefree jest,
I might once more call your love from out the past
And hold you closely to my side—lest,
Again between us the figure stand and fast
Would bind my hands and from me turn your face away,
Making once more my day a night and my night a day.

Ah, love, if we could turn Spring into last Spring again,
Or if I could toss my heart away and make it new;
If I could drink deeply of some draught to ease the pain,
Or become more callous, less kind and far, far less true . . .
Less true to ideals, to love and you.

Perhaps I will, then my brain will cease to ache,
And this sad frenzied chaos I will not prolong;
Then for yours, or mine or hers or each one's sake,
I will wave farewell to you, singing Love's Swan Song.

Singing Love's Swan Song, so that this may truly be,
That never again will false love take hold of me;
I may be mad, but which is the maddest of we three,
Is it you? Or I? Or is it she?

GENEVIEVE TAGGARD
1894–1948

Just Daylight

Men follow women whom they would not follow;
And women yield who do not want to yield;
Wounds here are given, hardly to be healed;

(Oh, better, better, better to be dead
Than so to lie in such an alien bed.)

Married

Your face from my face slips,
Lover of my lips.
Holder of my heart,
For all our close companionships,
We are apart.
Apart, apart, we are apart.

Crying beauty leaves me dumb,
Your fire, cold and still.
I watch the hours of morning come,
And always will,
With this dull agony in my heart—
We are apart.

Strong, solemn, stupid-kind;
Parting, we leave behind
Silence, where our foot-steps sound
Dead on the hollow ground.

With a singing river I used to run
Wild with wonder: now
There is no river, there is no sun,
Only an old vow.

And this dull chant goes through my head,
And this dull moan sinks in my heart:

Half of my body must be dead,
We are apart.

For Eager Lovers

I understand what you were running for,
Slim naked boy, and why from far inland
You came between dark hills. I know the roar
The sea makes in some ears. I understand.

I understand why you were running now
And how you heard the sea resound, and how
You leaped and left your valley for the long
Brown road. I understand the song

You chanted with your running, with your feet
Marking the measure of your high heart's beat.
Now you are broken. Seeing your wide brow
I see your dreams. I understand you now.

Since I have run like you, I understand
The throat's long wish, the breath that comes so quick,
The heart's light leap, the heels that drag so sick,
And warped heat wrinkles, lengthening the sand. . . .

Now you are broken. Seeing your wide brow
I see your dreams, understanding now
The cry, the certainty, wide arms,—and then
The way rude ocean rises and descends. . . .

I saw you stretched and wounded where tide ends.
I do not want to walk that way again.

ROBERT HILLYER
1895–1961

From "Sonnets": XIV

A while you shared my path and solitude,
A while you ate the bread of loneliness,
And satisfied yourself with a caress
Or with a careless overflow of mood.
And then you left me suddenly, to press
Into the world again, and seek your food
Among the mortals whom you understood,
Instead of learning in the wilderness.

Now you return to where you fled from me,
And find me gone. You call me from afar,
And call in vain; I can not turn to see
You loveliness, beloved as you are.
Inexorably I move from sphere to sphere,
Nor wait for any soul, however dear.

A Failure

Evening has come, young man;
What have you done today?

I have fashioned a younger man
Out of the ageless clay.
He will pass invisible
Through crowds in the market square;
They will say, "Did you hear a bell?"
They will say, "How queer to smell
Incense in open air!"
Wherever he plants his feet,
Wherever he skims his heel,
The air will go mad and sweet,
The asphalt will skirl and reel.
They will say, "We can hear the beat

Of a mighty revolving wheel
In a powerhouse far off."

Young man, that is not enough.

A Letter

Dear boy, what can this stranger mean to you,
   Blown to your country by unbridled chance?
That he should drink the morn's first cup of dew
   Fresh from the spring, and quicken that grave glance
Wherein as rising tides on hazy shores
   Rise the new flames and colours of romance?

Ah, wise and young, the world shall use your youth
   And fling you shorn of beauty to despair,
The sum of all that fascinating truth
   That you have gleaned, hands tangled in brown hair,
Eyes straining into contemplative fires,—
   This truth shall not seem truth when trees are bare.

The hunger of the soul, the watcher left
   To brood the nearness of his own decay,
Dully remarking the slow shameless theft
   Of the old holiness from day to day,
How youth grows tarnished, wisdom changes false,—
   Till one bends near to steal your life away.

Yet who am I to turn aside the hand
Outstretched so friendly and so humbly proud,
   Heaped up with beauty from the sunrise land
Of hearts adventurous and heads unbowed?
Only, look not at me with changing eyes
When we must separate amid the crowd.

ROBERT McALMON
1895–1956

Ero-Somnambulism

The peacock cackles discordantly
down the stairs, strutting.
Erotically
my somnambulistic spirit
rides his lofty tail
stridently asserting erection.

Rhododendrons
white as white on ebony
gesticulate
in the hushed darkness
of slippery waters
on moving sidewalks
towards the old mill.
There are insidious whisperings
of deep incarceration
and unspeakable malpractices.

Night is an amphora
the universe pours itself into.
With entities swept in waterfalls
and earth upheavals
my soul, apathetically protesting
slips in with the gooey conglomeration.

Moonlight crackles in the night,
stars moan,
cylindrically revolving.
Some break away to split the sky
into which suave vapours snap
mending the tortured rent.

At Daylight
my ego regains its sceptre
and solemnly majestic
intolerant of the foolish night

conquers a hummingbird
and feeds on pollen.

The Mother

Mother sits before the sewing machine.
She will never believe that shirts she sews
are not better and cheaper than ones I buy.

She will never believe that my welfare
is not better served where she can work for me.

Her hands are old and wrinkled.
It is not fair that I must pity her.
I want my life, and did not will
that her last years should all be bound
in mother love for me.
What she has not, what she has missed,
I can not help. Her love's my prison,
and my pity is the lock.

My body is here,
but will that make her last years happy,
and when she's gone
what will I have to fasten to, if I am old?

My blood is a fire in me.
I do not know why my flesh is not burned to ashes.
My will has become black gropings,
Pity is a merciless master.

Taunt to the Egoist

Fan your tail to the silver twilight,
gorge in pomp, my dove.

As for myself,
I shall disrobe
to grovel in the ashes.
How adorable is my humility,
so utter in its simplicity,
surely wrought
as small ivory in Chinese hands.

Green and gold
and the changing rays of purple
pulsate in your plumage, my dove.
Strut. Show the world your splendour.

As for myself,
I take great pride
in knowing that my plainness conceals me.
Someday the pod of me will burst
then you will see
how fertile are the meek and humble.

BERNICE KENYON
1897–?

The Letter

"Therefore take comfort from this sheet of paper
On which your lover has written words of light;
And then destroy it—burn it at a taper
Held in a trembling hand, on a chill night."

Darkness shuts in—the night is cold—my fingers
Are cold too. The cold clutches at my heart.
There is no mortal warmth at all that lingers
Here in your letter; and no skillful art

Has set the feeling of life down with the writing.
I am aware only of what you say—
And here you write forever of feasting and fighting—
And what are they, in this cold ?—and what are they?

Nothing of you comes nearer for my reading. . . .
Do you know what this night is like ?—But you cannot know.
There are dark winds over the world; they are moving and speeding,
Forever bringing the cold; and they blow and blow,

Rattling my windows, shrilling the air, and sighing;
Making a sound of lost things in a storm—

Pursued things—hurt and wild—running and flying. . . .
I will burn your letter up to get me warm!

Here is the candle. . . . Never does flame mount quicker
Than in white paper, snapping, and turning it black;
The fire spurts—shrivels—dies in a final flicker . . .
And the cold—the terrible cold—comes creeping back.

A Woman Like a Shell

You are the worn sea-haunted shell
That lapping tongues of brine and sand
Have ravaged—once the citadel
Of a shy beast that loved the swell
Of water beating on the land.

Nothing could live within you now;
Your bones are chalk, your blood is drained.
Yet the fair shape will still allow
Echoes that tell your life, and how
And why the living substance waned.

Possession, now, to roving men—
Home-set, they listen long to hear
The old sea-roar and thunder, when
Your emptiness gives back again
The loud blood racing in the ear.

Mediaeval

If you ask me why she is lovely, I shall answer:
It is because of the stately way she has of moving,
Making a stir of air that is sweet like the stir of arras—
Taking her lightly-measured steps with a regal bearing.

She is one that you cannot know by the face uplifted,
Nor by the flutter of hands above rich-patterned fabric;
She is a woman wearing a mask of delicate laughter—
She who is small and bright and calm in the ancient manner.

If you ask me what she has known, that a mask conceals her,
Checking the sting of tears and the motion of lips that tremble,

I shall say she is sad, and has been sad too often—
Making her proud and strange, who today has tears for no one.

Now there is none would dare disturb the mask she is wearing;
Let her alone—beware of a secret scorn beneath it;
Count it enough that she is lovely and small and slender,
Here where the light grows warm, as it falls and clings around her.

JOHN WHEELWRIGHT
1897–1940

Apocryphal Apocalypse

For Waldo Frank

Wisemen to glossators unknown
when the Assisian or the Galilean
entered to the death which made his life
lustless in hope to find with keener sperm
have said:
"We liked him, but we found him hard to chat with.
His conversation bored us more than talk."
You gluttons for seedless speech and Vegex meat
who fondle terms to dull their definitions
and chew in vain each mouthful more and more
of day by day to find water taste sweet:
though sunk in boredom beyond excavations,
dose yourselves with bottled conversation's
pedantic antidote to boredom's poison.
Made of the Dictionary your Book of Truth
to hear the Apocalypse of Wheels with puckered lips:

Beware, beware like dogs with indoor faces
all fops and frumps who think it good, or better
for every man to follow his ideal:
anti William Carlos Williams Oscar Williamses
(less Apollonian than plumbers, laureate)

Waldos, un-Emersonian frank
Imbecile in paradisian beatitude
who ruminate on something . . . something
which men who lack a more definite term call Holy, Holy
wholly holy, hale, and wholly wholesome.
Combatting thought with thought's own element
Pied Pipers fop flute the Youth towards Baby's cave.
But above all Bores, the Hegelian Yes-Man Frump
beware who reconciles thought's hostile poles with smiles
(synthetic smiles) to prove his platitude
quite true: "Evil is the shadow side of Good."
God-The-Eternal-Bore-of-Bores—subsists
in see-saw half-affirmation
(as A.E. and E.A.
Robinson have said at greater length
who each caught deaths of cold from Cosmic Chill)
but the Truth lives in contradictions of the flesh.
Transfigurated bone can cast no shadow.
Something there is that does not love a Bore.

Phallus

Friends need not guard each other as a jealous
Moslem must segregate his odalisque,
no more than one need see the symboled phallus
while meditating at an obelisk.
   If we could be together day after day,
   companionship, pointed with entering wedge
   compact, whittled by common task and play
   inevitable and slow, would split the pledge
   which kisses tallied once in valediction:
   that our hidden selves in separation meet.
   The corollary's simple contradiction
   May render yet the contract obsolete.
Habit is evil,—all habit, even speech;
and promises prefigure their own breach.

Adam

Subject alone to lonely and sincere
allegiance to crown-and-robeless liberty,
he can submit to no authority,—

yet he is wise in all he does revere,
and loveable, because his will is clear
and beautiful, because his mind is free.
In him, all admirable traits appear
and he is kindly, for he owns no fear.

   A youthful Adam, fresh from Genesis,
   standing in memory, with pectoral muscles bright
   alabaster, dusted by morning's light;
   comprised the Sodomites' antithesis,—
   and, could I be as he looked in my sight,
   from friendship would arise a trinity.

ELSA GIDLOW
1898–1981

The Beloved Lost

'Tis not alone that you have gone from me:
All the hungry, fragile roots of hope
Are blasted by a Thing I cannot name;
And I am desolate, remembering

The rare kiss, the intimate silent climbing
From passion to a wordless comprehension.
Even my peace of heart, born of long pain
Dies, drowned in a turbulence of sorrow.

Life today is like a glass reflecting
Nothing more than my own grieving eyes,
Or like a goblet that I sit and stare at,
Empty of all but stains of last night's wine.

Conquest

Yea, I have reached cruel and strange heights
And the road is one I would not travel again
For any wealth of wisdom, or any gift

Within the generous power of gods or men.
Yea, I have conquered! Yea, I should exult
And love my strength and drink my loneliness
Like wine, a very crag among proud crags,
Superbly calm in austere barrenness.
Yet peace may be a lie and strength a curse,
Conquest makes melancholy history,
And she whose victim is her own poor heart
May soon regret the bitter victory,
So, with a pride that half my nature scorns,
I wear my courage like a crown of thorns.

Love Dies

I watched her every movement as she died,
    Feeling as far away and as detached
As if she were not mine. I watched her cringe
    When Death's shadow crawled over the latched
Gate, and Death crouched, waiting, there.
    I watched her shaken body, sigh-torn,
The pitiful veined eyelids shut on tears,
    And hardly wondered that I did not mourn.
And then there came a gusty sweep of sobs,
    And then silence and slowly opened eyes
That I met very calmly, only thinking:
    Love is very lovely when she dies.

Then the latch slipped, the gate swung open
    Letting Death in, and there flew in with Death
Flocks of fluttering velvet-feathered laughters
    That nested in Love's hair, and drank Love's breath
Until she gasped no more. And she was dead.
    And no change in anything around her:
No new sorrow in the wind's voice
    Or grief on the day's face when it found her.
And I half wondered why *they* were so calm,
    Why they did not care that love was dead,
What the silence meant, the vague hurt
    That quivered through me, and the vague dread.

"Yet I would not raise her if I could,
    For have I not the best of her to keep?"
But I suddenly wanted darkness, and a place
    To hide my heart's emptiness. And I wanted sleep.

ROYAL MURDOCH
1898–1981

The Earthling

What happens on earth
Takes away my breath—
O before my birth
And after my death!

Do seas dry up
And turn into sand,
And the big whales pup
Over ancient land?

Do tall waves lift
Where cities once stood?
Do continents drift
Like pieces of wood?

Shall sea-bottom shell,
That tiny shroud,
Beach high in a dell
Under billows of cloud?

Shall mountain crown
Lie prone as a plain
Washed utterly down
By snow and rain?

So small my place,
So little of me,
Is there still space
That such things be?

The grey-beard rocks
Hear eons tick by,
Worn are the clocks
Of eternity.

Dame Time must go
On a wobbly crutch

She is so slow—
But, ah, so much!

Is she a crone
Who loves to wheedle
As she sits alone
With her rusty needle—

My life her stitch,
Hasty and brittle,
The sewer is rich,
But I have little?

Or is she someone
Cleaning out bars,
With a broken glass sun
And a dust of stars?

Does she work for ages
To pay for a spree?
Whatever her wages
She doesn't suit me.

O mighty broom
That sweeps the sky,
Give me more room
To love and die.

She Walks Alone

All day for him the summer waves
Ran wildly laughing up the beach,
But now they hide in off-shore rocks
And hold their sullen tongues from speech.

He is gone, is gone, is gone.
Will he never come again?
Pacific isle, Tunisian sand,
Or lost in dark Italian rain?

All night for him the winter sea
Chanted praise upon the shore,
But now the choral voice is mute,
Stilled to a sob the distant roar.

My love, my heart, my boy is gone.
Will he never come again?
Pacific isle, Tunisian sand,
Or dead in bleak Italian rain.

The Thrall

At last I climbed one night of wind and blare
To seize you lip and thigh and breast and bone:
Behind a eucalypt the moon alone
Beheld the thief creep down the darkened stair,
Release the knotted gag of jetty hair
And set your naked feet on paving stone:
Just when he thought I had you for my own,
Unkissed, unharmed, I left you standing there.
A fool that hour gave liberty away:
Fool! Fool! how soon to realize
They are possessed for always who resign
Possession: captive now, who chose obey
The regal black defiance of your eyes,
I am forever yours and you not mine.

HART CRANE
1899–1933

Episode of Hands

The unexpected interest made him flush.
Suddenly he seemed to forget the pain,—
Consented,—and held out
One finger from the others.

The gash was bleeding, and a shaft of sun
That glittered in and out among the wheels,
Fell lightly, warmly, down into the wound.

And as the fingers of the factory owner's son,
That knew a grip for books and tennis
As well as one for iron and leather,—
As his taut, spare fingers wound the gauze
Around the thick bed of the wound,
His own hands seemed to him
Like wings of butterflies
Flickering in sunlight over summer fields.

The knots and notches,—many in the wide
Deep hand that lay in his,—seemed beautiful.
They were like the marks of wild ponies' play,—
Bunches of new green breaking a hard turf.

And factory sounds and factory thoughts
Were banished from him by that larger, quieter hand
That lay in his with the sun upon it.
And as the bandage knot was tightened
The two men smiled into each other's eyes.

C33

He has woven rose-vines
About the empty heart of night,
And vented his long mellowed wines
Of dreaming on the desert white
With searing sophistry.
And he tended with far truths he would form
The transient bosoms from the thorny tree.

O Maternal! to enrich thy gold head
And wavering shoulders with a new light shed

From penitence must needs bring pain,
And with it song of minor, broken strain.
But you who hear the lamp whisper thru night
Can trace paths tear-wet, and forget all blight.

Modern Craft

Though I have touched her flesh of moons,
Still she sits gestureless and mute,

Drowning cool pearls in alcohol.
O blameless shyness;—innocence dissolute!

She hazards jet; wears tiger-lilies;—
And bolts herself within a jewelled belt.
Too many palms have grazed her shoulders:
Surely she must have felt.

Ophelia had such eyes; but she
Even, sank in love and choked with flowers.
This burns and is not burnt. . . . My modern love were
Charred at a stake in younger times than ours.

LYNN RIGGS
1899–1954

Song of the Unholy Oracle

Be that placated
Monastic one—
Chill fingered, gated
From the sun!

Shrubs may be tended
With the shrunk wrist,
Oaks grow splendid
Unsunkissed.

Furrows long fattened
May turn from sleep
Sprouting, flattened
Worms shorten and creep,

Feverish earth—
Field, thicket, plain—
Come to birth
Without pain.

In the beginning,
This was your wish:

To feed unsinning
At the iron dish.

Be that lone diner
On the grubby root—
You who want no finer
Disastrous fruit!

Admonition in Ivory

Not your body, the marble flower,
Is so chastely of this hour,

Nor your mind discriminate
And so sensuously elate,

Nor your own exhaustible
Athletic ardor beautiful—

But the velvet delicate
Closing of an open gate.

Heed these slight and transitory
Hidden words admonitory!—

Lest you never learn the brittle
Texture of a sound, and little

Realize the insecure
Hingeing of an open door,

And never feel the strength of that
Fragile gate you struggle at.

Before a Departure

Before I go away,
This must be conceded:
Nothing is asked of anyone,
And nothing needed.

If you see me beckon
Comrades broad or gaunt,
Tall or short—I summon
What I do not want.

If you see me kneel,
Let it be understood:
Bowing is a habit
And prayer an attitude.

ROBERT FRANCIS
1901–1987

The Goldfish Bowl

The year is nineteen forty-one, the season winter.
The earth lies naked to the wind. The frost goes deep.
Along the river shore the ice-sheets creak and splinter.
Under the frost the tree roots and the woodchuck sleep.

The time is winter night, but in the swimming pool
Is summer noontime, noon by the electric sun.
The young men dive, emerge, and float a while, and fool,
And dive again. The year is nineteen forty-one.

The tropic water is safe-filtered and the room
Is air-conditioned, kept an even eighty-five.
Outdoors a shivering newsboy is proclaiming doom.
Inside the pool a naked youth is poised to dive.

The time is ten o'clock in nineteen forty-one.
Somewhere a bell upon a tower begins to toll
While hour by hour the moon, its fat face warm with sun,
Gloats like a patient cat above a goldfish bowl.

If we had known

If we had known all that we know
We never would have let him go.

He never would have reached the river
If we had guessed his going. Never.

We had the stronger argument
Had we but dreamed his dark intent.

Or if our words failed to dissuade him
Unarguing love might still have stayed him.

We would have lured him from his course.
And if love failed, there still was force.

We would have locked the door and barred it.
We would have stood all night to guard it.

But what we know, we did not know.
We said good-bye and saw him go.

Boy Riding Forward Backward

Presto, pronto! Two boys, two horses.
But the boy on backward riding forward
Is the boy to watch.

He rides the forward horse and laughs
In the face of the forward boy on the backward
Horse, and *he* laughs

Back and the horses laugh. They gallop.
The trick is the cool barefaced pretense
There is no trick.

They might be flying, face to face,
On a fast train. They might be whitecaps
Hot-cool-headed,

One curling backward, one curving forward,
Racing a rivalry of waves.
They might, they might—

Across a blue of lake, through trees,
And half a mile away I caught them:
Two boys, two horses.

Through trees and through binoculars
Sweeping for birds. Oh, they were birds
All right, all right,

Swallows that weave and wave and sweep
And skim and swoop and skitter until
The last trees take them.

GLENWAY WESCOTT
1901–1987

Magnolias and the Intangible Horse

> But no beast comes.
> —YVOR WINTERS

The magnolia bud
stained with plum,
not built to open
but to remain tubular. . . .

The watering place
full of white tubes
piled in pyramids,
where I stoop
in the wet air,
where I dream of the red horse
(nostalgia)—

his nose a spike
of chestnut flowers,
his tail and mane
silver-centred
curls, and his shell-hoofs
cutting
a mist of pebbles
between villages. . . .

In sorrow
the sun breaks the bud
to a flower
like a fallen bird,
feathers bent up
and out, star-shaped.

Mountain III: Coyotes

Dusk falls
with a single movement.

The sheep nod in the corral
fenced with cactus.
I crouch in my hut, playing
on the unpainted flute,
while the moon thickens.

The three dogs
lie by the door, slim as goats,
and the coyotes
come, to lure them away
with crooning
and shouts like bells
which break
on the forked rocks.

I fall on my
knees, weeping:
"They will leave
me alone, to go mad! Stay
here, they will tear
your lips and ears!"

They whimper and lick my face,
leap about
on their shadows
with stiff sharp feet.

Natives of Rock

The fire cut away
the soft forest
down to the rose-pink rock
harder than light.

Movement is not easy
in the mountain clearing
where all that is not stone
imitates and is above stone.

We ride so high
that we are embedded
in the air (O crystal)
and cry for love among aspens,

ferns that uncoil beneath—
cry discontent. At night
we lie down
on red granite

ledges, throat on throat,
mid polished berry rods,
eyes wide open
for the early rays' stir:

illusion of antelope
who make the horizon
quiver upon their lifted
spikes, and lap the dew.

LANGSTON HUGHES
1902–1967

Café: 3 a.m.

Detectives from the vice squad
with weary sadistic eyes
spotting fairies.
   Degenerates,
   some folks say.

   But God, Nature,
   or somebody
   made them that way.

Police lady or Lesbian
over there?
   Where?

Low to High

How can you forget me?
But you do!

You said you was gonna take me
Up with you—
Now you've got your Cadillac,
you done forgot that you are black.
How can you forget me
When I'm you?

But you do.

How can you forget me,
fellow, say?
How can you low-rate me
this way?
You treat me like you damn well please,
Ignore me—though I pay your fees.
How can you forget me?

But you do.

Impasse

I could tell you,
If I wanted to,
What makes me
What I am.

But I don't
Really want to—
And you don't
Give a damn.

COUNTEE CULLEN
1903–1946

Fruit of the Flower

My father is a quiet man
  With sober, steady ways;
For simile, a folded fan;
  His nights are like his days.

My mother's life is puritan,
  No hint of cavalier,
A pool so calm you're sure it can
  Have little depth to fear.

And yet my father's eyes can boast
  How full his life has been;
There haunts them yet the languid ghost
  Of some still sacred sin.

And though my mother chants of God,
  And of the mystic river,
I've seen a bit of checkered sod
  Set all her flesh aquiver.

Why should he deem it pure mischance
  A son of his is fain
To do a naked tribal dance
  Each time he hears the rain?

Why should she think it devil's art
  That all my songs should be
Of love and lovers, broken heart,
  And wild sweet agony?

Who plants a seed begets a bud,
  Extract of that same root;
Why marvel at the hectic blood
  That flushes this wild fruit?

Advice to Youth

For Guillaume

Since little time is granted here
    For pride in pain or play,
Since blood soon cools before that Fear
    That makes our prowess clay,
If lips to kiss are freely met,
    Lad, be not proud nor shy;
There are no lips where men forget,
    And undesiring lie.

Sacrament

She gave her body for my meat,
    Her soul to be my wine,
And prayed that I be made complete
    In sunlight and starshine.

With such abandoned grace she gave
    Of all that passion taught her,
She never knew her tidal wave
    Cast bread on stagnant water.

EDWIN DENBY
1903–1983

The Subway

The subway flatters like the dope habit,
For a nickel extending peculiar space:
You dive from the street, holing like a rabbit,
Roar up a sewer with a millionaire's face.

Squatting in the full glare of the locked express
Imprisoned, rocked, like a man by a friend's death,
O how the immense investment soothes distress,

Credit laps you like a huge religious myth.

It's a sound effect. The trouble is seeing
(So anaesthetized) a square of bare throat
Or the fold at the crotch of a clothed human being:
You'll want to nuzzle it, crop at it like a goat.

That's not in the buy. The company between stops
Offers you security, and free rides to cops.

Summer

I stroll on Madison in expensive clothes, sour.
Ostrich-legg'd or sweet-chested, the loping clerks
Slide me a glance nude as oh in a tiled shower
And lope on dead-pan, large male and female jerks.

Later from the open meadow in the Park
I watch a bulging pea-soup storm lie midtown;
Here the high air is clear, there buildings are murked,
Manhattan absorbs the cloud like a sage-brush plain.

In the grass sleepers sprawl without attraction:
Some large men who turned sideways, old ones on papers,
A soldier, face handkerchiefed, an erection
In his pants—only men, the women don't nap here.

Can these wide spaces suit a particular man?
They can suit whomever man's intestines can.

People on Sunday

In the street young men play ball, else in fresh shirts
Expect a girl, bums sit quietly soused in house-doors,
Girls in dresses walk looking ahead, a car starts
As the light clicks, and Greeks laugh in cafes upstairs.

Sundays the long asphalt looks dead like a beach
The heat lies on New York the size of the city
The season keeps moving through and out of reach
And people left in the kitchen are a little flighty.

Look at all the noises we make for one another
Like: shake cake bake take, or: ton gun run fun,
Like: the weather, the system, the picture of his brother,
And: shake hands and leave and look at the sun go down.

One Sunday a day-old baby looked right at my eyes
And turned its head away without the least surprise.

FRANK BELKNAP LONG, JR.
1901–1994

In Antique Mood

I am afraid, for every slender dream
Has burst its sheath, and were I now to blow
The ancient pipe the ancient god would seem
A form gigantic, and I fear him so.
His hoofbeats are too rhythmic, are too loud;
They clatter in my brain, and when at night
I draw the sheets, I seem to draw my shroud:
The goat would trample me if I should fight.

But you a steadfast, jealous watch will keep.
You tender me your lips and fallen hair
As safeguards: there is solace when I sleep
Beside you, O compassionately fair!
But even on your arms there falls a shade—
Dear, hold me close! I am afraid . . . afraid.

The Rebel

He walked in caverns, talked with eager men
Whose thoughts were bent on barter, gain and loss:
He saw the worlds which center in the toss
Of one small coin; and he was wretched then.
He hated cities and their iron marts;
He longed for palms against a sunset sky;
His only friends were lads with sea-tamed hearts;
He loved tall masts and great ships scudding by.

For there are men who never sail in ships,
Who cannot bide the thought of any land;

As children they awake with muted lips,
Amazed by endless leagues of sunlit sand;
As children they awake, and seeking, find
The black monsoon and gulls upon the wind.

A Time Will Come

A time will come when we shall share
   The wonder, dear, together,
Of flaming candles on a shrine
   In gray and golden weather.

And we shall kneel with avid eyes
   To watch a shining chalice
By children borne across the nave
   Of some cathedral-palace.

And we shall rise, and go away
   With eager lips that cling,
Unmindful of the strumming choirs
   And every living thing.

CHRISTOPHER ISHERWOOD
1904–1986

Mapperley Plains

By the swift ways of shade and sun
We trod the morning. Spring was white
And hushed in lovely pools of light—
But we were eager to have won
Mapperley Plains, so strange and fair;
Nor guessed what should await us there.

And strong noon bridged half Heaven in flame
And day swung down from blue to blue. . . .

We marched untired, for we knew
Daylight could never be the same,
Or Glory half so glad, as when
The weird plains seize the hearts of men.

Their beauty is the sword that cleaves
Youth, royally lived in pride and laughter,
From blank, prosaic Age. Hereafter
A bright day's ending . . . fallen leaves—
Mapperley Plains are years behind,
Their music dies within the mind.

The Common Cormorant

The common cormorant (or shag)
Lays eggs inside a paper bag,
You follow the idea, no doubt?
It's to keep the lightning out.

But what these unobservant birds
Have never thought of, is that herds
Of wandering bears might come with buns
And steal the bags to hold the crumbs.

On His Queerness

When I was young and wanted to see the sights,
They told me: "Cast an eye over the Roman Camp
If you care to,
But plan to spend most of your day at the Aquarium—
Because, after all, the Aquarium—
Well, I mean to say, the Aquarium—
Till you've seen the Aquarium you ain't seen nothing."

So I cast an eye over
The Roman Camp—
And that old Roman Camp,
That old, old Roman Camp
Got me
Interested.

So that now, near closing-time,
I find that I still know nothing—
And am not even sorry that I know nothing—
About fish.

RICHARD BRUCE NUGENT
1906–1987

Narcissus

—And as he gazed there seemed to grow
The sound-soft beauty of pale Echo;
Petaled breasts began to show
On the image pictured below.

And the beauty of it pained him so,
The smile so double sexed and slow,
Faint fair breasts and pale torso,
Male into female seemed to flow,—

Bastard Song

For H.F.

Since I am neither truly one, nor really true the other,
Can you not see that I must be the third—the first two's brother?
For it is true I am not black and just as true not white,
But when the day gives sudden way, dusk stands 'tween it and night
And dusk is just as true a thing as either night or day
And if the dusk smells faint of musk, turn not its scent away—
Night perfumes dusk's pallor—day etiolates the night:
My love for you is love for you though neither black nor white.

Yes, it's love I offer you and hope that you will keep.
This love you see is true, from me;—but no—it is to weep.
For you—pale white—cannot trust love from whom you've loved
    too long
And yet deride with untaught pride—my love is far too strong
So what thing can I offer you? What gift is there to give?
Not even dreams, or so it seems—for you refuse to live.
So this I offer now to you is weak with right and wrong—
Half dark, half light, half black, half white—a truly Bastard Song.

Who Asks This Thing?

I walk alone and lone must be
For I wear my love for all to see—

It matters not how close our hearts appear to be.
Since I tell my love in song for all to know—
It matters not how close our hearts may seem to grow—
Love must not be blind or small or slow,
But that I wear my heart for all to see
Means I am bound while he is, sadly, free.
He walks alone who walks in love with me.

W. H. AUDEN
1907–1973

From "Five Songs"

What's in your mind, my dove, my coney;
Do thoughts grow like feathers, the dead end of life;
Is it making of love or counting of money,
Or raid on the jewels, the plans of a thief?

Open your eyes, my dearest dallier;
Let hunt with your hands for escaping me;
Go through the motions of exploring the familiar;
Stand on the brink of the warm white day.

Rise with the wind, my great big serpent;
Silence the birds and darken the air;
Change me with terror, alive in a moment;
Strike for the heart and have me there.

From "Twelve Songs"

Dear, though the night is gone,
The dream still haunts to-day
That brought us to a room,
Cavernous, lofty as
A railway terminus,
And crowded in that gloom

Were beds, and we in one
In a far corner lay.

Our whisper woke no clocks,
We kissed and I was glad
At everything you did,
Indifferent to those
Who sat with hostile eyes
In pairs on every bed,
Arms round each other's necks,
Inert and vaguely sad.

O but what worm of guilt
Or what malignant doubt
Am I the victim of;
That you then, unabashed,
Did what I never wished,
Confessed another love;
And I, submissive, felt
Unwanted and went out?

Lullaby

Lay your sleeping head, my love,
Human on my faithless arm;
Time and fevers burn away
Individual beauty from
Thoughtful children, and the grave
Proves the child ephemeral:
But in my arms till break of day
Let the living creature lie,
Mortal, guilty, but to me
The entirely beautiful.

Soul and body have no bounds:
To lovers as they lie upon
Her tolerant enchanted slope
In their ordinary swoon,
Grave the vision Venus sends
Of supernatural sympathy,
Universal love and hope;
While an abstract insight wakes
Among the glaciers and the rocks
The hermit's sensual ecstasy.

Certainty, fidelity
O the stroke of midnight pass
Like vibrations of a bell
And fashionable madmen raise
Their pedantic boring cry:
Every farthing of the cost,
All the dreaded cards foretell,
Shall be paid, but from this night
Not a whisper, not a thought,
Not a kiss nor look be lost.

Beauty, midnight, vision dies:
Let the winds of dawn that blow
Softly round your dreaming head
Such a day of sweetness show
Eye and knocking heart may bless,
Find the mortal world enough;
Noons of dryness see you fed
By the involuntary powers,
Nights of insult let you pass
Watched by every human love.

HUBERT CREEKMORE
1907–1966

Always Overtures

Always are endings, always overtures—
Scenario of nonsense, acts of dismay,
The quick, the slow curtain, the interlude—
A macaronic, tragi-comic play.

Turbid cities of our homeland lighted
Magic faces over cocktail bars—
Fading faces, downy sacrifices
To defenders, giddiness of wars.

The sudden friends, now old ones are so scattered,
Dwindle with the footlights in the trough.
You saw what could have been (essential magnet)
If rules of battle gave you time enough.

Austral islands, school-book islands, press
Their jungles round each camp, press to blind
The weeding eye. You have them now, just as
You did—the tangled faces far behind.

Man talk with your friends, sweettalk your girls,
But someone leaves, someone is left, endures
The jungle of characters, the jig-saw scenes,
The always endings, always overtures.

Lament

That uniform bed, whereon two bodies lie
in grotesque swooning love, and slay all time
with piercing promises, follows their game
of knitted limbs with vague and slow dismay.
It sees them rising now, and Time, reborn,
in vigor of new youth draw each one taut
with days gone and to come. Another coat
with that one from the needle—(one now torn,
and sewn from a ragged world)—falls over each,
constricts their minds as tailors do their reach.
Hovel of love and tomb of shortdead Now,
the bed may cry *Cannot you choke the doubt
of fawning life and to my beggar mate
my corpse?* But none will hear; none can obey.

It's Me, Oh Lord, Standing with a Gun

They crouch in the barge and the palms roll close,
Green echo, high over sand, of waves,
Of gray jelly-fish in smoke puffs whose
Invisible sting is swift and leaden.
  They crouch, tongue-dry, in the boat,
And all the world is a puny beach-head:

World of clean-sliced hemispheres,
Of latitudes of love and crime,
Peopled with the mental smears
Of medieval magic, thinning
   To a short horizon
Under war's tremendous engine.

That glittering hierarchy down
Through which the war blood streams, and great
Einsteinian logistics, drown
Upon this coast of conquest. Here is
   All of war, compact.
It is simple. It is death-fear.

Undiscriminating death
Appraises his approaching guests,
Uniform in gear, beneath
Which shiver bodies, black and white skinned,
   But uniform in value
As currency of life. Their insight

Penetrates the island's pull,
Magnetic jointure of here-after.
Across the rail, the Negro full
In death's face stares and blinks, beside him
   Son of owners of slaves,
Floating to a mortal hyphen, tongue-tied.

And the hyphen joins the puzzled past:
The tired way down which they came,
Twin exiles of historic trust—
And fades in the jungle's blinding chaos.
   For on that final range
Men sprawled, too patient in the wave lay,

Letting the gently anxious foam
Entomb their scars in sand. No scales
Enamel the minds of two from whom
All memory soon may flee. The Negro
   And the Southern man
Reflect how inner bondage subtly

Links them to oppose what fought
At home between them: tenant house
Of jerried boards, and house it wrought
Of moonbeam pillars; loom of clod-veined

Overalls that wove
Tradition's silky gown. The drained blood

Mirrors doubly self and war,
Retreating in the glasses to
Extinction. The Negro fighting for
A freedom fraud, the white for freedom
   Mortgaged to mistrust,
Fight to shield the bigot's long breed.

And while the boat rolled on the waves,
Palm surf roaring at their face,
The Negro felt, not as on slaves,
The white hand on his arm, and heard him:
   "We can do it, can't we?"
And some familiar thing was lost words.

The strakes grate on the shore, defy
Horizon turned foreground of slaughter.
Whether I, the Negro, lie
Here or return, by all these tokens,
   Medals are for white men,
Jim Crow life for me and my folk.

Upon the coral shingle they leap
And rush the smoking jungle. Round
Their legs the salt-curls break and seep,
Crumbling soon the mold of foot-prints.
   Streaks of red, shell-studded,
Blot in sand, in waves are washed mute.

LINCOLN KIRSTEIN
1907–1996

October

October on the waxed leaf, color
Like the spilled running glaze on a jar;

Inhaling the chilled air, smelling cider,
Dark down the day goes, October-colored; far
Under the hills, away from other Octobers
He lies. . . . Once I came into the room,
Found him making love to my sister.
Do you, he said, love your sister?
I said, Why I guess so, he: Well I do very much.
None of us were embarrassed, nor am I now
Thinking of him changing his shirt-studs
For dinner, or taking a bath with the clean
Underwear spread out on a chair.
How many times more facing the sunset,
Feeling October take me by the ears
Can I help remembering the gilt air in his hair
On his temples? Or ready for football-games
All our bags and us in the car, he ran back to the house
Calling, Christ! I'd almost forgotten the whisky!

Salesman

He got into York, Pa. about seven in the evening,
Inspected the Railroad Hotel, the Star,
Finally put up at the Central, bathed and ate.
A town he'd never been in before, bare
Like a rented room. No one there he knew.
No stores open till morning. Nor was he tired.
Walked around, stared at the streets,
The lighted fronts, the knees of one girl, her companion's eye.
Recalled friends afar. He whistled several bars,
Turned back to his hotel. Night-Clerk, Bell-Boy
Bade him good-night.
He stood, hand on his collar's brink,
Wondering at the car-tracks three floors below.
Tomorrow there were the things he had to do.
Tomorrow night he'd be starting home.
Day after tomorrow he'd have been in York,
Refreshed by the one day break.
Almost, with a sense of peril averted, he stepped back
From that black window: went to bed.

Blackmail

It's a good thing you burnt those letters:
Gee: some of them would sound terrible in court.
The time you were sore about the Corcoran Company
The time you were so cuckoo about Queenie.
Not that they were dirty, or silly or in bad taste.
Some of them were good letters.
I know what you meant. They knew what you meant.
But just suppose. . . .
The bell should ring, and there standing buttoned,
Would be two cops with warrants.
What the hell I've done? I ain't done nothing.
That's all right, Mister. Come along with us.
This would be too ridiculous: Wait a minute.
Call up George. He knows Mr. La Grange.
Call up Uncle Dick: He knows that man on the *Times*.
Get a hold of Forrester! He knows the District Attorney.
It would be no use.
No one would recognize you. Your name would be changed.
Your finger prints would even not be yours,
On account of your crime.
You would also be clapped in a cell and your face
Would greet your wife from the City edition.
Others now are in a similar set-up.
They lack the friends you'd lack.
They are more patient since more wise
To realize the nothing they can do.
Whatever it is, it's bigger than we are,
I'd pay anything as long as it didn't get me down.
But *It's* full-fed: *It's* not taking any.
The lad caught short, the lass caught short,
The man railroaded on a big mistake.
Lots of places you don't want to be found dead in:
Phone-booths, cafés and some back-yards.
What would you be doing there?
Innocent, O sure: only the circumstantial shock.
It's better, said the judge, that many go free,
Than one unguilty one be hung.
It's fairer, said the Mayor, if everyone be fed
Than any hunger.
I agree. I think you agree. To tempt luck
Here's a man solemn with lack of bread,

He's quite unkempt and eager for our proof.
We can spare him as much as he might spare,
If we were friendless, homeless and at sea.
Only we don't or can't or won't.

PARKER TYLER
1907–1974

Ode to Hollywood

The movie, the history of flutter and twitter, the
Voice of the bird was dumb and transformed there,
 The voice of the bird was pluralled.

The light of the person was exiled and fastened
To the dark of the person, and flowing-imaged.
 The person was broken and knitted.

The river, the fire and the libelled ocean
Roared in a voice that was coarser than nature,
 Surprising, swift and surgical.

The simple refrain of a touched paper came
Toward us like an actor from the ensemble
 For a tiny, arrogant symphony.

Now the garden of Garbo, the silver garden,
That intimate accurate moon of behavior
 Where Greta forever walks:

As children, omnivorous through time, O
We worship there: overjoyed at the
 Remoteness, the tallness.

A terrific comforting nostalgia
Unreels in us; celluloid memory invades us;
 Our flesh is unravelled by inches.

Perforce sitting like Egypt to envision Egypt,
Griffith's stage-struck Babylonia
 Once more comes near the gazer.

Gish like a lily hypnotized into life, takes
The first silent step of nearness and shuddering
   Comes closer, comes closer than

She who gave birth: so the birth of the close-up!
At a look from the camera, walls fall away from
   DeMille's white bedrooms with Gloria.

And Charlie, the most super-sensitive, who
Stumbles, ended end-up in the deathless
   Black-and-white suit of art's elegance.

Lubitsch brought lightness, the French the mature;
Shakespeare's land gave the arabesque vowel,
   Russia the esperanto iris.

More permanent than presidents, the Vampire,
Whose sin never, at worst, was venal, was Theda;
   And Pauline demolished her perils.

We have not been cheated of the mask of Venus,
Marlene, for a thousand nights and one; and Bette,
   Jitterbug of tragediennes, lives.

The millimeter has come to the library,
To the memorial of esthetics: the museum;
   The medal of continuous hushed honor.

And now comes the magic of Lumière in
A snug dream of a theatre, the silliness and
   Wonder of old reflections.

Look there, at the face of Rudolph hugging
The heaven of wives; perhaps the bridegroom at last cometh
   Unto the shamed hell of husbands!

We can learn how futile it is in nature
To imitate the mind, whose perpetual life is
   Rewinding, and springing, and blurring. . . .

Still, forever from that city of incredibly
Rapid and beautiful and fragile movement,
   The kiss in perpetuum mobile!

The Erotics

   The location
Of the lone dark room from which they struggle forever is

Hidden, humming, hammered to the earthquake, menacing
 The lovers

Whose homes are heated, anchored. The erotics are white heavers
And squirters, black blisterers and purpling contagions.

 The whore
And the richest roué, the social criminal, are better
Than evil and worse than good, they are the crucified,
 The artists

Whose content is sex, whose forms are theatrically
False and winsome, bitter, all clotted with fought fevers.

 The woman
And the man begin single, double everything and murder
The double, hate repetition, always love the same with
 The oath.

"I take thee" is given grown in a blurring of kiss, ended
In a brick of beauty, severed in a rose of bed: O

 The lyric
Cheating! The bride and bridegroom are stunned from winking
At coming, going; there, where it is too spacious,
 The traveller

In the erotic lands goes on elbows; back; knees; sleeping
In all but one place. The son soul-slaughtered, the mother defaced,

 The uncle
Of unctuous gifts, find room for their secrets and time for
Their favorites. The mad farmer who is a weathervane for
 The actress

En route to the actor, is the truest King of the Arctic
And the lily homosexual for all his one-eyed idiocy is

 The millionaire
Erotic. Futile to shun the boast in music's sober speaking!
What? Preserve candor, proportion, the thinking ability and
 The democracy?

Yes. Erotics are feminine, bored, drinkers of the glorifiers
The glorified: curved lords of lymph, the great girls, lady-killers

 The man
With his moon, the priest with his paradise, the satan with

His satin, red and reversible body (alas) Heaven's
   Harry

Himself with his harp of hurt, the horsehilled hugger:
He's startlingly human, distorted as only nature

   The Platonist
In her incredible rut, her bag of broken beauties, .
Distorts that she surprise us; the flirting dad, the cancers,
   The libidos,

It is so close! In looking at it we are the air it breathes
Or look so far from upper air, the forest is a scab,

   The sea
A simper. . . . . With those, the pillow is a hand of dreaming
Fists; those sigh! reach in! stretch out and hover thick in
   The images.

His Elegy

I shall be calm about us, about the terrific,
   Finger-pointing
Exclusion under the tolerant, smiling mask
Of society. Yes, others are calm, too, I know,
   But it is hard

For a man to make a girl of his ego, it is
   Difficult—
So much so!—to begin over again even the
Simple work of nature, twisting the clay for
   The cruel, complex

Sake of beauty, and facing mother or sister or
   Wife, not too
Agreeable or understanding, or too lenient
About it all, showing them themselves in another
   Skin, another form,

Another happiness. Some little boys are very
   Angels of etiquette,
Mocking their sisters, putting them to shame
Not out of malice, but envying the curls, and the
   Face of the female.

Verily, there are others, famous, of similar
  Character,
Who shape their manhood vilely, not for deity's
Sake, or darling's, merely to dictate unceasingly,
  To feel nothing.

But hot inhumanity: Aphrodite who withheld.
  However, rape,
Whether real or abstract, leads to nothing
Save perhaps in a poem, perhaps in pretenses
  Of the gentle poet.

From birth, we are slaves eager to rear such
  A pyramid
Of fictitious flesh that no infant or ancient
(Both old in looking) may derive from the look
  Or the gesture

Any history for the book as so secretly
  Our backs turn
To the truth! And with our false, thousand-eyed
Flesh helpless toward love of the lie, we then
  Make love to the lie.

Even though we poets may grow sick at thinking
  Of the torture
Common to all the genders, and then bundled
In that divine ague go home, absolutely sure
  Of Narcissus,

So fluid and flashing our world of beauty,
  We are certain . . .
Waiting for us deep in the mirror (all women
Over his face making a mask) is Narcissus,
  Criminal,

Weeping hysteria at our optimism, his male voice
  In flat prose
Saying, "You are guilty." I have answered, "How
Can we not be—famous for our feelings—having
  Seen another

Version of you, bewildered Hermaphroditus?
  Having seen in the fit
The fairy in the midst of the gay dancers,

Daring to be the gayest, the guilt seeming,
  For Cinderella,

Too much; so we preferred it. We prefer our
  Pumpkin and
Cinders to the adorable slipper of glass, that
Which at the highest peril, madness or jail,
  We would get into."

The pale and melancholy prince of guilt is
  Somewhere,
Somewhere the Hamlet of our sexuality in his
Elsinore of women. Meanwhile, we are in danger
  Of being snobs,

We who dictate to nature her most precious
  Example
Of play. Each tremendous, happy, masculine
Morning, we arise naked to the sun of that
  Paradox;

The whole world, since we are male, seeming
  Passive before
Us, and we know the abominable flattery
Of showing in the light our mother's possession
  In the black

Bedroom. How surely we were hers! Indeed, the
  World was
Conquered by half of us while the other half
Waited, lying awake; or, as half lies awake in
  Us now, we

Sleep on our backs, or as half sleeps if, on
  Our bellies,
We conceal, or if we love: kneeling without prayer.
Oh certainly we're forgiven, else even the
  Several wits of

Our rich arts could not save us from suicide.
  Death hovers
Impersonally over us, and we meditate, often,
How clean and holy and unworshipable is
  The killed soldier,

Far beyond our reach: and how the dead's live woman
  Often thrills to

Some delightful, induplicable, dear pang of
Experience from which we are fabulously,
   Fairly, excluded.

Even as others we are bored, bored horribly
   With great life, soon
Soon to vanish. . . . What is there to do but be
Sexual or revolutionary; make money; enjoy, over
   Again, the female?

The conversation flags, and insidious, heartbroken
   Socrates,
Whose pricelessly beautiful gymnasium
We inherit inside us, falls expressionless.
   Like a muscle,

The soul glistens, and hurdles; the hemlock's
   Husband
Continues silent. He will never speak again.
Something dreadful has happened. Melancholy
   Overwhelms us.

FREDERIC PROKOSCH
1908–1989

The Masks

Some sit by ferns and gaze across their valley
Counting the swallows loving on the gravel
Or walk along the rock beach, recall
A night beside the effigy in the garden,
The desire, the scent, the fall;

Or touch with closet fingers odorous volumes,
Children forever, clogged with solitude
Doze in the greenhouse, tremble at a rose,
Dream of their mothers when the winter darkens,
The wind, the big wind, blows.

Yes, in their Austrian houses sit the poets
And suffer at the passing of their heroes
Or in the Greek café beyond the noise
Of cheat and blackmail watch the panther-bellied
Girls, and the pensive boys;

Or wild grammarians traveling by the railway
Swift to the yellow cities on the Caspian
Blush, tremble; or the sisters who alone
Shed tears and on the entry of the Countess
Like owls rise and are gone.

Even among the natives those from Italy
Scatter and read their pages of an ancient
Epic, a great one, and with sterile hips
Dance; or in Utah weep before a mirror
With sensitive opened lips

Or in the ivied chamber count their syllables,
Stir toward the casement, watch the athletes passing;
Analyse love, as delicate as frost,
Talk to their girls in scholarly whispers, curious
Shift their grey eyes, are lost.

Some grow adroit at turning wheels, big women
Patient and proud deep in the Russian ices;
Or dream of Shelley, wishing he were here;
Nieces of millionaires, the undesired ones,
Year after maddening year

Grow stronger, glimpse at last the longed-for quiet
And talk with artists under April willows,
Find refuge in a masquerade of mind,
A pose, a flight toward dusk, smile like albinos,
And grow remote, grow blind.

The bones melt and the spirit breaks, the opium
Crosses the eastern sea and brings relief; and
Europe grows slim and pale; and we who loved
Her histories walk the city, wait and wonder,
Watch and are moved.

The Dolls

I found them lying on the shore,
Sweet shapes, pearl-lipped and crescent-eyed:

Night after night their hands implore
Pathetic mercies at my side.

They reach into my secret night
With pale and terrifying arms
And offer in a dark delight
Their subtle suicidal charms,

Gently they sigh into my mind
Wild words half uttered, half unsaid,
And when I dream of death I find
Small tears of glass upon my bed.

They are the children of desire,
They live on fear, they are my deep
And buried thoughts with eyes of fire,
They are the furies of my sleep.

The Piazza

Labyrinth, lonely corridors of our spirit
Who wind through winter and night: neither the white
Death of the stagnant centuries, nor the enormous
European fevers may thread and solve your allures.
I gaze from the edge of vast America
Toward the three continents twined in a common terror
Whose creatures still implore their nocturnal heroes:
A phrase toward the infinite, there as here: no more.

No more, it is all the same, all: nothing
Distinguishes my passion from those innumerable
Shapes in pairs or trios or utter isolation
Covering the city, in parks or story upon story,
Crossing the midnight seas, locked in huge prisons,
In taverns, towers, trenches awaiting the fire,
In chambers marked by the secret signs of the Romans
Or veiled from the vigilant Chinese constellations:

In which I rejoice: O darling, my limbs are happy
With power and delight in the uniform ways of man.
These lips which I love to all are lovely, these golden
Regions which hold my eyes and palms like a magnet
Are cast by the epochs of desire into such fragrance;
This gesture, lit by the intricate stars of summer,

Was dear to millions in equally still and desperate
Twilight, hot with the murderer breath of love.

GALE WILHELM
1908–1991

A Group of Sonnets

1. Arabesque
Often—
in these long afternoons
of drowsing autumn—
when silence, like a bird,
is poised on bright blue wings,
I feel that we—
more minute than two grains of sand—
are held, unaware,
in the hand of sleeping Time. . . .

2. Second Arabesque
If you were the tree,
looking forever seaward
over the brown shoulder of a dune,
I should be the rain—
and pray for an eternity
of Springs. . . .

3. Third Arabesque
If this shadow,
lying so close beside me,
should take sudden, pulsing identity,
you, who are silent,
would not hold your aloofness
in such proud, crystal fingers.

Quest

Night passes over,
a brushing silence deepens,
and all that happened in the afternoon,
the swift waking,
the swift unbelievable dream,
that too whispers away
with only a thin sound of grief.
You lie sleeping here
and yet not sleeping
against my heart
that is heavy and still
with answered questions.

CHARLES HENRI FORD
1909–2002

Baby's in jail; the animal day plays alone

Baby's in jail; the animal day plays alone,
tame as the animal baby behind the bars of the crib:
the cub whose nose has not yet dipped
in the reek of excitation,
whose claws have not unbound the hide of habit,
nor scratched at pride, the skin,
and tasted sensation's blood.
Baby will come to grief and love.
Visitors to the family zoo
do not go to see a vegetarian tiger.

If the clover's leaves are four,
good luck's just behind the door.
If your hand goes through a mirror:
the glass is dear, but bad luck's dearer.
Swipe a horsehair from his tail, drown it in a waterpail:
it takes thirty days to make

horsehair turn into a snake.
You want a new dress, I do too.
You bite a butterfly, I'll chew a leaf.
Baby will come to love and grief.

Somebody's Gone

There may be a basement to the Atlantic
but there's no top storey
to my mountain of missing you.

I must say your deportment took a hunk
out of my peach of a heart.
I ain't insured against torpedoes!
My turpentine tears would fill a drugstore.

May I be blindfolded before you come my way again
if you're going to leave dry land like an amphibian;
I took you for some kind of ambrosial bird
with no thought of acoustics.

Maybe it's too late to blindfold me ever:
I'm just a blotter crisscrossed with the ink
of words that remind me of you.

Bareheaded aircastle,
you were as beautiful as a broom made of flesh and hair.

When you first disappeared
I couldn't keep up with my breakneck grief,
and now I know how grief can run away with the mind,
leaving the body desolate as a staircase.

January wraps up the wound of his arm

January wraps up the wound of his arm,
January, thieving as a boy, hides the jewel,
sunset, bright bleeding equation.

Day has written itself out, a giveaway, a poem
that balks like a horse before the ditch of night.

Tomorrow, the gash will be an eye:
a drop of dew will travel up his cheek,
like a tear that has changed its mind.

PAUL BOWLES
1910–1999

Scene III

Sometimes the fever comes back and I can see the mountains,
the morning heavy with nuns walking
and the hypodermics of hunger,
the rapacious trees, the false waterfalls shining with spiders,
the vines of silence.
I see the same deaf mountains, their mouths stuffed with snow,
and I move my fingers a bit; even so,
I need help.

Sometimes the fever strolls at evening in the suburbs,
Sometimes there is only one mountain, right above our heads.
At noon the rain begins. The horses hide among the rocks,
And the idiot sea is there.
I need help from time to time.

"That day two thousand men perished there on the endless shore."

> For us: sharks, tin, stagnant water.
> Eight sicknesses come in the night
> as the scorpion clings to the ceiling.
> For us: barbed wire, open mouths, dry blood,
> the hairy flowers of the tarantulas
> and the constant sightless eye
> of time, frozen in the air.

> The wind in fragments drops
> down the mountain passes.
> We must scream without respite—
> he who stops is lost.

Blessed Are the Meek

Blessed be god and I
Blessed be all his angels and all my thoughts
The roofs are wet with night rain
I am undergoing a deep change
My slippers have frayed tops

Blessed be all gods and myself in all my moods
All my clothes may become shreds but I shall sleep through it
While my curtains sweep over the windowsills it can rain
And I can keep undergoing a deep change
If I walk down a road in the provinces I shall meet a beggar
His feet will be on the earth but I shall not care at all
Even if his feet have been wet by the night rain
It is on all the engines of the forest
It glistens on every leadpipe in the meadow oh blessed be god and I
Every smokestack in the wilderness is covered with night rain
We have ice god and I

Love Song

The head is where the cricket sings
The cheeks are what the teeth will bite
The lake is where the lover flings
The other in the dead of night
The lips are where the blood goes in
The eyes are what the fingers claw
Knowing now what might have been
Will the lips tell what the eyes saw?

ELIZABETH BISHOP
1911–1979

Casabianca

Love's the boy stood on the burning deck
trying to recite "The boy stood on
the burning deck." Love's the son
    stood stammering elocution
    while the poor ship in flames went down.

Love's the obstinate boy, the ship,
even the swimming sailors, who

would like a schoolroom platform, too,
     or an excuse to stay
     on deck. And love's the burning boy.

Chemin de Fer

Alone on the railroad track
     I walked with pounding heart.
The ties were too close together
     or maybe too far apart.

The scenery was impoverished:
     scrub-pine and oak; beyond
its mingled gray-green foliage
     I saw the little pond

where the dirty hermit lives,
     lie like an old tear
holding onto its injuries
     lucidly year after year.

The hermit shot off his shot-gun
     and the tree by his cabin shook.
Over the pond went a ripple.
     The pet hen went chook-chook.

"Love should be put into action!"
     screamed the old hermit.
Across the pond an echo
     tried and tried to confirm it.

The Gentleman of Shalott

Which eye's his eye?
Which limb lies
next the mirror?
For neither is clearer
nor a different color
than the other,
nor meets a stranger
in this arrangement
of leg and leg and
arm and so on.

To his mind
it's the indication
of a mirrored reflection
somewhere along the line
of what we call the spine.

He felt in modesty
his person was
half looking-glass,
for why should he
be doubled?
The glass must stretch
down his middle,
or rather down the edge.
But he's in doubt
as to which side's in or out
of the mirror.
There's little margin for error,
but there's no proof, either.
And if half his head's reflected,
thought, he thinks, might be affected.

But he's resigned
to such economical design.
If the glass slips
he's in a fix—
only one leg, etc. But
while it stays put
he can walk and run
and his hands can clasp one
another. The uncertainty
he says he
finds exhilarating. He loves
that sense of constant re-adjustment.
He wishes to be quoted as saying at present:
"Half is enough."

PAUL GOODMAN
1911–1972

The Cyclist

The young Master of the Wheel at Danbury
absently, both hands, fondling his prick
through traffic thoughtfully—up on the walk
(the curb was broke an inch) before me *was*,
and alighted even as the wheels ceased.
I who ride like a ferocious fireman
thank heaven for this breath of breeze of art,
the hottest noon that ever made Route 6
mirror the forest upside down. But he
arrived with the swoop of a swallow.
I'd speak with him, except his only lust
is in his speedy ease. Now everywhere
by moments and through rips, through the brilliant
curtain of July I spy the Way
whereon we deviate but do not err.

Out of the Tulip Tree

Out of the tulip tree Haskell his green eyes
        tossed yellow blossoms to the girls below
        standing with upturned faces in a row.
It clouded over, wind began to rise,

it grew obscure, the leaves turned white,
        the air was quiet, full of tiny noises,
        the girls vanished with their screaming voices.
"Come down," I shouted, "Haskell, before light-

ning strikes the tree and you are shaken out
        by swaying boughs this way and that!"
        "Catch!" he commanded, "catch! catch!"
and he tossed down a rubber ball, I caught,

and he aloft and I on the ground under
        threw the white sphere back and forth, amid

the gusts of wind and strings of rain, silently
amid the bursts of lightning and the claps of thunder.

Ballade to Jean Cocteau

Martyrs of the crimes of sex,
    Sappho, Hyacinth, and she
who fucked the Bull, and Oedipus Rex,
    these are not by Jean and me
    blotted out of memory
but wept and named, so all may read
    and know them and ourselves and ye.
To heaven was raped Ganymede.

Read, all, and pay respects
    of etiquette to outlawry.
Don't look away, fate protects
    these names from shame: Pasiphaë
    was mounted not for luxury,
the boy drowned in the pool for need,
    and Sappho jumped into the sea.
To heaven was raped Ganymede.

Jean and I meet among wrecks
    cast by froth and cut from tree
and vanishing in the vortex.
    His hair is white prematurely
    and I say to him from what I see,
"O poet of the winter sun indeed!"
    but who am I is yet to be.
To heaven was raped Ganymede.

The clawed and wingèd angel, the
    Eagle, did not make beauty bleed
lifting him over field and sea,
    to heaven was raped Ganymede.

WILLARD MAAS
1911–1971

Poem

anonymous calling
of bodies assails us

beneath the far weather
the mint-green snake
sings through water

be brave for hot deeds

upstanding trunks
of holy trees

          the musical
light of sleeping breasts

o burden of eyes

of arm of fire

          and the split rock
bubbling a froth of lilies

            shaken

the mouths
        of white-fleshed saints

the dust whirls stars
where their feet have fled

Poem

o rivers of my flesh
warm channels of the bone

run swiftly

        is love sweeter
under the summer-wet willow

                        swiftly
darkness to darkness

under the elm
under the elderberry

                listen

music of a woman
where no woman is

                love
somewhere is unfolding

love

Poem

        the great arm
sprung from the deep
earth
        lifting
the dark eagle
talons of flame
strength of a million
red suns in his heart
our brothers
                o proud
fierce hand of humanity
facing the iron sky
and the bleak world
with breasts of music
fall
        the towers
the stone walls
and false heroes
of power
                topple

the gold temple
and purple myth
of empire and state

the arms of the red suns
beat with wings of vengeance

over the ashes of oblivion
the paper shards
run the swift feet

brothers o brothers

greet the hot spring
of your triumph
with steel songs
of creation
        speak
comrades of victory
with mouths of love

brotherhood eternal

MAY SARTON
1912–1995

From "Encounter in April": 1

We came together softly like two deer
Their horns in velvet still, erect and slight,
Their fur like silk, their large eyes amber-clear,
Startled and dazzled in each other's light.
We stood quite still together face to face,
Untrembling, unaware, remote from love,
Beguiled there simply by each other's grace,
Not moving—O we did not want to move.
We stood quite still like two deer in a wood
Knowing a silence exquisite and wild,
Chilled into crystal the mercurial blood,
The heart fierce and transparent as a child:
We came together softly in great wonder
Not dreaming of this lightning-love, this thunder.

From "Sonnets": 6

I picked love from the bough on which it swings,
I tasted of the pomegranate-vine.
I plucked the fire and sweetness where it hangs,
I tasted love—it does not taste like wine.
It is a fruit that swells and turns to seed.
It is a pomegranate ripe too soon,
A brilliant fruit upon a barren reed,
Rich to the rotting, turning red to brown—
I tasted it, the sweetness and the fire,
And it was not like wine nor even bread:
Love never was fulfillment of desire.
Love is not anything that has been said.
I curse it, knowing well that the same thirst
Will turn me back to bless what I have cursed.

Strangers

There have been two strangers
Who met within a wood
And looked once at each other
Where they stood.

And there have been two strangers
Who met among the heather
And did not look at all
But lay down together.

And there have been two strangers
Who met an April day
And looked long at each other,
And went their way.

JAMES BROUGHTON
1913–1999

Papa Has a Pig

Papa has a pig.
And a big pig too.
Papa plays a piggy-toe that I can't do.
O Papa has the biggest pig you ever did see.
He gave only ten little piggies to me.
Papa has the star of all the swine,
Papa shines stern in the sty.

Papa goes to market.
And I stay home.
Papa doesn't tickle his toes all alone.
O Papa has the fattest pig you ever did feel.
My ten little piglets just pinch and squeal.
Papa has the star of all the swine,
Papa shines stern in the sty.

Papa has a pen.
And a big pen too.
Papa rides a piggy-back that I can't do.
O Papa stands out in the pig-feet race.
My ten little wiggles don't go any place.
Papa has the star of all the swine,
Shine, Papa, shine in the sty.

Mrs. Mother Has a Nose

What a big nose Mrs. Mother has,
the better to smell her dear.
Sniff sniff sniff it comes round the door,
detective of everything queer.

Two big noses Mrs. Mother has,
the better to quell her dear.
"I smell something odd, I smell something bad,
what is that smell in here?"

Thee big noses Mrs. Mother has,
they grow and grow in the night.
Sniff sniff sniff her naughty naughty dear!
And she also can smell with her ears.

Junior's Prayer

Now I lay me down to sleep,
I pray the Lord to help me out.
I'm flat on my back and left alone,
so God bless nobody, please keep out.

If I should die and fall asleep
how will I run away from home?
If I should wake before I die
will still be in the dark alone?

Now I lay me down to sleep.
But keep me awake, Lord, keep me awake!

ROBERT FRIEND
1913–1998

Impossible Blue

Yes, brood on those islands to which the stranger
comes, the barbarous coast, the reefs like fangs,
the Circe-like power of the drowsy palms;
and from your brooding rise, the pale discoverer
upon whose eyesight the horizon breaks
with that far country. Seek the impossible blue,
skies to match the color of your illness,
white surf that washes out the sight of cities.
At last lay down your head.

                    To sleep give over,
o unconsolable who dare not see

the world as beautiful with the greatness
of bravery. O lunatic lover, foundered in your own eyes,
creeping along night pavement, clawing the buildings
as the streets whirl with the lights and faces.
Behold: picket lines point out the meaning;
each morning breaks with men's decision to act,
real as bread and the mouth of the beloved,
real as guns.

        Belief like this betrays you into action.
Do not believe: neither in the power of love
nor in any power that makes a plan for life. Coddle
your loneliness—project it through the night.
Make stars your symbol: all worlds are lonely—
the shuddering planet signals through the dark,
unanswered. All men are lonely gathering in the night
to keep each other warm. Cling to that sick thought
which gives excuse for flight. Wish the cool green

and the translucent blue, soft gleam in ocean gloom,
the languid wave. "I have lost all innocence to believe."
Not innocence but courage lost when the first skies
fell and heaven earth became. Hands
dropped lifeless down then, eyes turned to the past;
self pity began then, and the posing on the rack.

And that searching and heaving out of the night,
longing for islands. Goodbye then.
When you are wrecked upon that shore, feed on the waves
and the mountains' music. May you not die deceived.
May the albatross bring you beauty and false tears
to fright the spectre trampling on the years.

Strangers

Dead as the door where no friend knocks you are,
and call a brother by the name of death.
Drink with him as the beer glass bubbles to tears,
feed deep deep upon his whorish eyes.

Offer the first stranger your naked night;
his eyes will open like a frozen sun,
or close into a world as distant as the pole.
Look in the glass and see yourself alone.

For each is in his grave with a private door,
and no one turns the lock but the faithless hand;
smiling or weeping he must be what you are,
or throw away the key, you are your own whore.

Take him then—though his words cannot reach
or hands touch to where you lie. You
cannot reproach, who loving, leave no land behind,
being his stranger who must prove just as untrue.

Meaning

These lips hard on your lips to kiss the world
away, and in each other's eyes to read
each night a meaning. Each night beyond drawn blinds
the panicky streets between the oblong tenements
run to the black river. White flares search
the blind sky from the topmost towers in a wide arc,
swing out, swing back. What do they hope to find?

What do we hope to find? The lonely trains
rattle along the tracks long after day is over.
And we renew ourselves, seek to cast off
the world: again these kisses and these circling
arms, our selves a centre while the earth
wheels round, leaks in with roar of midnight trains
dying in distance, fainter and fainter heard,
and steady movement of the solemn clock
ticking towards death.

               Light under the shades,
footsteps on the stair, voices in the hall
defeat our love. The moment like a wave
breaks upon the grimy shores of morning,
and we are stranded facing another day.
This love is solitary that will die this death;
it weeps on your breast, gathers loneliness
of all men who at the self-same hour
lying behind dark shades in a rotting house
shut out the light of history, shut out that love
which giving of itself gives to itself,
creates new worlds. That is our meaning;
and when I'll read it in the eyes of men,

sharing their lives with them, our purpose one,
I'll read it clear in yours.

MURIEL RUKEYSER
1913–1980

Letter, Unposted

> My love, my love, my love,
> why have you left me alone?
> —JAMES JOYCE

If I could write   :   Summer waits your coming,
the flowers are colored, but half-alive and weak,
earth sickens, as I sicken, with waiting,
and the clouds print on the dull moon a dark and blotting streak.
If I could write   :   no energy is kinetic,
storm breaks nor foot falls until you arrive,
the trees thrive, but no fruit is born to hang
heavily   :   and the stale wind continues to drive
all pausing summer before it into the distance
from which you, shining, will come. . . . But summer lives,
and minds grow, and nerves are sensitized to power
and no winds wait, and not tree stands but gives
richly to the store of the burning harvest   :
the door stands open for you, and other figures pass,
and I receive them joyfully and live   :   but wait for you
(and sometimes secretly watch for wrinkles, in my glass).

The Handclap

The body cannot lie, but its betrayals,
narrower actions, cross even frontiers of night,
and your most delicate treason falls in a quick stroke,
          undercuts sleep.

Now, if I bodily sometime betrayed myself,
the foolish play's curtain drops on your active exposure,
grotesque as a peepshow, definite as the axe
        in instant effect.

The toppling high tree lets fall its heavy side
green on the air, goes anyway down to ground
after a clap of weight resting—but we descend to
        imperfect peace.

Here's war!—body betrayed, but all nerves still exerted
to rise up whole, grasp the perpetual sun.
Echo the shock, handclaps of fact composing
        a blackest pattern,

a tyrant pace to dance, clatter of anger
spanking the fury up to publish treason,
ranting and clapping madness; while the dim
        blood groans forever love.

Drunken Girl

Do you know the name of the average animal?
Not the dog,
  Nor the green-beaded frog,
Nor the white ocean monster lying flat—
  Lower than that.
The curling one who comes out in the storm—
The middle one's the worm.

Lift up your face, my love, lift up your mouth,
Kiss me and come to bed
  And do not bow your head
Longer on what is bad or what is good—
  The dead are terribly misunderstood,
And sin and godhead are in the worm's blind eye,
We'll come to averages by and by.

ALICIA KAY SMITH
1913–?

Before the Dawn

This is the time
To let you go,
This still, cool hour
Before the dawn.
And waking so
Later in a world grown bright
Each will know
It was a dream
And turn again
To seek the night.

Identity

Read to me the poem I love:
The one we found that rainy night
When first I saw the firelight
Touch curls upon your brow;
Read of those who love,
But find their starlight
Deep in wells, as we do now.

It is Reality now

Dear, it is Reality now, this Dream
   That used to stretch and sigh
     And curl up on our counterpane
     Between us; it might have lain
   Here always. It did not try

To seek another shelter. It was
   Content with us. So still it kept
     Nor tossed, nor stayed awake
     Nor mumbled in its sleep to break
   Our rest. With quiet breath it slept.

Who was it then who suddenly moved,
    And cried, and at a finger's touch
        The Dream leapt up till it was flame
        Higher than our room? And it became
So real we could not disregard it overmuch.

OWEN DODSON
1914–1983

Drunken Lover

This is the stagnant hour:
The dead communion between mouth and mouth,
The drunken kiss lingered,
The dreadful equator south.

This is the hour of impotence
When the unfulfilled is unfulfilled.
Only the stale breath is anxious
And warm. All else is stilled.

Why did I come to this reek,
This numb time, this level?
Only for you, my love, only for you
Could I endure this devil.

I dreamed when I was
A pimply and urgent adolescent
Of these hours when love would be fire
And you the steep descent.

My mouth's inside is like cotton,
Your arm is dead on my arm.
What I pictured so lovely and spring
Is August and fungus calm.

O lover, draw away, grow small, go magic,
O lover, disappear into the tick of this bed;

Open all the windows to the north
For the wind to cool my head.

Midnight Bell

This cannot be the hour for oral speech:
Words vying with the wind, with private sounds
Of other lovers striving on the beach,
With waves: the sand sniffers, the hounds.
No, this is quiet in between the long
Sentences, the lengths of speech at will.
Let the eyes remember, the ears catch the songs
We sing deep in the bone, in the still
Unoutward parts, that have their resurrection
In themselves. Cancel the mouth of poetry and prose;
Be eager now to seek the dark confection
In the flesh and feed until desire goes,
Until we sleep, until we cannot tell
Why midnight walked and did not ring her bell.

The Reunion

I loved the apple-sweetness of the air
And pines that settled slanting on the hill,
Indians old and soft with needles there,
Where once we stood, and both so strangely still.
We must have surely known what other days
Would come in other flaming autumn's flame.
And even though we walk through different ways
To different hills that hill remains the same.
Watch every splendor, envy all the sky,
But recognize the days we knew, and hear
The simple sounds we heard. As birds that fly
Southward to warmth, we shall come back one year.
The little teeth of time will make no mark
On any stone, on any leaf or bark.

DUNSTAN THOMPSON
1918–1975

This tall horseman, my young man of Mars

This tall horseman, my young man of Mars,
Scatters the gold dust from his hair, and takes
Me to pieces like a gun. The myth forsakes
Him slowly. Almost mortal, he shows the scars
Where medals of honor, cut-steel stars,
Pin death above the heart. But bends, but breaks
In his hand, my love, whose wrecked machinery makes
Time, the inventor, weep through a world of wars.
Guilt like a rust enamels me. I breed
A poison not this murdering youth may dare
In one drop of blood to battle. No delight
Is possible. Only at parting do we need
Each other; together, we are not there
At all. Love, I farewell you out of sight.

In All the Argosy of Your Bright Hair

Whom I lay down for dead rises up in blood,
Drawn over water after me. His wavering
Footfall echoes from the ocean floor. Blow,
Ye winds, a roundabout. These bully sailors flood
My eyes with tears, treacheries. But his voice shivering
North in lamentation is all I now know—
Whose million miles, once worth gales to be glad,
Tell me last look was best photograph I had.

When that damask duke took my heart for hound,
I dogged him with praises, with poems, a beggar's homage.
His blue eyes, fencing like a dance of swords,
Ringed me from foemen, were night lights. I found
He turned my head from death's entrancing image,
Gold in the desert sun, who sang: "What words
You want, I have." He saved me from my own hand
And the five assassins nervous for the grandstand.

My whole life in gratitude does him no good,
Whose happiness was dancebands, beer, and baseball,
Talked love to be polite. But the soldier boy
Grows up, goes after the goddess in the barbed-wire wood
Who sells him secrets for a firing squad. This tall
Young man, this blond young man, his mother's joy,
Must kill her first, his father next. He shall ride
To the top of the hill where three thieves died.

The whores of Wardour Street, the Soho whores:
"Give us a light, dearie." But I have no match.
Now the inconsolable year hazes with twilight.
Only the cold phantasmal rose burns out-of-doors.
Inside, the lamps are lit. If I should watch
All autumn nights, I'd see no ghost. My light
Fingered friend stole the world away. Imperilled heirs,
You of the equal sadness, give him your prayers.

Return of the Hero

The hero, the hero as stranger, comes home again,
Waking the wanderer, the moonstruck leviathan sea.
He passes the places where the dreaming submarine
Lay like a lover waiting, awaiting break of day.
  He has seen everything, he has gone everywhere,
  And his heart, his sad heart, is heavy with the war.

Always on water was danger, was death. The one-range pipes
Played by the sailors played panic, preyed on his run
Away, run away, if only he dared to run away, hopes.
Then the suicides shooting like stars where more friendly men,
  For cries from the gulls were as nothing to the shrill cry
  Caught in his throat as he thought of himself, the undrowned
   boy.

The islands were enemies, and the unfeathered palm trees,
"Where no bird sings" he said to someone a world far off,
Told more than he wanted to know, told the dazing craze
Of the sun and the gin and the high pitched hysteric laugh.
  On leave, but with no one to love, for the tropical girls
  Bartered with souvenirs, he went dizzily down companionway
   hells.

What was the name of his ship? Did it matter? Sex
And the boredom of being together were always the same.
He commanded a crew who were thieves but charming. "The luck's
Against me" he wrote in a letter, and grieved for a different time.
    Honest, dishonest, each was the other, and none to judge
    Save himself; but he, so the poet insisted, was over the edge.

The salt in his blood, in his eyes, mocked the ocean as poems
Mocked the dead by enjoying their deaths. "O lost," they began,
But would he be lost to even the artful collector of dooms,
Heigh, ho, the wind and the rain? Who cared if he never came in
    The door smiling, honest, dishonest, his smile no more false
    Than a rhyme? O lost, the living, unliving, was somewhere
      else.

Alone. He was all alone. The best-friend-ever controlled
Only his own disaster, wrote only his own citation out,
Somehow surviving the day on paper, to note how often he failed
To be true, and how these forbidden heroics clotted his ink with
      hate.
    No, the hero as friend was stranger than fiction, was real,
    Never to be forgiven for this, the laurel crowned chance to kill.

If friendship were fake—which the poet affirmed and denied,
While he went from one bed to another in search of himself,
Until for the last time, or was it the first, he woke up the dead
To tell them "I've fallen in love," and half joking, half
    Serious, sang them to sleep again—if friendship were fake,
    The hero reflected, his hand on the rail, then love was the
      rock.

But nothing was certain. He had seen them, the eager excited
      youths,
Go white as the sail-white surf for all their sunburn but say
Not a word, not one of their sleeptalking tyrant words, though the
      myths
Of the mariner, home and happiness, blew up in the darkling sky,
    And fluttered a moment like signal flags taut on the air,
    Then fell, the crumpled and traitorous messages, from deck to
      shore.

God betrays no one, or so he was told. Not a diamond devil
      suspires
In the baths of the ice of absence, but went there on fire with pride.

He considered the mass men crossing their deaths with a raft of
  prayers
As they drowned to the clanging of gongs; and considered the poet,
  afraid
  For his poems, when the roller-coaster became his master, who
   confessed
  His ridiculous sins aloud, and for once was drunkenly unamused.

Faith was their gift, but never his own, the glittering present not
  found
Under the tree at Christmas. Like toys for a princely pauper, this
  bright
Childlike thing must delight at a distance the unpossessed. He
  resigned
To the saint and the sinner their fabulous fortune, their brilliant
  conceit
  Of being the followed, the agents who watched for a sign of
   the hand
  Which might mean the masked murderer, which might mean
   the only friend.

Alone. He is all alone. No one follows and no one is there to wait.
Behind him the past extends like the bone-filled, the rusty steel-yard
  sea.
Ahead lies the future, the land of a make-believe, pity, and wit,
Where he must meet the guilt haunted chandlers, pirates who
  sculled away.
  He looks at his sailors, he looks at his ship, he takes the last
   look
  At himself, and then, all alone, he goes down to the clamorous
   dock.

Dazzled from the blazing, the bedazzling sea, he wonders where he
  is,
The stranger, the hero, the young man returning from the sundown
  war.
Others will tell him, he supposes, and already he can hear huzzas
Ring in the avenues, but lightly, but lightly, as though women were
  To welcome the armless, the cripples, the blind, and the
   laughing mad.
  He is still whole, or seems so, and yet too often he thinks of
   the dead.

ACKNOWLEDGMENTS

Every effort has been made to find the owners of copyright for the poems included in this anthology. The editor gratefully acknowledges the following permissions and sources for the poems and apologizes for any that he may have inadvertently missed.

"Paoa's Proclamation to Hiiaka"and "Paoa's Lament for Lohiau," from *Pele and Hiiaka: A Myth from Hawaii* by Nathaniel B. Emerson (Rutland, Vt.: Tuttle, 1978). "Shark Hula for Ka-lani-'ōpu'u" and "Chant of Welcome for Ka-mehameha," from *The Echo of Our Song: Chants and Poems of the Hawaiians,* eds. and trans. Mary Kawena Pukui and Alfons L. Korn (Honolulu: University Press of Hawaii, 1973). "Song [I will not chase the mirage of Maná]," from *Unwritten Literature of Hawaii: The Sacred Songs of the Hula,* ed. and trans. Nathaniel B. Emerson, reprinted in *Bureau of American Ethnology Bulletin* 38 (1909). "Kawaleo's War Chant" and "Kamapuaa's Chant," from *Fornander Collection of Hawaiian Antiquities and Folk-Lore . . . ,* Memoirs of the Bernice Pauahi Bishop Museum, series 1, vol. 4, by Abraham Fornander (Honolulu: Bishop Museum Press, 1916–17). "Hiiaka's Lament for Hopoe," from *Hawaiian Legends of Volcanoes* by W. D. Westervelt (Boston: Ellis Press, 1916). "Song of the Alyha's Skirt," "Song of the Hwame," and "Song of the Boy Who Paints Dice," from "Institutionalized Homosexuality of the Mohave Indians" by George Devereux, in *Human Biology* 9 (1937): 498–527. "A Hogan-Building Song of Be'gočidí" and "A Stalking Song of Be'gočidí," from "The Agricultural and Hunting Methods of the Navaho Indians" by W. W. Hill, in *Yale University Publications in Anthropology* 18 (1938). Used by permission of Yale University Press. "Békotsídi's Song of Blessing," from *Navaho Myths, Prayers and Songs, with Texts and Translations* by Washington Matthews, ed. Pliny Earle Goddard (Berkeley: The University Press, 1907). Reprinted in *Publications in American Archaeology and Ethnology* 5.2 (1907). "There was a cowboy named Hooter," "A cowboy named Bill," and "Young cowboys had a great fear," from "Cowboy Sexuality: A Historical No-No?" by Clifford P. Westermeier, in *Red River Valley Historical Review* 2 (1975): 92–113. "The Lavender

Cowboy" from *Cowboy Songs and Other Frontier Ballads*, rev. and enl. ed., by John A. Lomax and Alan Lomax (New York: Macmillan, 1938). "The Little Bunch of Cactus on the Wall," from *Songs of the Cowboys* by N. Howard (Jack) Thorp (New York: Potter, 1966). "Riding Song," from *Songs of the Cattle Trail and Cow Camp* by John A. Lomax (New York: Macmillan, 1927). "Devotee's Song," "Lesson Song," "Invisibility Song," "Priest's Song," "Song Announcing Death," "Song of Reproach," "Song of Allegiance," and "Song Requesting Protection," from *Voodoo Heritage* by Michel S. Laguerre (Beverly Hills, Calif.: Sage, 1980). "Friar Anselmo," "The Whipporwill and I," and "The Fountain of Youth" by Horatio Alger, Jr., from *Alger Street: The Poetry of Horatio Alger, Jr.*, ed. Gilbert K. Westgard II (Boston: Canner, 1964). "Five Songs," copyright 1934 and renewed 1962 by W. H. Auden, "Twelve Songs," copyright 1937 and renewed 1965 by W. H. Auden, and "Lullaby," copyright © 1972 by W. H. Auden, from *W. H. Auden: The Collected Poems*. Used by permission of Random House, Inc. "Sonnet on a Portuguese," "The Eyes," and "Mnemonic System for Psycho-analysts" by Leonard Bacon, from *Rhyme and Punishment* (New York: Farrar and Rinehart, 1936). "Six Songs of Khalidine," "Lullaby," and "First Communion" by Djuna Barnes, from *A Night Among the Horses* (New York: Liveright, 1929). "The Love of Judas," "Double Being," and "Love's Comrades" by Natalie Clifford Barney, from *Poems and Poèmes* (New York: Doran, 1920). "To One Who Waits," "A Mountain Soul," and "The Victory" by Katharine Lee Bates, from *Selected Poems*, ed. Marion Pelton Guild (Boston: Houghton, 1930). "Casabianca," "Chemin de Fer," and "The Gentleman of Shalott" by Elizabeth Bishop, from *Complete Poems* (New York: Farrar, Straus and Giroux, 1969). Sonnets XXXIII, LV, and LXXII by George Henry Boker, from *Sonnets: A Sequence on Profane Love*, ed. Edward Sculley Bradley (Philadelphia: University of Pennsylvania Press, 1929). "Scene III," "Blessed Are the Meek," and "Love Song" by Paul Bowles, from *Next to Nothing: Collected Poems, 1926–1977* (Santa Barbara, Calif.: Black Sparrow Press, 1990). "Papa Has a Pig," "Mrs. Mother Has a Nose," and "Junior's Prayer" by James Broughton, from *Packing Up for Paradise: Selected Poems, 1946–1996*, ed. Jim Cory (Santa Rosa, Calif.: Black Sparrow Press, 1997). Used by permission. "The Ballad of a Dancer," "The Earth-Clasp," and "Ghost" by Witter Bynner, from *Selected Poems*, ed. Robert Hunt (New York: Knopf, 1936). Reprinted by permission of the Witter Bynner Foundation. "Sonnet [Alas, that June should come when thou didst go]," "Antinous," and "Asphodel" by Willa Cather, from *April Twilights (1903)*, ed. Bernice Slote (Lincoln: University of Nebraska Press, 1903). "The Lost Pardner," "My Enemy," and "The Smoke-Blue Plains" by Badger

Clark, from *Sun and Saddle Leather* (Boston: Chapman and Grimes, 1935). "The Pictured Eyes," "Her Mouth," and "The Heart's Desire" by Esther M. Clark, from *Verses by a Commonplace Person* (Topeka, Kan.: Crane, 1906). "Isolation," "The Tryst," and "To a Friend" by James Fenimore Cooper, Jr., from *Afterglow* (New Haven, Conn.: Yale University Press, 1918). "Episode of Hands," "C33," and "Modern Art" by Hart Crane, from *Complete Poems and Selected Letters and Prose*, ed. Brom Weber (Garden City, N.Y.: Doubleday, 1966). "Lament" by Hubert Creekmore, from *Personal Sun: The Early Poems* (Prairie City, Ill.: Village Press, 1940). "It's Me, Oh Lord, Standing with a Gun" and "Always Overtures" by Hubert Creekmore, from *The Long Reprieve*, copyright © 1946 by Hubert Creekmore. Used by permission of New Directions Publishing Corporation. "Fruit of the Flower," "Advice to Youth," and "Sacrament" by Countee Cullen, from *Color* (New York: Harper, 1925). "Toward the Piraeus," "For Bryher and Perdita," and "At Baia" by H. D., from *Collected Poems, 1912–1944*, ed. Louis L. Martz (New York: New Directions, 1983). "Infatuation," "Soiled Hands," and "We Three" by Mercedes de Acosta, from *Archways of Life* (New York: Moffat, Yard, 1921). "The Battle of the Passions," "Phantoms," and "The Suicide" by Walter de Casseres, from *The Sublime Boy* (New York: Seven Arts, 1926). "The Subway," "Summer," and "People on Sunday" by Edwin Denby, from *The Complete Poems of Edwin Denby*, ed. Ron Padgett, copyright © 1986 by Full Court Press. Used by permission of Random House, Inc. "Her breast is fit for pearls," "Going—to—her!," and "Precious to Me— She still shall be," from *The Poems of Emily Dickinson*, ed. Thomas H. Johnson (Cambridge, Mass.: The Belknap Press of Harvard University Press, 1955). Reprinted by permission of the publishers and the Trustees of Amherst College. Copyright © 1951, 1955, 1979 by the President and Fellows of Harvard College. "Drunken Lover," "Midnight Bell," and "The Reunion" by Owen Dodson, from *Powerful Long Ladder* (New York: Farrar, Straus, 1946). "You! Inez!," "The Gift," and "I Sit and Sew" by Alice Dunbar-Nelson, from *The Works of Alice Dunbar-Nelson* (New York: Oxford University Press, 1988). "The Love Song of St. Sebastian" by T. S. Eliot, from *Inventions of the March Hare: Poems 1909–1917*, text copyright © 1996 by Valerie Eliot, editorial matter and annotations copyright © 1996 by Christopher Ricks, reprinted by permission of Harcourt, Inc. "Hysteria" by T. S. Eliot, from *Collected Poems 1909–1962* (New York: Harcourt, 1963). "Eyes that last I saw in tears" by T. S. Eliot, from *Collected Poems 1909–1962*, copyright 1936 by Harcourt, Inc., copyright © 1963, 1964 by T. S. Eliot, reprinted by permission of the publisher. "From Frodmer's Drama *The Friends*" by Ralph Waldo Emerson, from *Journals and*

Miscellaneous Notebooks, eds. William H. Gilman et al. (Cambridge, Mass.: Belknap Press, 1960). "Love and Thought" and "Friendship" by Ralph Waldo Emerson, from *Complete Poetical Works* (Boston: Houghton, Mifflin, 1918). "Beneath this beauty," "Love That Never Told Can Be," and "Parting" by John Erskine, from *Collected Poems 1907–1922* (New York: Duffield, 1922). "Baby's in jail; the animal day plays alone," "Somebody's Gone," and "January wraps up the wound of his arm" by Charles Henri Ford, *Flag of Ecstasy: Selected Poems*, ed. Edward B. Germain (Los Angeles, Calif.: Black Sparrow Press, 1972). "The Goldfish Bowl" by Robert Francis, from *The Collected Poems*, copyright 1976 by Robert Francis. Used with permission of the University of Massachusetts Press. "If we had known" by Robert Francis, from *Come Out Into the Sun*, copyright 1965 by Robert Francis. Used with permission of the University of Massachusetts Press. "Boy Riding Forward Backward" by Robert Francis, from *The Orb Weaver*, copyright 1971 by Robert Francis and reprinted by permission of Wesleyan University Press. "Impossible Blue," "Strangers," and "Meaning" by Robert Friend, from *Shadow on the Sun* (Prairie City, Ill.: Decker, 1941). "Tobias Holt, Bachelor" by Henry Blake Fuller, from *Lines Long and Short: Biographical Sketches in Various Rhythms* (New York: Houghton, 1917). "The Dahlia, the Rose, and the Heliotrope," "Absence of Love," and "The One in All" by Margaret Fuller, from *Life Without and Life Within; or, Reviews, Narratives, Essays, and Poems*, ed. Arthur B. Fuller (Boston: Roberts Brothers, 1874). "The Beloved Lost," "Conquest," and "Love Dies" by Elsa Gidlow, from *Sapphic Songs: Seventeen to Seventy* (Baltimore, Md.: Diana, 1976). "Ballade to Jean Cocteau," "A Cyclist," and "Out of the Tulip Tree" by Paul Goodman, from *Collected Poems*, ed. Taylor Stoehr (New York: Random House, 1973). "A Mona Lisa" and "For the Candle Light" by Angelina Weld Grimké, from *Black Sister: Poetry by Black American Women, 1746–1980*, ed. Erlene Stetson (Bloomington, Ind.: Indiana University Press, 1981). "El Beso" by Angelina Weld Grimké, from *Shadowed Dreams: Women's Poetry of the Harlem Renaissance*, ed. Maureen Honey (New Brunswick, N.J.: Rutgers University Press, 1989). "[To Carlos Menie]" by Fitz-Greene Halleck, from James Grant Wilson's *The Life and Letters of Fitz-Greene Halleck* (New York: Appleton, 1869). "Song [The winds of March are humming]" and "On the Death of Joseph Rodman Drake, of New York, Sept., 1820" by Fitz-Greene Halleck, from *Poetical Works*, ed. James Grant Wilson (New York: Greenwood, 1969). "Un Recuerdo—Hermano—Hart Crane R.I.P.," "K. von F.—1914—Arras-Bouquoi," and "He Too Wore a Butterfly" by Marsden Hartley, from *Collected Poems: 1904–1943*, ed. Gail R. Scott (Santa Rosa, Calif.: Black Sparrow Press, 1987). "The Knock

Alphabet," "Dwelling-Places," and "To My Shadow" by Thomas Wentworth Higginson, from *Afternoon Landscape: Poems and Translations* (New York: Longmans, Green, 1889). "Sonnets" and "A Letter" by Robert Hillyer, from *Five Books of Youth* (New York: Brentano's, 1920). "A Failure" by Robert Hillyer, from *Gates of the Compass: A Poem in Four Parts Together with Twenty-Two Shorter Pieces* (New York: Viking, 1930). "Café: 3 a.m.," "Low to High," and "Impasse" by Langston Hughes, from *The Collected Poems of Langston Hughes*, copyright © 1994 by The Estate of Langston Hughes. Used by permission of Alfred A. Knopf, a division of Random House, Inc. "Mapperley Plains," "The Common Cormorant," and "On His Queerness" by Christopher Isherwood, from *Exhumations: Stories, Articles, Verses* (New York: Simon and Schuster, 1966). "A Caged Bird," "Together," and "Flowers in the Dark" by Sarah Orne Jewett, from *Verses* (privately printed, 1916). "The Letter," "A Woman Like a Shell," and "Mediaeval" by Bernice Kenyon, from *Meridian: Poems 1923–1932* (New York: Scribner's, 1933). "October," "Salesman," and "Blackmail" by Lincoln Kirstein, from *Low Ceiling* (New York: Putnam, 1935). "Song of the Sun," "The Song of the Earth Spirit," and "Old Age Song" by Hasteen Klah, from *Texts of the Navajo Creation Chants*, ed. Mary C. Wheelwright (N.p.: Peabody Museum of Harvard University, n.d.). Reprinted by permission. "In Antique Mood," "The Rebel," and "A Time Will Come" by Frank Belknap Long, Jr., from *A Man from Genoa and Other Poems* (Athol, Mass.: W. Paul Cook/Recluse Press, 1926). "The Masker," "Song of Young Burbage," and "Ordeal by Fire" by Haniel Long, from *Poems* (New York: Moffat, Yard, 1920). "Belated Love," "Understanding," and "Remonstrance" by Samuel Loveman, from *The Hermaphrodite and Other Poems* (Caldwell, Idaho: Caxton Press, 1936). Reprinted by permission. "Orientation," "Crepuscule de Matin," and "The Letter" by Amy Lowell, from *The Complete Poetical Works of Amy Lowell*. Copyright © 1955 by Houghton Mifflin Company. Copyright © renewed 1983 by Houghton Mifflin Company, Brinton P. Roberts, and G. D'Andelot Belin, Esquire. Reprinted by permission of Houghton Mifflin Company. All rights reserved. "Songs to Joannes: XIII," "Lunar Baedeker," and "Faun Fare" by Mina Loy, from *The Lost Lunar Baedeker*, ed. Roger L. Conover (New York: Farrar, Straus and Giroux, 1996). "Poem [anonymous calling]," "Poem [o rivers of my flesh]," and "Poem [the great arm]" by Willard Maas, from *Fire Testament*, 2nd ed. (New York: Alcestis Press, 1935). "The Love of a Man" and "One" by Douglas Malloch, from *Tote-Road and Trail: Ballads of a Lumberjack* (Indianapolis: Bobbs-Merrill, 1917). "The Bachelor" by Douglas Malloch, from *Come on Home* (New York: Doran, 1923). "Ero-Somnambulist," "The Mother," and "Taunt to the

Egoist" by Robert McAlmon, from *Not Alone Lost*, copyright © 1937 by New Directions Publishing Corp. Used by permission of New Directions Publishing Corporation. "Absence," "The Barrier," and "Adolescence" by Claude McKay, from *Selected Poems* (New York: Bookman Associates, 1953). "Monody," "C—'s Lament," and "After the Pleasure Party: Lines Traced Under an Image of Amor Threatening" by Herman Melville, from *Collected Poems*, ed. Howard P. Vincent (Chicago: Packard, 1947). "My Heritage," "A Memory," and "Infelix" by Adah Isaacs Menken, from *Infelicia*, in *Collected Black Women's Poetry*, vol. 1, ed. Joan R. Sherman (New York: Oxford University Press, 1988). "Friends," "Pilots," and "Rebellion" by Scudder Middleton, from *Upper Night* (New York: Holt, 1927). "I, being born a woman and distressed," "Night is my sister, and how deep in love," and "I too beneath your moon, almighty Sex" by Edna St. Vincent Millay, from *Collected Poems*, ed. Norma Millay (New York: Harper, 1956). "The Earthling" "She Walks Alone," and "The Thrall" by Royal Murdoch, from *Gargantua's Mouth* (New York: Fine Editions, 1946). "An Artificial Tragedy" by Wilbur D. Nesbit, from *A Book of Poems*, subscription edition (Evanston, Ill.: Bowman, 1906). "The Trail to Boyland" and "The Four Guests" by Wilbur D. Nesbit, from *The Trail to Boyland and Other Poems* (Indianapolis: Bobbs-Merrill, 1904). "Narcissus," "Bastard Song," and "Who Asks These Things?" by Richard Bruce Nugent, from *Gay Rebel of the Harlem Renaissance: Selections from the Work of Richard Bruce Nugent*, ed. Thomas H. Wirth (Durham, N.C.: Duke University Press, 2002). All rights reserved. Used by permission of the publisher. "The Beach," "A Character," and "The Explorer" by David O'Neil, from *A Cabinet of Jade* (Boston: Four Seasons, 1918). "She wrote it," "The Master-Mistress," and "The Sonnet Begs Me" by Rose O'Neill, from *The Master-Mistress* (New York: Knopf, 1922). "The Dead have mourners plenty," "Dawn at Abbazia," and "[Poem: I–VII]" by Persis M. Owen, from *Blue Seas and Barren Sand* (Boston: Gorham, 1933). "Safe Secrets," "Prologue," and "In New York" by William Alexander Percy, from *Collected Poems of William Alexander Percy* (New York: Knopf, 1943). Copyright 1943 by Leroy Pratt Percy. Used by permission of Alfred A. Knopf, a division of Random House, Inc. "The Masks," "The Dolls," and "The Piazza" by Frederic Prokosch, from *The Assassins* (New York: Harper and Brothers, 1936). Copyright 1936 by Harper and Brothers. Reprinted by permission of HarperCollins Publishers Inc. "Song of the Unholy Oracle," "Admonition in Ivory," and "Before a Departure" by Lynn Riggs, from *The Iron Dish* (Garden City, N.Y.: Doubleday, Doran, 1930). Copyright 1930 by Lynn Riggs. Used by permission of Doubleday, a division of Random House, Inc. "The Secret" and "The Door" by Jessie

B. Rittenhouse, from *The Secret Bird* (Boston: Houghton, 1930).
Copyright 1930 by Jessie B. Rittenhouse Scollard, renewed 1958. Re-
printed by permission of Houghton Mifflin Company. All rights re-
served. "Myself" by Jessie B. Rittenhouse, from *The Door of Dreams*
(Boston: Houghton, 1918). "Letter, Unposted," "The Handclap," and
"Drunken Girl" by Muriel Rukeyser, from *Collected Poems* (New York:
McGraw-Hill, 1978). "Infidelity," "Imeros," and "Hope" by Edgar Sal-
tus, from *Poppies and Mandragora* (New York: Harold Vinal, 1926).
"To W.P.," "Apollo in Love or the Poet Lost in the Platonist," and
"Dedication of the Later Sonnets to Urania" by George Santayana,
from *Complete Poems*, ed. William G. Holzberger (Lewisberg, Pa.:
Bucknell University Press, 1979). Used with permission of Associated
University Presses. "Encounter in April," "Sonnets," and "Strangers"
by May Sarton, from *Encounter in April* (Boston: Houghton Mifflin,
1937). Copyright 1937, and renewed © 1965 by May Sarton. Re-
printed by permission of Houghton Mifflin Company. All rights re-
served. "The Lesbians," "The Swimming Pool," and "Tea Making" by
Antoinette Scudder, from *Italics for Life: Collected Poems* (New York:
Exposition, 1947). "The Garden," "Sumer Is Icumen In," and "The
Dark Mirror" by Edward Slocum, from *Lads o' the Sun: Memories*
(N.p.: Ladslore Series, n.d.). "Before the Dawn," "Identity," and "It is
Reality now" by Alicia Kay Smith, from *Only in Whispers* (Portland,
Maine: Falmouth, 1947). "Two Loves," "The Magic Streets," and
"Fulfilment" by Logan Pearsall Smith, from *Songs and Sonnets* (Lon-
don: Elkin Mathews, 1909). "Anonyma: Her Confession," "Holyoke
Valley," and "To Bayard Taylor" by Edmund Clarence Stedman, from
Poetical Works, household edition (New York: Houghton, 1891). "Lift-
ing Belly" by Gertrude Stein, from *Lifting Belly*, ed. Rebecca Mark
(Tallahassee, Fla.: Naiad, 1995). "America" and "Your Own" by Ger-
trude Stein, from *Bee Time Vine and Other Pieces [1913–1927]* (New
Haven, Conn.: Yale University Press, 1953). "Expectation," "Utopia,"
and "The Secret Well" by Charles Warren Stoddard, from *Poems*, ed.
Ina Coolbirth (New York: Lane, 1917). "On the Town," "Beloved,
since they watch us," and "The Messenger at Night" by Richard Henry
Stoddard, from *Poems*, complete edition (New York: Scribner's, 1880).
"Just Daylight" by Genevieve Taggard, from *Words for the Chisel* (New
York: Knopf, 1926). "Married" and "For Eager Lovers" by Genevieve
Taggard, from *For Eager Lovers* (New York: Seltzer, 1922). "The
Torso," "L'Envoi," and "To a Persian Boy" by Bayard Taylor, from
Poetical Works, household edition (New York: AMS, 1970). "To a Pic-
ture of Eleanora Duse in *The Dead City*," "Song [You bound strong
sandals on my feet]," and "What do I care" by Sara Teasdale, from
Collected Poems (New York: Collier, 1966). "This tall horseman, my

young man of Mars," "In All the Argosy of Your Bright Hair," and "Return of the Hero" by Dunstan Thompson, from *Lament for the Sleepwalker* (New York: Dodd, Mead, 1947). "Indeed indeed, I cannot tell," "I'm guided in the darkest night," and "I knew a man by sight" by Henry David Thoreau, from *Collected Poems*, ed. Carl Bode (Chicago: Packard, 1943). "Haunted" by Charles Hanson Towne, from *The Quiet Singer and Other Poems* (New York: Dodge, 1908). "Vision" by Charles Hanson Towne, from *Today and Tomorrow* (New York: Doran, 1916). "A World of Windows" by Charles Hanson Towne, from *Selected Poems* (New York: Appleton, 1925). "Ode to Hollywood," "The Erotics," and "His Elegy" by Parker Tyler, from *Will of Eros: Selected Poems, 1930–1970* (Los Angeles, Calif.: Black Sparrow Press, 1972). "2. Samuel, I. 26," "The Master Key," and "Children of Lilith" by George Sylvester Viereck, from *The Candle and the Flame* (New York: Moffat, Yard, 1912). "John" by Willard Austin Wattles, from *Lanterns in Gethsemane: A Series of Biblical and Mystical Poems in Regard to the Christ in the Present Crisis* (New York: Dutton, 1918). "Only a Cloud Dissolving" and "How Little Knows the Caliph" by Willard Austin Wattles, from *Iron Anvil* (Manchester, Maine: Falmouth, 1952). "Magnolias and the Intangible Horse," "Mountain III: Coyotes," and "Natives of Rock" by Glenway Wescott, from *Natives of Rock: XX Poems, 1921–1922* (New York: Francesco Bianco, 1925). "Legend" by We'wha, from *The Zuñi Indians* by Matilda Coxe, reprinted in *Bureau of American Ethnology Annual Report* 23 (1901–02). "Apocryphal Apocalypse," "Phallus," and "Adam" by John Wheelwright, from *Collected Poems of John Wheelwright*, ed. Alvin H. Rosenfeld (New York: New Directions, 1971). Copyright © 1971 by Louise Wheelwright Damon. Used by permission of New Directions Publishing Corporation. "In Paths Untrodden," "City of Orgies," and "We Two Boys Together Clinging" by Walt Whitman, from *The Complete Poems*, ed. Francis Murphy (New York: Penguin, 1975). "Love and Death," "Lyric Love," and "To a Woman" by Helen Hay Witney, from *Sonnets and Songs* (New York: Harper, 1905). "A Group of Sonnets" by Gale Wilhelm, in *Overland Monthly and Out West Magazine*, December 1930: 358. "Quest" by Gale Wilhelm, in *Frontier* 13 (November 1932): 48. "To—," "The Annoyer," and "The Confessional" by Nathaniel Parker Willis, from *Poems: Sacred, Passionate, and Humorous* (New York: Arno, 1972).

THE CONTRIBUTORS

HORATIO ALGER, JR.
1832–1899

Known best as a writer of juvenile fiction, Alger wrote over a hundred books exemplifying a "rags to riches" plot. The oldest child of a Unitarian preacher, he was born in Revere, Massachusetts. He graduated from Harvard in 1853, and after a brief time at Cambridge Divinity School, he became a teacher at several boarding schools, returning to Cambridge Divinity School and ordained a minister in 1861. His earliest novels were directed toward adults, but in 1864, he published his first juvenile fiction, *Frank's Campaign; or What Boys Can Do on the Farm for the Camp*. In 1866, encouraged by the success of his juvenile fiction, he resigned his post as minister and moved to New York City and published, a year later, his most successful novel, *Ragged Dick; or Street Life in New York with the Boot-Blacks*. Many of his novels were initially published in serial form in magazines of the time.

W. H. AUDEN
1907–1973

Born in York, England, of an upper-class family, Auden attended Christ Church at Oxford, from which he graduated in 1928. His first collection, *The Orators*, appeared in 1928, followed by *Poems*, which established his career. Friend of Stephen Spender and Christopher Isherwood, he traveled extensively through Germany, Iceland, China, and Spain. In 1939, he immigrated to the U.S. where he met his life partner, Chester Kallman. Considered one of the greatest poets in English of the twentieth century, Auden published a large number of collections of poetry, with *The Age of Anxiety* being perhaps his most famous, but he also wrote large amounts of critical pieces, opera libretti, and other works. He died in Vienna.

LEONARD BACON
1887–1954

Born in Solvay, New York, Bacon attended St. George's in Newport, Rhode Island, before entering Yale, from which he received a B.A. in 1909. He taught for some time at the University of California, Berkeley, while publishing a string of books of poetry, beginning with *The Scrannel Pipe* in 1909 through *Rhyme and Punishment* in 1936. His work was noted for its satire. He also translated the heroic, epic poems of several countries, such as *The Song of Roland* and *The Lay of the Cid*. He married in 1912, when he was thirty-five.

DJUNA BARNES
1892–1982

While her literary ability often competes with her social celebrity, Djuna Barnes was an important, if overshadowed, figure among the U.S. expatriates in Paris during the 1920s and 30s. Born north of New York City, Barnes grew up on Long Island. Her formal education was scanty. She was living in Greenwich Village in the year her first book, *The Book of Repulsive Women*, a collection of poetry, was published (1915). She had affairs with men, was married to Courtenay Lemon from 1917 to 1919, and possibly had a relationship with Mary Pyne. In Paris, she formed relationships with Thelma Wood and Natalie Barney. Although she never abandoned poetry, by the 1930s, Barnes had included fiction to her repertoire, and it is for her fiction that she is most often now remembered, particularly *Nightwood* (1936).

NATALIE CLIFFORD BARNEY
1876–1972

Although Barney's fame now rests more on her social life—and her notoriety—than on her literary work, she was, nevertheless, a well-known poet, playwright, essayist, and fiction writer among the U.S. expatriates in Paris. Born in Ohio to wealthy parents, her family moved to Washington, D.C. During her childhood, she learned French from her French governess, and she was able to settle in Paris in 1902 after her father's death left her financially independent. There, she eventually met and formed a relationship with Renee Vivien, an Anglo-American, who was also bilingual and as at home in Parisian society as Barney. Barney's books include a number of memoirs. She appeared as characters in a number of thinly disguised autobiographical novels by her lovers, including Liane de Pougy's *Idylle saphique* and

Renee Vivien's *Une Femme m'apparut*—as well as in work by her friends: Collette's *Claudine s'en va*, Radclyffe Hall's *The Well of Loneliness*, and Djuna Barnes' *Ladies Almanack*. Her *Pensees d'une Amazone* outlines her thoughts on lesbianism and is perhaps her most well-known book today.

KATHARINE LEE BATES
1859–1929

Best known as the author of the song "America the Beautiful," Bates was an educator, scholar, editor, poet, and a writer of prose ranging from travel books to children's fiction, and an advocate for women's education. Born in Massachusetts, the youngest of five children of a minister father, Bathes was formally educated and began writing as early as 1876 when she entered Wellesley College. After several teaching positions, she returned to Wellesley as an instructor and later received an M.A. from Oxford (1891). Of her scholarly work, her *The English Religious Drama* and her *American Literature* are best known. Bates relates her experiences with lifelong companion Katharine Coman in her poetry.

ELIZABETH BISHOP
1911–1979

Born in Worcester, Massachusetts, Bishop's father died when she was a child, her mother was institutionalized, and she went to live with her maternal grandparents in Nova Scotia. In her senior year at Vassar, she met poet Marianne Moore, who would become not only a friend but a huge influence on Bishop. Having graduated in 1934 and being independently wealthy, Bishop was able to travel extensively for the next three years. Her first collection, *North and South*, appeared in 1946, and it received the Pulitzer Prize for poetry in 1955 when it was reissued as *Poems: North and South*. Bishop had several lovers, among them Marjorie Stevens and Lota de Macedo, whom she met in Brazil and with whom she would live until de Macedo's suicide in 1967. Bishop remained in Brazil for three years after de Macedo's death, then returned to the U.S. where she died in 1979 from a cerebral aneurysm.

GEORGE HENRY BOKER
1823–1890

Called a patriot and a diplomat as well as being a major poet and playwright, Boker grew up in Philadelphia, graduated in 1842 from the College of New Jersey (which came to be called Princeton University), and married Julia Riggs in 1844. Four years later, his first volume of poetry, *A Lesson of Life*, was published, as was his first play, *Calaynos*, which was produced the following year. His other plays include *The Betrothal*, *The World a Mask*, and others. In 1856, he issued his *Plays and Poems*. His *Poems of the War* was published in 1864, followed by *Konigsmark, The Legend of the Hounds, and Other Poems* (1857) and other books. His posthumous *Sonnets: A Sequence on Profane Love* was one of the chief literary events of its time.

PAUL BOWLES
1910–1999

Bowels is best known for his novel *The Sheltering Sky* (1949), which was recently made into a movie, but he was a proficient as a story writer, translator, travel writer, autobiographer, scriptwriter, and poet. Born in New York City, he attended the University of Virginia only briefly then studied music with composer Aaron Copland in New York City. He went to Paris in 1931, and for most of the rest of his life lived as an expatriate, writing scores and music reviews. In 1938, he married lesbian author Jane Bowles, and by 1947, he had abandoned his interest in music for literature.

JAMES BROUGHTON
1913–1999

Born in Modesto, California, Broughton received his B.A. from Stanford University in 1936 and later studied at the New School for Social Research in New York City. He married in 1962, fathered a son and a daughter, and was divorced in 1978. He held numerous and differing jobs, from merchant marine to professor. Although principally a poet, whose work was seminal in the early years of Gay Liberation, he also wrote six plays and was an experimental filmmaker, with nearly twenty films to his credit.

WITTER BYNNER
1881–1968

Author of eighteen volumes of poetry, plays, and essays and of numerous other books of translations, Bynner was also an editor, pacifist, translator of Chinese poetry, advocate of Native American and African-American cultures, and an amateur actor. Born in Brooklyn, he graduated from Harvard in 1898, became an editor at *McClure's Magazine*, and arranged for the first U.S. issue of A. E. Housman's poetry. His first collection was published in 1907, followed by the publication of two one-act plays, and in 1915, his second volume of poetry, *The New World*. He was the chief instigator of the Spectra Hoax, a joke on the literary establishment of the time. He met Robert Hunt, his lifelong companion and many years younger, in 1930. During Bynner's failing health, Hunt died of a heart attack in 1964. Bynner died four years later after a serious stroke left him mentally and physically disabled.

WILLA CATHER
1873–1947

Born in Gore, Virginia, Cather moved with her family to Red Cloud, Nebraska, nine years later. Its diverse population and prairie would later influence her work, especially her fiction. She attended the University of Nebraska, Lincoln, and in 1892, a Boston journal, *The Mahogany Tree*, published "Peter," a story she'd written. Thereafter, she wrote fiction on a regular basis. She left Red Cloud in 1896, bound for Pittsburgh where she worked as an editor, and it is in Pittsburgh that Cather met Isabelle McClung, with whom Cather lived. During this time, Cather's first book, *April Twilights*, her only collection of poetry, was published. It was expended into a larger edition and re-issued two decades later. Author of twelve novels, four story collections, and two volumes of essays, Cather became one of the most highly acclaimed novelists of the twentieth century, especially for *My Ántonia*, *A Lost Lady*, *The Professor's House*, and *Death Comes for the Archbishop*. In 1922, she was awarded the Pulitzer Prize.

BADGER CLARK
1883–1957

Born in Albia, Iowa, Clark attended public schools in South Dakota, where his family had moved, before attending, but not graduating from, Dakota Wesleyan University. He was chiefly a poet, one of the most popular of his day, to which the brisk sales (and many reprintings) of his books attest. Because of the subject of much of his verse, Clark was quickly identified as "The Cowboy Poet," although he also wrote a novel, *Spike*. Among his collections of poetry are *Sun and Saddle Leather* (1915) and *Grass Grown Trails* (1917), his most popular books.

ESTHER M. CLARK
1876–?

Born on a farm in Neosho County, Kansas, Clark attended the University of Kansas, working toward a degree in English. She would be employed there later in the Extension Department. Her books include *Verses by a Commonplace Person* (1906) and *The Call of Kansas and Other Verse* (1909).

JAMES FENIMORE COOPER, JR.
1892–1918

Born in Albany, New York, Cooper, who was the grandson of the noted U.S. novelist, died twenty-six years later at Fort Dix, New Jersey, the same year in which his only book, *Afterglow*, a collection of poems, appeared.

HART CRANE
1899–1933

Born in Garrettsville, Ohio, Crane never attended a university, although he had read voraciously from his childhood on. He moved to New York City rather than becoming involved in his father's business, candy manufacturing, where he would become associated with some of the most visible literary figures of his time. His relationship to both parents was, in a word, dysfunctional to the extreme, with his mother's manipulation and bouts with mental illness the cause for his own illnesses, including alcoholism. On his way back to New York from a trip to Mexico, he committed suicide by leaping from the deck of his ship. His book-length poem *The Bridge* (1930) is perhaps his best-known work; his first collection was *White Buildings* (1926).

HUBERT CREEKMORE
1907–1966

Born in Water Valley, Mississippi, Creekmore was known as a writer of many genres. He was a translator (*Juvenal's Satires*), an editor (*The Little Treasury of World Poetry*), a novelist (*The Welcome*), and a poet (*The Long Reprieve*).

COUNTEE CULLEN
1903–1946

Born Countee Leroy Porter in Louisville, Kentucky, Cullen's early background is obscure. He was adopted by the Rev. and Mrs. Frederick Cullen of New York City in 1918. Theirs was a comfortable home that would provide a foundation for the spiritual interests that would later emerge in his work. One of the first black poets to achieve national recognition (Paul Laurence Dunbar was the first) and one of the best-known poets of the Harlem Renaissance, Cullen was influenced by Keats and wrote in traditional forms. His poems address personal issues of love, as well as racial injustice and black pride. He was briefly married to Yolande Du Bois, daughter of W. E. B. Du Bois, and to Ida Roberson for a brief period before his death. His first collection, *Color* (1925), was issued when Cullen was an undergraduate at New York University and was followed by *Copper Sun* (1927) and *The Medea and Some Poems* (1935), as well as fiction, journalism, and plays.

H. D.
1886–1961

Born Hilda Doolittle, but also writing under the pseudonym John Helforth, H. D. was the prime force in Imagism, the first important movement in poetry of the twentieth century and an important influence in the development of Modernism. She was raised in Bethlehem, Pennsylvania, and attended Bryn Mawr for two years, becoming friends with Marianne Moore and William Carlos Williams. Briefly engaged to Ezra Pound, she later met then married Richard Aldington. In 1918, H. D. separated from Aldington and became the lover of Winifred Ellerman, also a writer, whose pseudonym was Bryher and who had been married to Robert McAlmon. The two raised H. D.'s daughter. H. D.'s literary experimentation during these years and after has earned her a great deal of praise and attention, culminating a year before her death when the American Academy of Arts and Letters presented her with its Award of Merit Medal, the first time a woman had received it. She wrote both novels—*Paint It Today* (1921), *Asphodel* (1922), *HERmione* (1927)—and poetry.

MERCEDES DE ACOSTA
1893–1968

Born in New York City of Cuban parents, de Acosta was lover of Greta Garbo, Marlene Dietrich, Isadora Duncan, and others and eventually married painter Abram Poole. She designed sets and costumes in Hollywood, as well as wrote film scripts for over ten years. Her first book, *Archways of Life*, was a collection of poetry (1921). Two of her plays were produced—*Sandro Botticelli* (1923) and *Jacob*

Slovak (1927)—and her tell-all autobiography, *Here Lies the Heart*, appeared in 1960.

WALTER DE CASSERES
1881–1900

Son of David and Charlotte (Davis) de Casseres, and brother of nationally recognized author Benjamin, de Casseres attended public schools in Philadelphia. He committed suicide when he was nineteen, and his brother had his only collection of poems published posthumously.

EDWIN DENBY
1903–1983

The most influential dance critic of the twentieth century, Denby contributed to all the important dance and literary magazines, and newspapers, of his day, among them *Ballet* and *Dance Magazine*. He wrote a number of important books, mostly on dance, but also on artists (such as De Kooning). His collection of poetry, *In Public, in Private* (1948), was the first of several, which would culminate in his *Complete Poems*, published posthumously.

EMILY DICKINSON
1830–1886

The "Belle of Amherst," Dickinson lived most of her life in isolation in that Massachusetts town, although she had attended the Mount Holyoke Female Seminary briefly. Nevertheless, she kept up an active correspondence with many individuals, including family members and Thomas Wentworth Higginson, editor of the *Atlantic Monthly*. During her life, she expressed her love for her sister-in-law Susan in many poems and letters. She died in Amherst, and her first volume was published posthumously in 1890.

OWEN DODSON
1914–1983

Born into poverty in Brooklyn, New York, Dodson's father was a freelance journalist and director of the National Negro Press Association who introduced his son to Booker T. Washington, W. E. B. Du Bois, and James Weldon Johnson. A scholarship allowed Dodson to attend Bates College (Maine); a fellowship allowed him to attend Yale Drama School in 1936. After teaching at various colleges, he joined the Navy. He had written a number of plays that were produced and received with praise by this time. In 1944, he was appointed to the prestigious Committee for Mass Education in Race Relations at the American Film Center. He later taught at Howard University, and among his students there were Amiri Baraka, Earle Hyman, Debbie Allen, and Ossie Davis. After writing his first, and best-received collection of poetry, he turned to the novel.

ALICE DUNBAR-NELSON
1875–1935

Born in New Orleans, Dunbar-Nelson's racial heritage was Creole—a mixture of African-American, Native American, and European American. Three years after graduating with a bachelor's in education from Straight College in 1892, her first book, *Violets and Other Tales*, a collection of stories, poems, and essays, appeared. She earned her living as a teacher then married Paul Lawrence Dunbar in 1898 after a long correspondence with him. Their marriage ended four years later, and she returned to teaching. She was to marry two more times. Although she is perhaps best known now for her fiction and other prose, during her life, Dunbar-Nelson was considered a leading poet and was associated with members of what has been called the Harlem Renaissance. Her work was included in many notable journals and anthologies, but most importantly in *The Book of American Negro Poetry* (ed. James Weldon Johnson). Not only a writer, Dunbar-Nelson was a feminist and an early worker in the Civil Rights movement.

T. S. ELIOT
1888–1965

Destined to be one of the most influential poets of the twentieth century, Eliot was born in St. Louis, Missouri, and attended Harvard. After graduating in 1910, he attended the Sorbonne, and in Paris met and formed a relationship with Jean Verdenal, who was killed in World War I and to whom Eliot dedicated his first book, *Prufrock and Other Observations* (1917). Eliot finally settled in England in 1914. He married Vivienne Haigh-Wood the following year and worked in London, eventually for Lloyd's Band. The publication of his first major poem, "The Love Song of J. Alfred Prufrock," marked the beginning of his career (and his huge influence on all poets in English who followed him), extending to the publication of *The Waste Land* and culminating in the appearance of *Four Quartets*. He was also an influential critic and playwright. He left his first wife in 1933 and married

Valerie Fletcher twenty-three years later. He received the Nobel Prize in Literature for 1948 and died in 1965.

RALPH WALDO EMERSON
1803–1883

Best known for his essays and poetry and as a founder of the Transcendental movement, Emerson was the son of a Boston Unitarian minister. He attended Harvard Divinity School and became a minister in 1829 (despite his doubts on traditional Christian teachings). In 1832, he resigned, moved to Concord, and traveled extensively in Europe. After returning to the U.S., he began writing the works on which his reputation rests, including addresses he delivered at Harvard Divinity School, which became the initial drafts of some of the essays for which is he best known: "Self-Reliance," "The Over-Soul," and "The Poet." In the 1840s he became associated with *The Dial*, a journal devoted to the Transcendentalist movement, in which a number of his poems appeared. His influence has been extensive (including Melville, Whitman, Dickinson, Hawthorne, Thoreau, and others). His *Complete Works* fills twelve volumes.

JOHN ERSKINE
1879–1951

Erskine's fourteen books include the novel *The Literary Discipline* (1923) and *Sonata and Other Poems* (1925). He was a professor of English at Columbia University and co-editor of the influential *Columbia History of American Literature*. A respected musician, he was president of Julliard for ten years, beginning in 1928.

CHARLES HENRI FORD
1909–2002

Ford's most famous work was a novel, the product of his collaboration with Parker Tyler, entitled *The Young and Evil*. He contributed to the leading journals of his day, among them *Transition*, *Poetry*, and *Pagany*, and lived much of his life as an expatriate in Paris.

ROBERT FRANCIS
1901–1987

Francis was born in Upland, Pennsylvania, and attended Harvard University from which he received his A.B. (1928) and his Ed.M.

(1926). Although he occasionally taught at summer writers' conferences and lectured at universities throughout the U.S., he devoted most of his energy to writing. He spent his life reclusively, reducing his wants and needs in order to live on his small income.

ROBERT FRIEND
1913–1998

Born in Brooklyn, New York, Friend's parents were Russian immigrants. He attended Brooklyn College, Harvard, and Cambridge, and eventually taught literature in the U.S. as well as in other countries. In 1950, he emigrated to Israel, where he taught English and U.S. literature at the Hebrew University. He was a translator (the poetry of Leah Goldberg and S. Y. Agnon, as well as the posthumous *Found in Translation: A Hundred Years of Modern Hebrew Poetry*) and a poet in his own right, publishing ten collections during his life, which culminated with the publication of his *Collected Poems.*

HENRY BLAKE FULLER
1857–1929

Considered by some (such as Theodore Dreiser) to be the originator of U.S. realism, Fuller was born into a wealthy Chicago family, second cousin to Margaret Fuller. As a young man, he began working first in a store, then in a bank. In 1879, he toured Europe for a year, the first of several trips abroad. By 1885, his father died, and Fuller had to return to Chicago. He published his first book, about his experiences in Italy, under the pseudonym Starton Page, to much acclaim in 1890, an event that made him one of the more prominent of Chicago's writers. His most famous book, however, is *The Cliff Dwellers* (1893), a novel of social self-consciousness. Besides eight novels, three travelogues, a collection of twelve plays, and a volume of satirical sketches, Fuller published a book of his lengthy, narrative poems at mid-career.

MARGARET FULLER
1810–1850

Best remembered now as a social critic, Sarah Margaret Fuller was an early feminist, co-founding editor (with Ralph Waldo Emerson) of *The Dial*, a Transcendentalist journal, and is often ranked with Edgar Allan Poe as the finest literary critic of her time. Her *Woman in the Nineteenth Century* (1845) is regarded as the first full-length treatise on feminism in the U.S. Although she had many attachments among the young women she knew, in the mid-1800s she traveled in Europe and, in Rome where she settled, she met Giovanni Angelo d'Ossoli, with whom she had a son and later married. Because of a war between France and Italy, they fled the country for the U.S. Their ship sank off Fire Island, and only their son's body was recovered.

ELSA GIDLOW
1898–1981

Born in Hull, England, Gidlow moved to Canada with her family when she was a child. Her formal education was sporadic at best, although she read voraciously. She had her first relationship at sixteen and moved to New York City in 1921, where her first book, *On a Grey Thread,* was published and is considered by some to be the first openly lesbian collection of poetry in the U.S. In New York, she worked as an editor and met her first life partner, with whom she remained for thirteen years. In the mid 1920s, Gidlow moved to San Francisco and met Ella Young, with whom she shared most of her life. She supported herself as a freelance journalist. She died after a series of strokes.

PAUL GOODMAN
1911–1972

Regarded during his life as a social critic and political thinker, as well as the leading philosopher of the "New Left," Goodman was born and raised in New York City. His father abandoned his mother shortly before Goodman's birth. He earned his Ph.D. in philosophy at the University of Chicago and wrote numerous studies including the very popular *Growing Up Absurd.* Along with a steady stream of books of social criticism, Goodman produced a large literary corpus, which included five novels, four volumes of *Collected Stories,* and the posthumous *Collected Poems,* as well as plays and literary essays. His fiction often presented bisexual characters, their experiences paralleling his own, while his poetry was often overtly bisexual, perhaps even gay, in focus. He was married and had a son.

ANGELINA WELD GRIMKÉ
1880–1958

Born in Boston, her father was a prominent lawyer, diplomat, man of letters, etc., and son of a white man and a slave; her mother was the daughter of a white Methodist minister and his white wife, both of whom discouraged their daughter's marriage. When Grimké's parents' marriage failed, her mother left with her, but returned her to her father four years later. Grimké never saw her mother again. Her first poem was published when she was thirteen, in 1893. Following it, Grimké published a large number of poems in important literary journals and anthologies of the time, but never a book of them during her life. She is considered by most literary historians to be a significant figure in what is often referred to as The New Negro Renaissance in the arts, which included Countee Cullen, Langston Hughes, and Claude McKay.

FITZ-GREENE HALLECK
1790–1867

During his life, Halleck was a very popular and respected poet of satire and sentimental lyrics. Born in Connecticut, he became a member of New York's Knickerbocker circle of literati, including James Fenimore Cooper, Washington Irving, William Cullen Bryant, and others. His first poem was published when he was nineteen, and after moving to New York City in 1811, Halleck met Joseph Rodman Drake, a doctor and poet, with whom Halleck published a sequence of satires on New York society under the joint pseudonym "Croaker & Co." (Some were written individually: Drake as "Croaker" or Halleck as "Croaker, Jr.") His ten principal books include the book-length poem *Fanny*, a collection of the "Croaker & Co." work entitled *Poems*, and his best-selling *Alnwick Castle, with Other Poems*, which sold out almost as soon as it appeared. A version of his elegy on Drake is inscribed on Drake's tombstone.

MARSDEN HARTLEY
1877–1943

An important early modernist painter and leader in the postimpressionist and expressionist schools of painting, Hartley was also a poet. Born in Lewiston, Maine, as Edmund Harley, he adopted his stepmother's maiden name as his first name. At sixteen years old, he moved to Cleveland, where he won a scholarship to the Cleveland School of Art and then a grant for study at the New York School of Art. His first published poems appeared in 1918 and his poetic activity was intense for two years thereafter. Around 1931 or 1932, he again began to write poetry intensely. A spiritually-inclined artist, he was profoundly influenced by the death of his lover, Lt. Karl von Freyburg, a German soldier who died in WWI, and the accidental drowning of three young friends. He published only three books of his poetry during his life: *25 Poems* (1923), *Androscoggin* (1940), and *Sea Burial* (1941).

THOMAS WENTWORTH HIGGINSON
1823–1911

Born in Cambridge, Massachusetts, Higginson's father died when he was ten. He was raised by his mother and aunt. Henry Wadsworth Longfellow and Margaret Fuller were family friends, and Higginson entered Harvard when he was thirteen, later attending Harvard Divinity School. He married and was noted as a writer of many genres—essays, criticism, history, biography, autobiography, fiction, and translation, as well as poetry. He also exercised his strong interest in women's rights and abolitionism. He is best remembered for his *Margaret Fuller Ossoli* and for acting as Emily Dickinson's mentor and for co-editing the first collection of her work.

ROBERT HILLYER
1895–1961

Hillyer represents the quintessential "man of letters." In his literary career that lasted forty years, he was a professor of English, editor, translator, essayist, novelist, and poet, and he published sixteen volumes of his poetry. Born in East Orange, New Jersey, he attended Harvard, from which he graduated in 1917, the year his first collection, *Sonnets and Other Lyrics*, was published. After graduating, he joined an ambulance service and was sent to France, joining the American army after the U.S. entered the war. In 1920, he published two books of poetry, *The Five Books of Youth* and *Alchemy: A Symphonic Poem*. In 1953, he married Jeanne Duplaix. After publishing over a dozen other books of poetry, his *Collected Poems* appeared in 1961, the year of his death.

LANGSTON HUGHES
1902–1967

One of the best-known authors of the twentieth century, Hughes was born in Joplin, Missouri, but went to live with his grandmother in Kansas when his parents separated. After attending Columbia University for a year, he traveled extensively, and later received his bachelor's degree from Lincoln University. By 1930, his first novel had been published and had won the Harmon gold metal. He lectured nationwide thereafter, but lived in New York City, becoming involved with the political Left. In 1953, the HUAC, chaired by Joseph McCarthy investigated him. Known during his life primarily as a poet, he captured the everyday of African-American existence, ignoring no experience. The blues and jazz were chief influences of his poetics, and among his best-known books is *Montage of a Dream Deferred* (1951).

CHRISTOPHER ISHERWOOD
1904–1986

Known almost exclusively as a novelist, Isherwood was born in Cheshire, England. He attended, but never graduated from, Corpus Christi, Cambridge. A friend of W. H. Auden since their childhood, the two traveled extensively together, their life in Berlin setting the stage for his *The Berlin Stories,* which became the basis for the play *Cabaret,* which was made into a film. He collaborated with Auden on three experimental plays and in 1939 immigrated with him to the U.S. Settling in Los Angeles, he wrote film scripts. In 1953, he met his life partner artist Don Bachardy.

SARAH ORNE JEWETT
1849–1909

The middle of three daughters, Theodora Sarah Orne Jewett was born in Maine to a wealthy physician father. As a child, she was stricken with arthritis and attended school sporadically. Instead, she accompanied her father on his house calls, meeting the locals and being introduced to the landscape, which would later provide her with the "local color" for which her fiction is noted. At nineteen, she published her first story, in the *Atlantic Monthly.* A short time later, she met Annie Fields, then the wife of the *Atlantic*'s editor. After his death, the two women became lifelong companions, living and traveling extensively together. Employing many pseudonyms, including Alice Eliot and Sarah C. Sweet, to name but two, Jewett's reputation as an author is based on her fiction—three novels, eleven collections of stories or sketches—including her most famous book, *The Country of the Pointed Firs.* Nevertheless in 1916, her only collection of poetry, *Verses,* was published posthumously. Jewett was sixty when she died of a stroke.

BERNICE KENYON
1897–?

Born in Newton, Massachusetts, Kenyon attended the Bennett School in Millbrook, New York, then Knox School in what is now Tarrytown, New York, and finally Wellesley College, from which she graduated in 1920. She wrote in several genres, but principally poetry, and supported herself through editorial work at, for example, Charles Scribner's Sons. She received the Masefield Poetry Prize in 1920. She married novelist Walter Gilkyson in 1927.

LINCOLN KIRSTEIN
1907–1996

Born in Rochester, New York, to the owner of Filene's Department Store, Kirstein attended Harvard, where he co-founded the magazine *Horn and Hound* for which he reviewed dance and theater productions. In 1934, he founded the School of the American Ballet, which would become associated with the Metropolitan Opera by the end of the following year. A dozen years later, he and George Balanchine created the Ballet society and, in 1948, became co-directors of one of the most important dance companies in the U.S., New York City Ballet. He wrote a number of dance books—*Dance* (1935) and *Movement and Metaphor* (1970), among others—as well as a collection of poetry, *Low Ceiling* (1935). He was married to painter Paul Cadmus' sister, and with Cadmus and photographer George Platt Lynes comprised the core of a circle of gay men who influenced aesthetics from the 1920s to the 1950s.

HASTEEN KLAH
1867–1937

Navajo *nádleehí* Klah, whose name means "left-handed" (*hasteen* is a term of respect), was born right after the forced relocation of the Navajos from their ancestral home to a desolate reservation near Fort Sumner, New Mexico. At an early age, he revealed his "two-spirit" (also called "berdache" or "gay") status, and he eventually became interested in religion, in healing, and in preserving the culture of his people. To that end, he memorized eight ceremonies, while most medicine men learned only one, perhaps two in their lives. In his early teens, he learned weaving—work reserved for women—and gained a large reputation as a master weaver, which paved the way for his exhibit at the World's Columbian Exposition in Chicago in 1893. He also became an expert at sand painting—work reserved for men—and eventually combined weaving and sand painting by using the imagery of painting on the blankets he wove. His friendship with the family that ran the nearby trading post lead to his friendship with Boston aristocrat Mary Cabot Wheelright, who began transcribing Klah's songs and myths in 1927, resulting in three separate collections of his work. In 1934, Klah returned to Chicago to show his sand-painting techniques and exhibit his blankets, where he met Franklin Roosevelt. He died of pneumonia at the age of seventy, a few months before the Museum of Navaho Ceremonial Arts—which he helped Wheelright to found in order to preserve Navajo culture in general and, more specifically, Klah's contributions to it—opened. (In 1976, it was renamed after Wheelwright.) Unlike most two-spirited individuals, Klah didn't cross-dress, except during specific ceremonies.

FRANK BELKNAP LONG, JR.
1901–1994

A protégé of H. P. Lovecraft, whose fame overshadowed his own achievements, Long is best known for his many volumes of science fiction novels, beginning with *The Horror from the Hills* (1931) and extending to the end of the 1970s. He won the Bram Stoker Award for his fiction, but his first published book was a collection of poems, *A Man from Genoa and Other Poems* (1923).

HANIEL LONG
1888–1956

Born in Rangoon, Burma, the son of a Methodist missionary, Long returned to the U.S. (to Pittsburgh) with his family three years later. They lived among the indigent, his father continuing to work with the poor and needy, and eventually they moved to Duluth and to Minneapolis. Long entered Harvard in 1907, where he was on the editorial staff of a student journal, attended the lectures of George Santayan, and met Witter Bynner. Long was a reporter during 1909–10, then for the next three decades, he was on the faculty of Carnegie Technology School (now Carnegie Institute of Technology), despite constant eye problems. He married in 1912 and fathered a son. In 1924, Bynner convinced Long to visit him in New Mexico (where Bynner had moved) for his health, and within five years Long had moved his family there permanently, where he would befriend Lynn

Riggs and May Sarton. Long's *Atlantides* marks his development as a mature poet and introduced into his work sexual love as a theme for the first time. While in the hospital recovering from heart surgery, Long died—three days after his wife's death.

SAMUEL LOVEMAN
1887–1976

No details about Loveman's life have survived him.

AMY LOWELL
1874–1925

Known as the leading member of the Imagist movement in U.S. poetry and as one of the literary ex-patriots during the beginning of the twentieth century, Lowell was first and foremost a poet, but she also was an anthologist, editor, translator, critic, biographer, reviewer, and a spokesperson for modern poetry. Born to an aristocratic family in Boston, the youngest of five children, Lowell was educated at home (a ten-acre estate called Sevenels) by governesses, then at private schools, and then during trips abroad. Her brother, Abbott Lawrence Lowell, was an eminent astronomer and president of Harvard University; poet Robert Lowell was her nephew. *Atlantic Monthly* published her first poem in 1910, her first collection (*A Dome of Many-Coloured Glass*) appeared two years later, and in 1913, she met a number of poets and fiction writers who would become influential in her life—and vice versa: H. D., Ezra Pound, Richard Aldington, and others. Her last collection, *What's O'Clock* (1925), won the Pulitzer Prize for poetry. She died of a stroke in the presence of her life companion, Ada Russell.

MINA LOY
1882–1966

Born in London, the first of three daughters, her last name was not Loy but Lowy. Although her family discouraged educating girls, her father sent her to Munich to study art in 1899. When she returned to London, she studied art with Augustus John, exhibited her work, and met the first of her two husbands. (She had four children.) She moved to Paris in 1903 and changed her name from Lowy to Loy. In 1916, she left her children with a nurse (planning to return for them later) and sailed to the U.S., where she quickly became a member of the New York avant-garde and met her second husband, Arthur Cravan, who would disappear without a trace in 1918. The death of her son Giles in 1923 was an even greater tragedy. In the 1920s and 30s, Loy ran her own design business and shop, selling her original lampshades and was friends with both Natalie Barney and Djuna Barnes. She published only five collections of poetry during her life, and most of those in the first decades of the twentieth century. Her most important book is the posthumous *The Last Lunar Baedeker,* a "collected" volume of her published and unpublished poems and short prose pieces. Her *Lunar Baedecker* (which was published by Robert McAlmon in 1923) became notorious when customs officials confiscated copies shipped to New York City because it was considered pornographic. She moved to New York City in 1936, then to Aspen, Colorado, in 1953, where she lived until her death.

WILLARD MAAS
1911–1971

No details about Maas' life have survived him.

DOUGLAS MALLOCH
1877–1938

Born in Muskegon, Michigan, Malloch was educated in public schools and married in 1898. If not a "literary" poet, he was, nevertheless, one of the most popular poets of his time and was given the dubious distinction of being a "Lumberjack Poet" by the popular press. He published eight collections during his life and served as president of the Society of Midland Authors and the Press Club of Chicago. He lived much of his life in Chicago.

ROBERT McALMON
1895–1956

One of the lesser-known, but most instrumental, members of the "Lost Generation," McAlmon's Contact Publishing Company brought the works of Hemingway, Stein, Loy, H. D., Pound, Williams, and Barnes, among many other, to the reading public. Born in Clifton, Kansas, the ninth child of an itinerant preacher, McAlmon moved to Greenwich Village after a short stint in the Air Force. He met and married English heiress Winifred Ellerman (whose pseudonym was Bryher). The couple moved to Paris and was divorced in 1926. Bryher became H. D.'s lover. An alcoholic by 1929, and increasingly alienating his former friends, McAlmon returned to the U.S. before his death. Although his first published book was a volume of poetry, his fiction is better known, but his memoirs (with Kay Boyle) bring him most attention today.

CLAUDE McKAY
1889–1948

Jamaican-born McKay (who was born Festus Claudius McKay and who used Eli Edwards as a pseudonym) is one of the most important figures of the Harlem Renaissance. A writer of fiction, essays, and autobiography, but best known today as a poet, his work promotes racial pride, challenges while authority, and acknowledges the conflicts of black peoples throughout the Western hemisphere. McKay moved to the U.S. after his first two collections of poetry (volumes written in Jamaican dialect) were published. In 1922, angered by and concerned over the intense racial prejudice he had witnessed in the U.S., he left for Europe, remaining there, visiting various countries until 1934. During his years in Europe, McKay's novel, *Home to Harlem*, became the first best-selling novel by an African-American writer.

HERMAN MELVILLE
1819–1891

Known now for his allegorical and realistic masterpiece *Moby-Dick*, the novella *Billy Budd*, and several short stories, Melville was virtually unknown when he died. Born and raised in New York, his father died when he was twelve, when Melville began working to help support the family, including a stint as a cabin boy and on a number of other journeys, including trips to Europe and the South Seas. His first novels were thinly disguised autobiographical accounts of his sailing experiences. Although he had some success as an entertaining writer (e.g., *Typee* and *Ommoo*), *Moby-Dick*, which he dedicated to Nathaniel Hawthorne, was a disaster in terms of sales and acceptance by the public. While writing the fiction for which he would be esteemed, he also wrote poetry, beginning in 1860, with his first collection, *Battle-Pieces and Aspects of the War*, published six years later, the year in which he also became a customs official, a job he held for two decades. Most of his books of poetry were self-published near the end of his life.

ADAH ISAACS MENKEN
1835–1868

An internationally respected actress, Menken was born Dolores Adios Fuertes near New Orleans, Louisiana. Her father died when she was a child, and she and her sister began to dance at the French opera house in New Orleans, becoming favorites with audiences. She soon began traveling with touring companies to Cuba, Texas, and Mexico, and taught French and Latin at a girls' school. In 1858, she made her acting debut in Fazio at the New Orleans Varieties, which lead her to work at major cities throughout the South. She made her London debut in 1864 at Astley's and in Paris at the Theatre de la Gaiete two years later. She married and divorced four times: one husband was a musician, another was a prizefighter, and a third was a journalist-humorist. She was extraordinarily beautiful and intelligent, according to reports. Her last stage appearance was in London in 1868, the year she converted to Judaism and in which she died. She was thirty-three. Her only collection of poetry, *Infelicia*, was published posthumously in 1873.

SCUDDER MIDDLETON
1888–1959

Born in New York City, Middleton attended Columbia University and later worked at the Macmillan Company, a publishing house. His books include *Streets and Faces* (1917) and *The New Day* (1919) and the screenplay for the film *The Love That Lives* (1917).

EDNA ST. VINCENT MILLAY
1892–1950

Writing some of the best-known and important lyrics of her time, as well as plays in verse, operas, and political commentary, Millay was born in Rockland, Maine, the eldest of three sisters. He mother divorced her father and became a nurse to support her daughters. Her first published poem appeared in a children's magazine when she was a child. Early in her life, she became friends with Witter Bynner, when he wrote her to praise her "Renascence," when it became her first published "mature" poem. She attended Vassar, where she wrote a great deal, acted in plays, and was introduced to feminism. Her first book, *Renascence and Other Poems*, appeared shortly after she graduated to very favorable reviews. She moved to Greenwich Village in hopes of becoming an actor; instead, to make ends meet, she began writing prose for a magazine under the pseudonym Nancy Boyd (later collected in book form by "Nancy Boyd" with a preface by Millay). In 1923, Millay was awarded the Pulitzer for *The Harp Weaver*, the same year she married Eugen Boissevain. In the following years, Millay's interests took a turn toward social criticism, focusing on feminism as well as international peace, although she never abandoned the writing of poetry. She translated Baudelaire's *Fleurs du Mal* with George Dillon, with whom she may have had an affair. Millay suffered a nervous breakdown in 1944 and died of a heart attack six years later.

ROYAL MURDOCH
1898–1981

Born on a ranch near Chino, California, Royal Murdoch eventually attended Pomona College. He taught for a while in the San Joaquin Valley, then traveled throughout Europe. Upon his return to the U.S., he attended Columbia University, where he earned an M.A., and won the Van Rensselaer Prize (poetry). In his later life, he divided his time between New York City (where he was a fur cutter) and Cuba or Mexico (where he wrote). His first collection of poetry, *Spring Night*, was issued in 1925, followed by three others, most recently *Key of C* in 1960.

WILBUR D. NESBIT
1871–1927

No details about Nesbit's life have survived him.

RICHARD BRUCE NUGENT
1906–1987

Important as an artist as well as a poet of the Harlem Renaissance, Nugent—who wrote under the pseudonyms of Bruce Nugent and Richard Bruce—was not widely published during his life, despite the appearance of his work in such anthologies and journals as *Caroling Dusk* (ed. Countee Cullen), *The New Negro* (ed. Alain Locke), *Fire!!*, *Crisis*, and *Ebony*. He collaborated with Locke in turning Locke's story "Sahdji" into a ballet. Nugent's work often intertwined the themes of religion (specifically Christianity) with homosexuality. In 1960, he co-founded the Harlem Cultural Council.

DAVID O'NEIL
1874–1947

An executive as well as a poet, O'Neil was born and raised in St. Louis, Missouri, and attended St. Louis University, Manual Trade School, and Washington University Law School from which he received the L.L.B. He married in 1903 and, although he contributed to all of the leading journals of the day (*Poetry, Little Review,* etc.), he only published a single collection of his poetry, *A Cabinet of Jade* (1918).

ROSE O'NEILL
1874–1944

O'Neill, who is best known as the inventor of the Kewpie doll, was also an illustrator as well as a writer. Born in Wilkes-Barre, Pennsylvania, the second of seven children, O'Neill attended parochial schools. She began selling illustrations to magazines in Denver and Chicago very early in her life, and when she was seventeen, moved to New York City to work more closely with the publishing industry there. At nineteen, she moved to Missouri, where her family had settled, and continued to work with New York magazines long-distance, from her family's home. In 1896, she returned to New York and eventually married an inventor, who was trying to produce a successful projector for the then-infant film industry. They divorced in 1901. The following year, she married a novelist whose work she had illustrated, and they were permanently separated in 1907. Beginning in 1909, when her Kewpies began appearing in women's magazines across the U.S., she became quite wealthy, her royalties for the dolls making her a millionaire. However, she was generous and became a patron to many charities and to many other artists and writers in need. When she died of a paralytic stroke in Springfield, Missouri, she was nearly penniless. She published four unsuccessful novels and a single collection of poetry, *The Master-Mistress* (1922).

PERSIS M. OWEN
?–?

No details about Owen's life have survived him.

WILLIAM ALEXANDER PERCY
1885–1942

The son of a senator of Mississippi, Percy entered the University of the South at Sewanee, Tennessee, at the age of thirteen. After he graduated, he spent a year in Paris, then he attended Harvard University's law school. In 1917, he joined the U.S. Army and, the following year, received the Croix de Guerre. Both Percy and his father were noted during their lives for opposing the Ku Klux Klan and for working for social equality. He adopted and raised his cousin Walker Percy (the contemporary novelist, who was also gay) and Walker's two brothers after their parents died, and thereafter, he seems to have abandoned the writing of poetry. His most famous work, *Lanterns on the Levee,* an autobiography, was published a year after his death.

FREDERIC PROKOSCH
1908–1989

Born in Madison, Wisconsin, Prokosch attended several universities in the U.S. and Europe and traveled extensively throughout Europe, Asia, and Africa. He was an acclaimed poet, publishing four collections, before he turned to the novel. He also translated the poetry of Friedrich Hölderlin and Louise Labé.

LYNN RIGGS
1899–1954

Riggs was born in what was then called the Cherokee Nation of Indian Territory (now Claremore, Oklahoma), the son of a white father and a Cherokee mother. His mother died of typhoid when he was three years old, and his father remarried half a year later to a woman who mistreated him. He attended the University of Oklahoma in 1920, but was diagnosed with TB his senior year and sent to New Mexico to get better. There, he began writing poems and the plays for which he would become known in the 1930s and 40s. He was accepted into the theater and film circles of his day, counting as friends Bette Davis and Joan Crawford, among many others. Much of his work reflects the abuse he suffered during his early years, not only abuse of a personal nature but also the strained relations between whites and Native Americans. One of his most highly acclaimed plays, *Green Grow the Lilacs,* became the Rodgers and Hammerstein hit musical *Oklahoma!*

JESSIE B. RITTENHOUSE
1869–1949

Born in Mt. Morris, New York, Rittenhouse attended the Nunda Academy followed by the Genesee Wesleyan Seminary, from which she graduated in 1890. She married at age fifty-five, after a long and successful career as poet, anthologist, translator, and critic. She was a pioneer in the movement to recognize U.S. poets who, heretofore, had been ignored by the American poetry-reading public in favor of British poets. She was one of the founders of the Poetry Society of America and founder and president of the Florida Poetry Society. Her three collections of poetry were *The Door of Dreams* (1918), *The Lifted Cup* (1921), and *The Secret Bird* (1930).

MURIEL RUKEYSER
1913–1980

Born in New York City, Rukeyser attended Vassar then Columbia and finally the Roosevelt Aviation School, where she learned to pilot an airplane. Working as an editor, she witnessed a large number of social injustices both here and abroad which were to influence her work. Despite her embracing political movements, and especially feminism, she obscured most of her private life—and her sexual identity. She was briefly married in 1945, had a son by a man who was not her husband, and had a number of women lovers. Her first collection was *Theory of Flight,* and her *Collected Poems* appeared a year before her death in New York.

EDGAR SALTUS
1855–1921

Considered anything but conventional during his life, Saltus's work is pessimistic and promotes the decadent movement of his time while rejecting the vapid sentimentality and the lame genteel literature his era produced. Acclaimed as an historian, novelist, and religious writer, he was also an essayist, biographer, critic, dramatist, and poet. He was married three times, and his third wife introduced him to theosophy and the occult, both of which later influenced his work.

GEORGE SANTAYANA
1863–1952

Spanish-born (Madrid), Santayana was among the most prominent philosophers of his time, although he also wrote criticism, fiction, essays, plays, an autobiography, and poetry. Moving to Boston when he was six to live with his mother (his parents had separated three years earlier), he eventually attended Harvard University and later taught there. Among his pupils were T. S. Eliot and Robert Frost. Santayana, who had never liked the U.S. in general, and Harvard in particular, moved to Rome in 1912. His one novel, *The Last Puritan*, was nominated for a Pulitizer Prize and was a best-seller in 1936.

MAY SARTON
1912–1995

Born Eleanor Marie Sarton in Belgium, her family immigrated to the U.S., settling in Boston, when she was three. After high school, she left home to become an actor with, first, New York City's Civic Repertory Theater, then with her own company, the Associated Actors Theater—both of which dissolved leaving her to focus on writing. Her first collection, *Encounter in April* (1937), was followed by five others, including her *Collected Poems* (1993). Her work was not limited to poetry. She published fiction, essays, and her journals, including *Journal of a Solitude* (1977). In 1945, she met Judy Matlack, her life partner of thirteen years. A teacher at many leading colleges and universities, she died of breast cancer.

ANTOINETTE SCUDDER
1888–1958

Artist, playwright, and poet, Scudder founded (with actor/director Frank Carrington) the Paper Mill Playhouse in 1934 in Newark, New Jersey. Her published collections of plays include *Maple's Bride and Other One-Act Plays* (1935) and *The World in a Match Box* (1949). Her volumes of poetry include *The Grey Studio* (1934) and *East Wind, West Wind* (1935).

EDWARD SLOCUM
1882–1946

No details about Slocum's life have survived him.

ALICIA KAY SMITH
1913–?

No details about Smith's life have survived her.

LOGAN PERSALL SMITH
1865–1946

Born in Millville, New Jersey, Smith was the son of wealthy Quaker parents. His mother was involved in the temperance and revivalist movements of the mid- to late 1800s and wrote several books. Walt Whitman and William James were family friends. Both parents became strongly involved in evangelism, taking their family to England on several visits, and finally settling there. Smith eventually attended Harvard then worked for a short time for the family's business, manufacturing bottles. At twenty-three, he moved to Oxford, where he studied under Walter Pater, and read Baudelaire, whose poetry influenced his. He moved to Paris thereafter, and his first book, *The Youth of Parnassus and Other Stories*, was published. His most important, and representative, book, *Trivia*, was a collection of what might be called prose poem-like aphorisms. It was followed by three other very similar books, all of which were later gathered together in one volume as *All Trivia*, a book that was reprinted ten or more times during his life. He also wrote biography, memoirs, and essays, as well as poetry.

EDMUND CLARENCE STEDMAN
1833–1908

Poet, anthologist, critic, scholar, Stedman was born in Hartford, Connecticut, a distant relative of Thomas Wentworth Higginson. His father died of TB two years later, and his mother moved him and his brother to Plainfield, New Jersey, to live with her parents. There, she began writing poetry in hopes of supporting her family. At age six, he was sent to live with his maternal uncle, a lawyer and classicist. (His brother would follow when he also turned six.) His mother remarried, had two daughters, and virtually abandoned her sons. In 1850, Stedman attended Yale, but never finished. He married in 1853, and by 1854, had bought and sold two newspapers and published his first poem, "Amavi." He moved to New York in 1855, becoming friends of Richard Henry Stoddard and Bayard Taylor, among others, and working on Wall Street. Five years later, his first collection, *Poems, Lyrical and Idyllic*, was published. Several others were to follow. Although first and foremost a poet, Stedman was also a talented anthologist, translator, critic, and literary historian. He died of a heart attack.

GERTRUDE STEIN
1874–1946

Born of German-Jewish immigrants in Allegheny, Pennsylvania, Stein moved with her family back to Europe when she was three, then to California a year later. Both parents had died by the time she was seventeen, and in 1903, she moved to Paris where she would live for most of the rest of her life. Four years later, she met Alice Toklas, her life partner whose identity Stein adopted to write *The Autobiography of Alice B. Toklas.* Her influence on other expatriate writers and artists of the time is legendary, and by 1909, she began publishing the books that were to influence each successive generation of writers after her, beginning with *Three Lives,* followed by *Tender Buttons* (1915) and many other volumes—poetry, fiction, and nonfiction. She died of cancer.

CHARLES WARREN STODDARD
1843–1909

Born in Rochester, New York, Stoddard lived most of his early years in upstate New York, except for a brief, and important, two-year period (1885–56), when his family moved to San Francisco. In 1857, he was sent home with his brother who was very ill to live with their rather Puritanical maternal grandparents. At fifteen, Stoddard returned to San Francisco, devoting himself to writing, especially poetry, which he almost immediately began publishing under a pseudonym, Pip Pepperpod. Among his friends were Bret Harte, Mark Twain, and Ambrose Bierce. In 1864, Stoddard traveled to Hawaii under his doctor's advice, and there, he seems to have had his first affair, with a young indigenous man, Kane-Aloha, which he would later describe in *The Island of Tranquil Delights* (1904). In 1867, his *Poems* was published, the only volume of poetry he issued during his life although he continued to publish poems in journals until he died. He traveled extensively during his life—Hawaii, throughout Europe, and in the Middle East—and eventually took several teaching positions. Although most of his relationships were with much younger men, he formed brief relationships with a few men closer to his age, including the painter Frank Millet with whom he lived in Venice. After many bouts with illnesses, he died of a heart attack.

RICHARD HENRY STODDARD
1825–1903

Stoddard's father, a sailor, was lost at sea when the boy was three. He and his mother were taken in, first, by his paternal grandparents, then by his maternal grandparents. By 1835, his mother had remarried, to another sailor, and they had moved to New York City, where his schooling was brief and sporadic. At fifteen, he began earning his living, as errand boy and other menial jobs. At eighteen, he apprenticed himself as an iron molder, but near his twenty-fourth birthday, he met Edgar Allen Poe and began to devote himself to writing. Soon he would also meet Bayard Taylor, Nathaniel Hawthorne, and Herman Melville, and others involved in literature. During this period, he began publishing his own poems and met the woman he would marry, Elizabeth Barstow Stoddard, a novelist. He published four collections of his poetry, beginning with *Poems* (1852), but also wrote literary journalism and edited anthologies.

GENEVIEVE TAGGARD
1894–1948

Although a poet highly respected during her life by literary as well as popular audiences, Taggard was also a story writer, reviewer, essayist, and editor of journals and anthologies, and biographer of Emily Dickinson. Born in Waitsburg, Washington, to schoolteachers, Taggard went to live in Hawaii with her parents, who had become fundamentalist missionaries, when she was six. In 1910, after her father suffered two bouts of an illness, they returned to the mainland to a life of near poverty. In 1914, she began the University of California at Berkeley, putting herself through school by part-time jobs. She became editor of *The Occident*, the school's literary magazine, and studied with Witter Bynner. After graduating in 1920, she moved to New York and took on editorial jobs. She married the following year and had a daughter in 1922, the same year her first collection of poetry, *For Eager Lovers*, appeared. Her development as a poet began with rhymed lyrics focusing on love and nature, through socio-politically focused poems, and culminating in her experimental work of the 1940s. She taught at several universities, most extensively at Sarah Lawrence, and married twice. In her later years, she worked with composers, putting her poetry to music.

BAYARD TAYLOR
1825–1878

Considered the best travel writer of his time and an exemplary poet, Taylor was born in Kennett Square, Pennsylvania, son of a farmer who later became the local sheriff, then justice of the peace. Taylor published his first poem when he was sixteen in the *Saturday Evening Post*. He couldn't afford a college education, so he became a printer's apprentice in 1844, the same year his first collection of poetry appeared. After touring through Europe at nineteen, he published at twenty-one the first of his many travelogues, which by 1855 had gone through twenty-six reprints and had established his name as a writer. He married a chronically ill woman in 1850, but she died two months later. He remarried in 1857, to the niece of a friend. In 1863, he published his first novel, and his last, *Joseph and His Friend,* a retelling of the homoerotic David and Jonathan tale, seven years later. He died in Germany after several illnesses.

SARA TEASDALE
1884–1933

One of the most popular U.S. poets from World War I until the end of the 1920s, Teasdale was born in St. Louis, the youngest child of a wealthy businessman. Sheltered, educated in private schools, led to believe she was fragile physically and in need of constant care (a chain of dependence that would enslave her all of her life), Teasdale joined an amateur art club, The Potters, when she was twenty, and took part in publishing and contributing to the club's journal. Her work caught the eye of influential publishers, and in 1906, the *Mirror* began publishing her work. By the next year, her first collection, *Sonnets to Duse and Other Poems,* appeared. She became friends of Jessica Rittenhouse, with whom she traveled in Europe, Genevieve Taggard, and John Hall Wheelock. The initial printing of her very popular third collection, *Rivers to the Sea,* sold out in three months, but such success notwithstanding, she forced herself to marry Ernst Filsinger, whom she didn't love, for the sake of financial security. Her indifference to the Modernist movement may have contributed to the decline in her career. Despite her many successes, which included eight collections of poetry and *The Answering Voice,* the first women-only poetry anthology published in the twentieth century, she was depressed much of her life. Only her relationship with a much younger woman, Margaret Conklin, during Teasdale's later life, relieved the gloom. Conklin became Teasdale's literary executor when the poet committed suicide with an overdose of sleeping pills, an event that became front-page news across the U.S.

DUNSTAN THOMPSON
1918–1975

Born in New London, Connecticut, Thompson attended schools in the U.S., England, and France before entering Harvard, where he edited *The Harvard Monthly*. He enlisted in the U.S. Army during World War II, and it was during his stint as a soldier that the poetry for which he would be known was published: *Poems* (1943) and *Lament for the Sleepwalker* (1947). After being discharged, he traveled extensively then moved to England where he lived until his death after a long illness. He also published *The Phoenix in the Desert* (1951), a travelogue, and a novel three years later (*The Dove with the Bough of Olive*). His posthumous *Poems, 1950–1974* was published in 1984 and was edited by Philip Trower, to whom he had dedicated *Poems* almost forty years earlier.

HENRY DAVID THOREAU
1817–1862

Born in Concord, Massachusetts, to a pencil manufacturer, Thoreau attended Harvard, from which he graduated in 1837, then worked with his father and taught school. In 1841, he lived at the home of his neighbor, Ralph Waldo Emerson, where he met a number of other writers, among them Margaret Fuller who published a number of his early poems in *The Dial*, which she edited. Four years later, he built a house on Walden Pond, which was on Emerson's land, and his life there became the basis of his most famous book, *Walden*. His late essay on civil disobedience, influenced Mahatma Gandhi and Martin Luther King, Jr. He died of tuberculosis.

CHARLES HANSON TOWNE
1877–1949

Born in Louisville, Kentucky, Towne was the youngest of six children. His father, a math professor, moved the family to New York City in 1880. Beginning in 1901, Towne became an editor, for which he was known during much of his life, working at various magazines, such as *McClure's Magazine* and *Harper's Bazaar*. In 1917, he worked to support the Allied cause against Germany, which included editing two anthologies of pro-war poetry. At the same time, his poetry was beginning to appear in many journals, including the *Saturday Evening Post*, culminating in this *Selected Poems* of 1925. He also wrote four novels to lackluster reviews; penned a literary column that appeared regularly in the *New York American* from 1931 until 1937; compiled an etiquette book for men, *Gentlemen Behave;* and during 1940–41, toured with a road-company production of *Life with Father*, playing one of three doctors. His autobiography appeared in 1943.

PARKER TYLER
1907–1974

Film and art critic Tyler was born in New Orleans, but soon moved with his family to Chicago where he attended the Latin School. He moved to Cleveland to become an actor at the Cleveland Playhouse after graduation, but four years later, he moved to New York where he was befriended by the literati of his day. He co-authored the seminal *The Young and Evil* (1933) with Charles Henri Ford. His most ambitious work *The Granite Butterfly* is a book-length poem (1945). His lifelong partner was Charles Boultenhouse.

GEORGE SYLVESTER VIERECK
1884–1962

Considered one of the most highly praised poets of the pre-World War I era, especially from 1907 to 1914, Viereck's work was considered a vehicle for the "modern" impulse. It represented to many, first and foremost, the Decadent movement that was, already at his time, on the wane. Viereck's paternal grandmother was a famous German actress whose son was born out of wedlock. Rumor had it that her paramour was Kaiser Wilhelm I, a rumor the poet promoted. His father and mother immigrated to the U.S. when he was twelve. In 1906, he graduated from the College of the City of New York, and soon thereafter, he subsidized the printing of his first collection of poems, *Gedichte*, a volume in German. His third book, *Nineveh, and Other Poems* (1907), his first collection in English, brought him fame. His first novel, *The House of the Vampire*, was published the same year. In 1911, his parents returned to Germany, but Viereck remained to edit his father's German-language magazine and then to found his own journal, *Fatherland*. He devoted himself in many way to strengthening U.S.-German relations. He married in 1915, and he and his wife had two sons. Between the two world wars, he wrote history and psychology, as well as poetry and fiction. At the outbreak of World War II, he was indicted then convicted of what amounted to being a

Nazi spy, although Viereck vehemently denied it. After a year he was released, only to be imprisoned again and was again released, this last time in 1947. After his youngest son was killed in a battle in Germany, Viereck's wife left him.

WILLARD AUSTIN WATTLES
1888–1950

Born in Baynesville, Kansas, into a farming family with connections in the lumber industry, Wattles eventually attended the University of Kansas, where he received the B.A. in 1909 and two years later the M.A. During his life, he was an educator, teaching at numerous colleges and universities throughout the U.S., but he was also a highly visible poet of his time. His three books were well received: *Lanterns in Gethsemane* (1918), *The Funston Double-Track and Other Poems* (1919), and *A Compass for Sailors* (1928). However, his best-known collection, *Iron Anvil* (1953), was published posthumously under the direction of his wife. Wattles also edited *Sunflowers: A Book of Kansas Poetry* in which he included Ester Clark's poetry.

GLENWAY WESCOTT
1901–1987

Born in Wisconsin, Wescott left the University of Chicago after not quite two years to travel in both the U.S. and in Europe. He settled near Nice, France, in 1925, for the next eight years, returning to the U.S. in 1933 and living in either New York City or rural New Jersey for the rest of his life. While his most creative period of his career was during his expatriate years of the 1920s, Wisconsin was his chief subject. In 1927, he won the prestigious Harper Prize for his novel *The Grandmothers*. While his reputation rests on his fiction, he also wrote drama, and his first two published books were collections of lyric poetry relying on Imagist techniques. His last novel appeared in 1945, and for the next forty-two years, he wrote lyric essays, as well as criticism and commentaries, and lectured.

WE'WHA
1849–1896

A Zuñi *ko'lhamana*, a word indicating a man has a "two-spirit" (also called "berdache" or "gay") status, We'wha was born the year in which the Zuñis received their first "official" American visitor, Lt. Col. John M. Washington's expedition which had been sent to secure the area at the outbreak of the Mexican-American War. Both of We'wha's parents died of smallpox, probably during the epidemic of 1853, and he and his brother where adopted by their father's sister, whose family was among the most wealthy at Zuñi. We'wha was a potter, weaver, farmer, a housekeeper and laundryman for local missionaries, and the "matron" of the mission school—and always worked to learn as much Zuñi lore and ritual as possible in order to preserve it. He often participated in various ceremonies. He not only became fast friends with anthropologist Matilde Coxe Stevenson, who transcribed much of the lore he had learned, he became her chief source of information about the Zuñis. In 1885, Stevenson brought We'wha to Washington, D.C., where he quickly became the toast of the town and, because he had cross-dressed, was identified in newspapers and other reports as an "Indian princess." He eventually met President Cleveland. We'wha died of heart disease.

JOHN HALL WHEELWRIGHT
1897–1940

Born into a wealthy Boston family, Wheelwright was known for his experiments with poetry and his strong Marxist leanings. While at prep school in Rhode Island, he was strongly influenced by, first, his father's mental breakdown then, two years later, his father's suicide, and his conversion from Unitarianism to Anglicanism. At Harvard, where he abandoned the Church's dogma but not his search for some sort of spiritual fulfillment, he became friends with Robert Hillyer, e. e. cummings, and others; and he was expelled for not attending classes and exams. Much of his work reveals his philosophical values in conflict with his emotional state, and his experimentation includes novels in poetry. His work was respected during his life while, at the same time, it confounded many readers. He also wrote verse drama and was a publisher of two poetry series: *Poems for a Dime* and *Poems for Two Bits*. He was killed in Boston when, crossing the street, a drunk hit him with his car.

WALT WHITMAN
1819–1892

The son of a constructor, Whitman spent most of his youth in Brooklyn, New York, then on Long Island. Never receiving a formal education, he was apprentice to a printer when he was twelve years old and worked as a printer. In 1836, he became a teacher and, in 1841, a journalist. By 1848, he had become the editor of the *New*

Orleans Crescent, but he returned to Brooklyn later that year and founded the *Brooklyn Freeman*. In 1855, he published the first edition of *Leaves of Grass*, which went through several editions during his life, growing larger with each. He worked in Civil War hospitals in New York City and Washington, D.C., for a number of years, then found a post as a clerk in the Department of the Interior, a job from which he was eventually fired because his poems were offensive to the then Secretary of the Interior. While visiting his family in Camden, New Jersey, in early 1870, he had a stroke and, unable to return to Washington, he remained there until his death. Peter Doyle was Whitman's partner for many years.

HELEN HAY WHITNEY
1876–1944

Sports enthusiast, art collector, philanthropist, and author, Whitney was born in New York City, the daughter of the U.S. Secretary of State under the McKinley and Theodore Roosevelt administrations. She attended Miss Masters' School at Dobbs Ferry, New York, and published her first collection, *Some Verses* (1898), a few years after graduating. Nine other collections followed, among them *Beasts and Birds* (1899), *The Little Boy Book* (1900), *The Rose of Dawn* (1901), and *Herbs and Apples* (1910). After marrying financier Payne Whitney in 1902, she gradually lost interest in literature, focusing her energies on horseracing instead. She soon owned and ran one of the largest steeplechase stables in the history of racing. She also gave prodigiously to many charities.

GALE WILHELM
1908–1991

Born in Eugene, Oregon, Wilhelm is best known for two novels— *We Too Are Drifting* (1938) and *Torchlight to Valhalla* (1938)—which, on one hand, are to some extent precursors to lesbian pulp fiction but which, on the other, are considered today to also be well-written works of fiction.

NATHANIEL PARKER WILLIS
1806–1867

Born in Portland, Maine, Willis showed an interest and talent in poetry at early age, which his father encouraged. He attended Yale, from which he graduated in 1827, becoming editor of Boston's *Amer-*

ican Monthly Magazine, the first of his many editing positions, two years later. In 1833, he became the first paid U.S. foreign correspondent for the *New York Weekly Mirror,* a leading newspaper of the day, writing about literature and art as well as social criticism and gossip columns. He quickly became the second best-known writer of travel sketches in the U.S., with only Washington Irving considered better. Willis was also a poet, publishing two collections during his life; an anthologist, introducing European authors to U.S. audiences; and a playwright.

AUTHOR INDEX

TITLE INDEX

JIM ELLEDGE
is a poet and Chair of the Department of English and Humanities
at the Pratt Institute in Brooklyn. His most recent books are *The
Chapters of Coming Forth by Day*, a novel in prose poems, and the
anthologies *Real Things* and *Gay, Lesbian, Bisexual, and
Transgendered Myths from the Arapaho to the Zuñi*.